Personal, Academic and Career Development in Higher Education

It is now widely recognized that graduates need to develop employability and career management skills in order to enter and thrive in a global knowledge economy. *Personal, Academic and Career Development in Higher Education* shows how engaging students in personal and career development experiences can result in powerful insights that translate into enhanced skills and attributes useful in all areas of life.

Personal Development Planning (PDP) is a method of recording achievements, identifying strengths and areas for improvement, reflecting on progress and setting clear goals and action plans. *Personal, Academic and Career Development in Higher Education* explores PDP in relation to SOAR, a curriculum enhancement model used flexibly to integrate personal and career development with good academic learning and employability.

Packed full of useful practical features, this book enables readers to improve students' abilities to relate their learning and achievements to the requirements of both tutors and employers, and ultimately transfer and apply those abilities in future careers of lifelong learning.

Personal, Academic and Career Development in Higher Education is essential reading for anyone involved and/or interested in implementing PDP, career and employability approaches in higher education and will be of particular interest to academics, those working in central support services departments, external examiners, quality assurance officers and policymakers.

Arti Kumar is Associate Director of the Centre of Excellence in Teaching and Learning (CETL) at the University of Bedfordshire, UK, and is a National Teaching Fellow.

D0023874

Personal, Academic and Career Development in Higher Education

SOARing to Success

Arti Kumar

Routledge
Taylor & Francis Group

LONDON AND NEW YORK

First published 2007
by Routledge
2 Park Square, Milton Park, Abingdon, Oxon OX14 4RN

Simultaneously published in the USA and Canada
by Routledge
270 Madison Ave, New York, NY 10016

Routledge is an imprint of the Taylor & Francis Group, an informa business

© 2007 by Arti Kumar

Typeset in Times New Roman by
Florence Production Ltd, Stoodleigh, Devon
Printed and bound in Great Britain by
Antony Rowe Ltd, Chippenham, Wiltshire

British Library Cataloguing in Publication Data
A catalogue record for this book is available from the British Library

Library of Congress Cataloging in Publication Data
Kumar, Arti, 1946–
    Personal, academic and career development: SOARing to success.
  I. Title.
  LB1027.5.K78 2008
  371.4′2–dc22   2007025392

ISBN10: 0–415–42359–7 (hbk)
ISBN10: 0–415–42360–0 (pbk)
ISBN10: 0–203–93834–8 (ebk)

ISBN13: 978–0–415–42359–5 (hbk)
ISBN13: 978–0–415–42360–1 (pbk)
ISBN13: 978–0–203–93834–8 (ebk)

For Bal, unintentionally instrumental in the formation of my own career identity; and for Sanjeen, Umesh and Manoj: perfect proof of my SOAR principles

Contents

Illustrations

Figures

Tables

Foreword

We live in a world where change is exponential and we are helping to prepare students for jobs that don't yet exist, using technologies that have not yet been invented, in order to solve problems that we don't know are problems yet. In short, we have a responsibility to prepare our students for a lifetime of uncertainty, change, challenge and emergent or self-created opportunity.

It may sound dramatic but the reality is that the majority of our students will have not one but several careers. They will have to change organizations, roles and identities many times. Many will have to invent their own enterprise in order to earn an income or create and juggle a portfolio of jobs requiring them to maintain several identities simultaneously. Most will be part of organizations that periodically have to transform themselves in order to survive and prosper. Preparing our students for a lifetime of working, learning and living in uncertain and unpredictable worlds that have yet to be revealed is perhaps one of the greatest responsibilities and challenges confronting universities all over the world.

Thinking about such things raises different questions to the ones we normally consider when we talk about employability, which tend to focus on what people know and understand now, rather than the sorts of capability, attitude, thinking and creativity that will enable them to prosper in an indeterminate and unknowable future. Ron Barnett argues that the essential features of performance in such a world are:

> understanding (how do we develop the knowledge to learn?), self-identity (what are the unique set of qualities, abilities, attitudes, behaviours and beliefs that we bring to our engagements with the world?) and action (what repertoire of actions give us control over our own destiny?).[1]

Barnett and Coat[2] criticize higher education for its preoccupation with a knowledge and skills agenda, while ignoring the fact that what really matters is an individual's will to get themselves out of bed in the morning to tackle the challenges the day will bring and have the confidence to do something useful with their knowledge and skills. 'Our main consideration has to be what I am calling a "being for complexity." . . . The dispositions of enquiry for surviving, for engaging with will, with enthusiasm, in this extraordinary world we are in.'[3]

The introduction of Personal Development Planning (PDP)[4] in UK higher education in the year 2000 represents a system-wide policy-driven attempt – grown from a small practice base – to focus more attention on the learner as an individual with a unique identity and set of qualities, dispositions and motivations that enable her to be and to act in this crazy world. But PDP is no more than a framework for learning through reflection and action. It needs to be given life, purpose and meaning by students and teachers as they interpret and use the ideas it contains in different learning contexts.

It is in the animation and meaning-making of PDP that SOAR has much to offer. SOAR stands for Self, Opportunity, Aspirations and Results. It is a comprehensive tool to help teachers operationalize and contextualize the ideals of PDP. Different parts of the tool have the potential to promote personal enquiry, the discovery or re-discovery of *self* and the *building of identity* through participation and active engagement with *opportunities* for learning within and outside the curriculum (so much useful learning gained from experience outside the formal curriculum is ignored in higher education). The learning processes that the tool supports helps learners to develop realistic *aspirations and intentions* that can motivate and help them achieve the *results* they desire and help grow confidence in their own ability to meet future challenges.

In discovering what SOAR is trying to do I was reminded of Stephen Covey's inspiring vision of 'self' consciously interacting with the world:

> Between stimulus and response there is a space.
> In the space lies our freedom and power to choose our response.
> In those choices lie our growth and our happiness.[5]

It seems to me that SOAR can help us become more aware of our decisions, actions and their consequences in responding to the continuous stream of possibilities, opportunities, challenges and problems we encounter every day of our lives.

But it is not just an isolated view of self that SOAR encourages. Embedded in the concept is a social constructivist view of learning in which an individual's understandings are shaped and developed further as a result of interacting with others in work, study, play and other social situations. This chimes well with growing interest in more holistic concepts of the higher education experience as a means of preparing learners for a lifetime of living, working and learning in a complex world – regardless of the disciplinary contexts in which they learn.

PDP was proposed and developed to open up new ways of helping students prepare for an increasingly complex and uncertain world. The implementation of PDP is a 'wicked problem'. By that I mean the problem or challenge continually emerges from all the technical, informational, social and cultural complexity that characterizes teaching and learning. Such problems cannot be solved through simple, rational, standard solutions because the problem definition and our understanding of it evolve as we continually gain new insights and new potential solutions are implemented. The creation of SOAR is a novel solution to the implementation of PDP based on the author's insights and experiences gained in facilitating PDP and guiding students in their career decision making.

When I helped develop PDP policy in 1999 I believed that it had the potential to put students as self-regulating independent learners at the heart of the higher education enterprise. The reality has been that PDP processes often emphasize the instrumental features of action planning, record keeping and reflection on action and performance, while other important features of self-regulated learning are often implicit and happen by default rather than design. All too often little consideration is given to the richness of the underlying motivations, values, beliefs, personal creativities and identity that underpin the sense of self-efficacy that drives and energizes what we do, particularly when we encounter the unknown. I am impressed with the possibilities that SOAR provides for recognizing and valuing the intrinsic motivations of learners rather than the extrinsic motivation of teacher assessment that currently overwhelms students' experiences and perceptions of learning in higher education.

SOAR is intended to inspire and if you are inspired by concepts it will certainly cause you to think about how you would facilitate the use of the ideas in your own teaching and learning contexts. Arti Kumar is to be commended for creating a tool that raises the profile of self in an academic world that all too often wants to treat learning and individuals' engagements with it as an abstract, emotionless experience, rather than the personally meaningful, emotion-rich experience it really is.

Professor Norman Jackson,
Director, Surrey Centre for Excellence in
Professional Training and Education, University of Surrey

Preface

This is a book about SOAR – a curriculum enhancement model you can use flexibly to integrate personal and career development with good academic learning and employability. SOAR is an acronym for **S**elf, **O**pportunity, **A**spirations and **R**esults: all essential, mutually supportive and dynamically related elements within this model, and I use it hereafter as shorthand for a process of personalized, holistic development. SOAR is not meant to devalue or compete with existing initiatives – rather to provide a complementary rationale and framework within which students can construct personal real-life relevance. The acronym itself is simple and positive.

The model allows much flexibility at local level in the sequence of delivery and interpretation of its variable elements. My aim is to enable staff in higher education (HE) to – in turn – enable students to achieve more of their potential. You can use many suggestions here to advance your own professional development while you apply the model for students' needs. You can tailor it to your subject or occupational field, or to the needs of special groups such as mature or international students.

Individuals can personalize this process to suit their circumstances and aspirations, through inbuilt requirements for reflection, action, analysis and lateral thinking. The focus on **S**elf enables individuals to discover and build their unique identity positively and proactively, through effective participation in learning **O**pportunities both within and outside the formal curriculum, and to form realistic personal **A**spirations based on sound information, achieving more intentional **R**esults as they move towards and beyond transition points.

In the diversity of student populations today we see the whole spectrum of abilities, attitudes and aspirations. Some may be capable of absorbing skills by osmosis from role models and their environment, but students' choices and chances of success are subject to many external variables – both assets and constraints. Enabling all students to realize their potential in line with realistic aspirations is too important to be left to chance or individual choice. Engaging them in formal experiences, using appropriate methods and resources, can result in powerful insights that translate into enhanced skills and attributes useful in all areas of life. The central focus here will be on developing students towards graduate-level employability and lifelong learning.

I have interpreted and broken down SOAR into a series of four thematic developmental stages (around the synergy within and between Self, Opportunity, Aspirations and Results), which iteratively build on each other. Each stage is facilitated by specific inquiry, information and guidance. The themes provide structure, direction and coverage for the design and delivery of formal interventions in curricula – equally applicable to programmes of study, modules/units, course components or assessment tasks. They are underpinned by a principled and productive set of concepts, and associated with practical learning and assessment activities that have worked with my students across different universities and subject areas.

Engaging students with SOAR elements in a coherent and continuous process (as set out in this book) can empower them to take control of, and deal constructively with, the variety of factors that influence their personal, educational and professional success in 'an age of supercomplexity' – a term coined by Barnett (1999) to express the idea that the information age has brought us a surfeit of data associated with *complexity*, but a situation of *supercomplexity* means that we are also faced with multiple frameworks of understanding, of action, and of self-identity (p. 6). He recognizes that every discipline and institution is currently challenged to educate 'for the formation of human being that is going to be adequate to conditions of supercomplexity' (p. 154).

There is no doubt that we need to prepare students better for transition into a world where work, life and employment conditions are changing, career concepts have changed, and students themselves have changed. Our practices in HE must accordingly shift their focus. My interpretation of SOAR elements is consistent with contemporary labour market realities, an emerging new personal and career management culture, and the needs of higher education institutions (HEIs) having to respond to new demands. In these circumstances, SOAR can lead to life-changing benefits for students themselves, for the institutions in which they study, the occupations they enter, the employers they work for, and for society at large. Can those of us who work in HE afford not to respond? This book does not just say 'why we should' but 'how we can' – but we will start, in Chapter 1, by looking at some specific drivers for 'why we should'.

Acknowledgements

The intellectual concepts and functional examples that have shaped this book come from many different sources over several years: my thanks go out to my students in three different universities, and my colleagues at the University of Bedfordshire and at the Association of Graduate Careers Advisory Services (AGCAS), the Centre for Recording Achievement (CRA), the Higher Education Academy (HEA), the British Association for Psychological Type (BAPT) and the Association for Psychological Type international (APTi). There is so much collective wisdom, so generously shared (especially at AGCAS) and this book is written in the same spirit of sharing and building on such material.

In particular I would like to thank my colleagues Rob Carman, Mark Atlay and Eileen Scott for their support and encouragement. I am immensely grateful to Peter Norrington for proofing and commenting on my drafts and organizing the references. In the course of writing I have been helped by guidance from editorial staff at Routledge, Taylor & Francis – Sarah Burrows, Meg Savin and Katherine Davey; and more recently by staff at Florence Production in Devon, UK.

For their specific contributions and permissions I wish to thank all those mentioned below:

Angus McDonald, for his guidance on the use of Profiling for Success materials – see www.teamfocus.co.uk for details on obtaining and using these useful online tests and questionnaires on Learning Styles and Type Dynamics Indicators.

Bill Law, for permission to reproduce his career-related figures and to interpret his theories in my own way.

Chris Jackson for allowing me to build exercises around materials with the permission of AGCAS, the copyright holder. For the latest version of this material, see www.prospects.ac.uk/.

Carl Gilleard and Dorothy Spry for providing specific quotes via personal email communication with me.

Diana Hawkins of OPP, for her advice on referencing OPP materials. OPP Limited is a company registered in England, with its headquarters at Elsfield Hall, 15–17 Elsfield Way, Oxford, Oxon OX2 8EP, UK. www.opp.co.uk.

Helfried Waleczek, for writing an insightful commentary (for inclusion in Chapter 6).

Jamelyn Johnson of CAPT for her advice and permission to reproduce 'Thinking about mental habits' (from *People Types and Tiger Stripes*, 3rd edition, by Gordon D. Lawrence); the 'Type and Communication' questionnaire (from *Talking in Type* by J. M. Kummerow, 2002); and free access to useful online material at www.capt.org/using-type/workplace.htm (see Chapter 7), Center for Applications of Psychological Type, Gainesville, Florida, 1993.

Joanna Myhill, for the information literacy self-audit questionnaire.

Julie Blant, for allowing me to present an outline of her research findings (in Chapter 12).

Katie Scott of Miles Morgan, Australia, for permission to visit and link to the Australian Blueprint for Career Development website – see www.milesmorgan. com.au/.

Linda Ernst, Linda Berens and Melissa Smith for permission to reproduce two excellent figures related to team work (7.2 and 8.2, in Chapters 7 and 8).

Maggie Sumner and Dr Helen Jones for contributing a case example (in Chapter 9).

Nancy Betz for sharing her research findings on 'career decision self-efficacy' and her copyright CDSE manual (see Chapter 10).

Neil Fleming, for permission to use the VARK Learning Styles materials from a link online, or in paper format, © Copyright Version 7.0 (2006) held by Neil D. Fleming, Christchurch, New Zealand and Charles C. Bonwell, Green Mountain Falls, Colorado (Chapter 6).

Norman Jackson for writing a brilliant Foreword for the book.

Peter Hawkins for permission to adapt and use his ideas and some of his material (Chapters 2 and 4).

Taylor Nelson Sofres, for providing a job advertisement and granting me permission to reproduce it as an exercise for students (in Chapter 11).

Dr Tom Angelo, for allowing me to link to his Teaching Goals Inventory (TGI).

The assignment briefs and marker sheets are similar to those I previously authored for a web-based learning resource; they have been reproduced here with permission from the University of Reading.

Figures 2.4 and 2.5 have been published on the HEA website in A. Kumar (2004) *A Resources Guide to PDP and the Progress File* (permission has been granted to reproduce these).

Finally, and essentially, this book would not have been written without the umpteen dinners cooked by my husband while I was researching, and writing, and . . . in need of sustenance – thanks, Bal!

Acronyms and terms explained

ABCD	Australian Blueprint for Career Development
AI	Appreciative Inquiry
AGCAS	Association of Graduate Careers Advisory Services (UK)
AGR	Association of Graduate Recruiters (UK)
BAPT	British Association for Psychological Type
CAPT	Center for Applications of Psychological Type (USA)
CDL	career development learning
CDSE	career decision self-efficacy
CMS	career management skills
CPD	continuing professional development
CRA	Centre for Recording Achievement (UK)
CV	Curriculum Vitae (Resumé in the US)
DLHE	Destinations of Leavers from Higher Education
DOTS	Decision learning, Opportunity-awareness, Transition skills, Self-awareness
EBL/IBL	Enquiry/Inquiry-based Learning
EI	emotional intelligence
FRBS	financial and related business services
GDP	Gross Domestic Product
GWB	General Well-being
HE	higher education
HEA	Higher Education Academy (UK)
HEIs	higher education institutions (i.e. universities and colleges of HE)
HESA	Higher Education Statistics Agency
HR/HRM	human resources/human resources management
ICTs	information and communications technologies
LCR	Life-Career Rainbow (a graphic representing Super's life-span, life-roles approach to career)
LSI	Learning Styles Indicator
NLP	neuro-linguistic programming
PDP	Personal Development Planning (a UK government agenda for HE)
PFIG	Progress File Implementation Group

PPAD   personal, professional and academic development
QAA   Quality Assurance Agency (a government body set up to ensure
          standards are maintained according to quality criteria in the HE
          curriculum)
QCA   Qualifications Curriculum Authority
RoA   Record of Achievement (the national Record of Achievement was
          launched by the UK Government in 1991 to motivate and support
          personal and career development planning all through life, but it
          has been used mainly in the schools sector)
SDS   Self-Directed Search
SMEs   small and medium-sized enterprises (usually classed as those with
          fewer than 50, or between 50 and 250 employees respectively)
SOAR   Self, Opportunity, Aspirations, Results (a process model for
          integrating personal, career and academic development – and the
          main formula for this book)
SWOT   Strengths, Weaknesses, Opportunities, Threats
TDI   Type Dynamics Indicator
TGI   Teaching Goals Inventory
USEM   Understanding (of subject), Skilful practices, Efficacy (beliefs),
          Metacognition
VARK   Visual, Auditory, Read/Write, Kinaesthetic (styles of learning)
VLE   virtual learning environment
WBL   work-based learning

Assessment centres: usually the last stage in an employer's recruitment process, where candidates are put through a set of activities that are carefully observed and assessed according to pre-defined job-related criteria.

Behavioural competency: effective behaviours defined against key job performance criteria, enabling trained assessors to collect objective information about candidates through various tests and exercises at assessment centres.

Criterion referencing: a student's performance or grade is assessed by comparing his or her achievement against clearly stated standards or criteria for expected learning outcomes. It is not determined by comparison with 'performance' of other students.

Formative assessment: identifies a student's strengths and development needs with the aim of giving feedback (usually in words rather than grades) to improve them.

Ipsative assessment: a measure of an individual's present performance compared with 'personal best' performance in the past – generally arrived at through self-assessment.

Meta-skills: generic over-arching ability – e.g. self-awareness or self-assessment skills enable students to reflect and identify their level of ability, interest and use of other skill-sets such as communication, IT, problem solving, etc. Meta-skills are therefore vital in understanding the extent to which skills can transfer between one context and another.

Summative assessment: generally in the form of final results, marks or grades given at the end of a module, unit or course, allowing the learner to move on to further study or training.

Part I

A theoretical and applied model

Integrating and enabling personal, career and academic development

Chapter 1

Introduction

Working in UK HE for the past ten years, I have been part of the many debates and challenges we are facing as a result of external agendas and internal pressures to prepare students for life and work in our times. Throughout the 1990s academic and support staff have been drawn into the increasing desire and drive to produce more 'rounded graduates' equipped to work in rapidly changing, high-tech workplaces, in a global knowledge economy. Many of us are designing and delivering innovative curricula to address these issues and to meet the increasingly diverse needs of different stakeholders, driven by increased governmental and institutional pressures. Often we are working with a smaller unit of resource to meet the expectations of large numbers of 'non-traditional' students in the context of widening participation policies, globalization and internationalization.

In 1996 the Council for Industry and Higher Education (CIHE, 1996) said, 'Most British people, most educators and most students now believe that it is one of higher education's purposes to prepare students well for working life.' Dearing (1997) made influential recommendations that stressed key skills and work experience. Further reports followed (e.g. Jackson, 1999; Knight and Yorke, 2003a), steering the HE system towards greater responsibility for the employability of graduates.

My experience is therefore based on responding to a series of UK reports and initiatives, the most significant of which is the Progress File, which defined requirements for all HEIs to offer Personal Development Planning (PDP) opportunities for their students. PDP is 'a structured and supported process undertaken by an individual to reflect upon their own learning, performance and/or achievement and to plan for their personal, educational and career development' (QAA, 2001b). Although the main general PDP principles were centrally prescribed by government (more fully discussed in Chapter 2), there is much scope for developing university-wide, innovative, local approaches.

Such flexibility challenges all of us who work with an increasingly diverse student population in HE to decide what will be feasible and effective in our situations, and experiment with it. A number of related initiatives (e.g. e-portfolios, career management skills (CMS), employability, work-related or work-based/

practice-based learning, transferable skills and transcripts, entrepreneurship, professional development) seem to be jostling with PDP for position within HE.

These initiatives are often approached as disparate interests and abilities, involving as they do new players or refocused staff roles with different perspectives. Staff on a university-wide basis can contribute to PDP as a 'structured and supported process', and academics accustomed to teaching subject disciplines have usually been given responsibility for developing and coordinating initiatives. Engaging students in PDP processes is very different to teaching a subject, however. It is also different from 'training', which starts with professional or employer needs. If anything, the subject is the 'self', and the process may be collectively enabled in real or virtual environments, but needs to be uniquely realized by each student.

In this respect, PDP can form the core of any learning and teaching strategy, because all learning requires an investment of 'self', and this investment is best thought of as being generic or trans-disciplinary. This involves using student-centred pedagogy, giving feedback, motivating, effective questioning, facilitating self-help through dynamic interaction – it does not rely on a one-way flow of telling and instructing. The tutors are there primarily to enable learners to locate and utilize their own resources and strengths.

The implementation of PDP is raising many issues: What is the structure? Who should support/lead? How should the key terms and concepts be presented to students, to reflect contemporary needs? What is the common ground on which curriculum approaches can be constructed? What strategies will encourage students to engage – to reflect and record their achievements, exploit the resources and support available, develop a range of skills and derive the wide benefits intended by PDP? Can disparate needs be met and integrated within a single coherent, structured model? Do they lend themselves to course design and delivery consistent with HE academic values? I believe they can and do. This book addresses such issues.

PDP benefits should be operational across the UK HE sector by now, but there is much anecdotal evidence to indicate varying degrees of success and failure. A number of recent developments are still adding impetus to PDP: Burgess (2004) recommends that the Progress File/PDP framework be incorporated into new degree classification systems that provide a more detailed transcript representing student achievement in more meaningful ways for employers and other stakeholders. At the time of writing there is much anecdotal evidence that PDP concepts are spreading across Europe as well, and transcripts are likely to evolve as they feed into the 'Bologna process' which is seeking to make academic standards and qualifications more comparable and compatible throughout Europe.

The Leitch Report confirms the increasing importance of 'economically valuable skills':

> In the 21st Century, our natural resource is our people – and their potential is both untapped and vast. Skills will unlock that potential. The prize for our country will be enormous – higher productivity, the creation of wealth and

social justice. The alternative? Without increased skills, we would condemn ourselves to a lingering decline in competitiveness, diminishing economic growth and a bleaker future for all. . . . This challenge is formidable. . . . There is consensus that we need to be much more ambitious, and a clear message that the UK must 'raise its game'. . . . We must begin a new journey to embed a culture of learning. Employer and individual awareness must increase . . . this will be the best investment we could ever make.

(Leitch, 2006: 6,7)

These issues are not confined to the UK – a great deal of money, time and effort has been invested in attempts to transform HE by governments the world over. They want the curriculum to foster in graduates (citizens and workers) the skills and personal qualities needed to both compete and collaborate in a global knowledge economy. The global marketplace is paralleled by the 'internationalization of HE' – a phenomenon that has arisen due to the increasing mobility of students and graduates worldwide. HE curricula must value diversity *and* create unity.

Rationale

Although this book is grounded in UK experience, the SOAR concepts on which it is based are widely applicable and relevant. I am aware through collaboration and consultations with educators in the USA, Canada, Australia and Western Europe that similar conceptual frameworks are used marginally in many culturally 'Western' countries. However I believe that the potential of the SOAR model to empower all students is not widely utilized within mainstream curricula. My interpretation can stimulate new ways of delivering the model to students, and can be replicated in developing countries too, as they have similar needs within a global knowledge economy.

The skill-sets and concepts involved in personal, professional and academic development (PPAD) are not mutually exclusive – there is considerable harmony, synergy and transferability in the relationships and dynamics between them. That synergy can be conceptualized and animated by the SOAR process, but first we must create a shared understanding of its concepts and clarify what seems to be an increasing complexity and diversity of demands.

In essence these requirements boil down to nothing more or less than the need to develop each student as a whole person, to enable individuals to find and lead the lives they want to live (as long as their aspirations are not illegal, immoral or unhealthy!). This book invites you to engage your students in more holistic development, through a SOAR model that enables them to value and exploit learning derived from a wide range of experiences and opportunities, and to view learning broadly for the linked purposes of personal growth, intellectual ability and preparation for future careers of rapid change and lifelong learning.

Through a focus on 'meta-learning', SOAR can provide solutions for key issues:

- enabling students to learn about learning: to assess their own learning in and through multiple contexts and identities;
- bridging across what seem like disparate and competing agendas;
- meeting the needs of different stakeholders (staff, students, employers, government);
- clearing conceptual confusion, which often acts as a barrier to productive partnerships;
- delivering holistic and integrated development to all students, leading to aspirations of lifelong learning and (graduate) employment;
- integrating initiatives that engage both staff and students in PDP–CPD (continuing professional development) processes;
- generating pedagogy and practical learning tools that result in holistic development applicable in all areas of life.

Readership

I speak to you, the reader, assuming you are in some way involved and/or interested in implementing PDP, CMS and employability approaches in HE. The book will be most relevant and useful if you are an academic: lecturer, personal tutor, coordinator or researcher; or if you work in a central, support services department: a careers professional, learning support /education developer, librarian or counsellor; or if you are an external examiner, quality assurance officer or policymaker.

External stakeholders (e.g. employers, professional bodies, policymakers) will gain ideas of what is being done and can be done to enhance curriculum development, and how they can contribute.

Staff working in other sectors (further education, schools) and in related departments such as work-based learning (WBL), placement offices, volunteer bureaux and job shops should find that the SOAR concepts and applications give their work a new coherence and relevance.

You should find material of interest in this book regardless of prior knowledge and experience. No specific ability will be assumed, but for the activities to work a conviction of their relevance and value, and an ability to facilitate (and model) optimistic developmental processes will be required. In sharing my experience of resolving the many tensions that can occur in this area, I hope you will find your own ways of integrating these principles into the design and delivery of interactive approaches that suit your subject, students and circumstances. As you apply this model you will gain a fuller understanding of content and process, and your students will bring the model to life with their personal experiences.

A parallel process and dual benefit is at work here, as subtext. If you use the SOAR model for students you will be able to apply the same principles to your own personal and professional development. The new UK National Professional Standards Framework proposed by the 2003 White Paper, *The Future of Higher Education*, has been launched by the HE Academy. It calls for the sector to demonstrate defined activities, core knowledge and values in supporting student learning. The intention is to apply it within CPD requirements for academic staff in HEIs, as is the case in most other industries.

When you are seen to be involved in and supportive of CPD processes yourself (for instance as preparation for your career reviews or performance appraisals), students perceive the value of PDP processes (reflecting, recording, improving) in a new light. They see the relevance of forming good habits that will have a tangible pay-off in the future as well.

In this respect, survey findings reported by Michael Arthur in *New Careers* resonate with me:

> Our exploration suggests that affirming the new careers, promoting knowledge accumulation, seeking out career communities, getting ahead of the problems and following the progress of people's career journeys can all be helpful to the individuals we seek to serve. So can seeing for ourselves the same career possibilities we see for others. Let us have fun, work well, learn new things, and support each other as we go. Let us be part of the new career landscape as well.
>
> (Arthur, 2003: 9)

In broad and general terms personal and career development may be thought of as a fundamental human need. Without doubt you will have applied the principles described in this book in your own life by default, if not by design; you therefore have the potential to engage learners in developmental processes, and may already excel in doing so. There are challenges, however. Many of us may have got our present jobs through random, unplanned experiences and influences, varying in the extent of their usefulness and relevance. Most of us grew up in a world where graduate jobs and their corresponding 'career ladders' were not as elusive as they seem today. We are under pressure now to go beyond the sort of happenstance we may have experienced, and to provide structured approaches that will progressively empower students to thrive in a rapidly changing, more uncertain world.

Relationship between 'SOAR' and 'DOTS'

SOAR is my broad, eclectic interpretation of a model which will be familiar to careers professionals in the UK, where it is popularly referred to as DOTS or new-DOTS, and typically understood as an acronym for Decision learning, Opportunity-awareness, Transition skills and Self-awareness. In practice the 'DOTS' are not usually 'joined up' in this order, however – a more logical way of introducing students to the elements within the structure of careers programmes is usually in the following sequence, which assumes that students need to develop skills and knowledge in these four areas:

1   **Self-awareness**: '. . . awareness of the distinctive characteristics (abilities, skills, values and interests) that define the kind of person one is and the kind of person one wishes to become.'

2   **Opportunity-awareness**: '. . . awareness of the possibilities that exist, the demands they make and the rewards and satisfactions they can offer.'

3   **Decision learning**: '. . . increased ability to make realistic choices based on sound information.'

4   **Transition skills**: '. . . increased ability to plan and take action to implement decisions.'

(Watts and Hawthorn, 1992)

Central to both the SOAR and DOTS models is the reflective-active dynamic between Self and Opportunity, the internal world of the self interacting with and reflecting on the external world of opportunity. The latter is a place to conduct inquiries, develop skills and experience, generate, clarify and test aspirations and achieve desired results. It is in making these connections that Aspirations (the A of SOAR) are formed and implemented, and Decisions are made (the D of DOTS). The Results achieved (the R of SOAR) through this process are implemented in particular at Transition points (the T of DOTS). The main result we are aiming for in HE is to enable students to develop their potential in a more holistic sense, towards graduation and beyond. In the SOAR model, Results drive personal change, transfer and transition skills, closing the feedback loop to a higher level of self-awareness.

The DOTS model is underpinned by social science theories that have evolved over the past century, attempting to explain career choice and identity in relation to changing times and perspectives (Watts *et al.*, 1996). The *new*-DOTS version recognizes that the DOTS cycle is not a one-off process at the point of transition from university; rather DOTS processes are recurrent in our times, when transitions within and between jobs are more frequent. There are current attempts to develop or generate career theories even further. I adopt a critical approach to theories in this book (and with students). I use them sometimes to inform practice, and often to encourage reflection, discussion and critical thinking. They are not to be regarded in a strict scientific sense as 'received wisdom'.

The DOTS model gives rise to both the process and content of many career development learning (CDL) programmes. The SOAR variant aims to:

1   re-focus DOTS in line with contemporary concepts and needs;

2   broaden the CDL framework to integrate personal, professional and academic development, thereby enhancing employability;

3   interpret SOAR elements against a broader range of theories, case studies and survey findings, focusing on positives (see next section);

4   link theoretical concepts with practical examples for you to experiment with in class and online;

5   show how appropriate pedagogy can develop a range of skills and attributes without diluting academic standards.

SOAR and the principles of Appreciative Inquiry

I like the notions that come from Appreciative Inquiry (AI) for their applications in positive self-development. Originally developed by Dr David Cooperrider and Suresh Srivastva (1987) in a paper they published at Case Western Reserve University in the US, AI was applied to organizational change, asking 'What is working well – and why? How can we replicate or do more of this, to create more successes in the future?' These questions are less threatening than a deficit model that asks 'What's wrong, and who is to blame? How shall we fix the problem?'

While the AI approach does not ignore problems, it sees 'problem solving' and 'conflict resolution' as deficit approaches that unduly emphasize negative issues. When people focus on identifying things that are 'wrong' and 'correcting problems' they ultimately slip into a negative culture of fault-finding and criticism. One approach many of us will be familiar with is a SWOT analysis, which attempts to identify both positive and negatives – Strengths, Weaknesses, Opportunities and Threats. AI reframes this to become a SOAR approach that focuses on the positives – Strengths, Opportunities, Aspirations and Results. The differences between SWOT and SOAR are mainly those of vocabulary and emphasis, but these differences can add up to much better attitudes and outcomes.

When I encountered the action research process and principles of AI it struck me that it was in harmony with the approach I was using. When students use SOAR to discover their strengths, they can align optimistically with opportunities that are suitable, generate aspirations congruent with their identified 'profile' and achieve better results. AI works by asking participants about their achievements, what has worked well for them or is working well now, and carrying their best practices (known) to travel forward into the future (unknown).

As Marcus Buckingham says in his books *The One Thing You Need to Know* (2005) and *Now, Discover Your Strengths* (Buckingham and Clifton, 2001), sustained individual success comes from both focus (on strengths) and the ability to filter the complex information and choices available in today's world of super-complexity. Finding, naming and claiming their strengths enables students to both focus and filter, to aspire and make appropriate decisions, and achieve effective results at transition points.

A word of caution: although I advocate focusing on strengths, we should not ignore our development needs. The focus on assets does not gloss over or underestimate the external constraints that often limit or determine our own and students' choices. I experienced this at the end of my degree (many years ago) when I was advised by a well-meaning programme leader to apply for high-flying, mega-buck jobs – all of which were impossible to reconcile with responsibility for my three boys, and restrictions on my ability to travel or move house. I was grateful for her interest in me and her confidence in my abilities, but there it ended.

For students who have disabilities or special needs, there is a wealth of information and guidance available in careers services and learning support units – but students need to have these services explained and signposted so that they feel encouraged to access relevant help early on. Through a SOAR process they may discover both the nature of their need and a means of accessing their inner resources. There are ways of dwelling positively on what is possible and what students can do rather than wallowing in problems and what they cannot do.

Assumptions underpinning the SOAR model

- Students are unique individuals full of potential.
- The world is full of opportunities, but access to these is unevenly distributed and differentially available to individuals.
- There is no single predetermined 'opportunity' that suits an individual in every way, and conversely there may be many choices that are suitable and possible.
- How students draw on their potential to seize different opportunities depends mainly on their motivation, ability and personality.
- To interact with the world in an effective way and make informed choices, students need to enhance self-awareness and self-efficacy in relation to external reference points such as tutors' expectations and employers' requirements.
- Focusing attention on each stage of the SOAR process as an optimistic inquiry and 'subjective reality' can make it 'appreciate in value'. A strong sense of self gives students a way of using holistic potential, a means to filter out unsuitable choices and to focus on those that fit them.
- This is a recurrent process, in a changing world. They will need to be flexible and review strategies as appropriate, but use their unique (and changing) profile to continually act as a guiding 'map' in their journey through life.

Structure of chapters

In Chapter 2 I define SOAR principles in relation to key concepts, intentions and implications related to PDP, CDL, employability and skills agendas. In the UK, staff working in these and other subject and functional areas could (and in some HEIs have) come together to collaborate in implementing PDP. However, conceptual confusion often acts as a barrier to productive partnerships in delivering the integrated benefits envisaged by the PDP agenda. This brings with it a fundamental need to coordinate, and create a common vocabulary with which to discuss and implement the main aims. For the purposes of this book, it is also fundamental to realizing the potential of the SOAR process.

The SOAR model has provided a structure for programmes I have designed and delivered successfully with students across many disciplines in different universities. In Chapter 3 I give an outline of a generic, accredited and assessed module designed for the penultimate year of degree programmes. I indicate how this can be tailored to meet the needs of different subjects, give examples of congruent teaching, learning and assessment methods, and suggest a way of scaling it up or down to different levels of study.

The SOAR elements then lend structure to the rest of this book. The focus on 'Self' (the S of SOAR) in Part 2 enables individuals to develop a range of skills and attributes associated with 'self-awareness'. This is essentially about articulating one's strengths within a 'Self-MAP' that can be used to navigate stages in the journey through life (Chapter 4). MAP provides an opportune acronym – it stands for Motivation, Ability and Personality, the main facets of an individual profile. Chapters 5, 6 and 7 are devoted to each of the MAP elements in turn.

The focus on Opportunity (the O of SOAR) in Part 3 takes 'Self' into the external world, and enhances the skills associated with 'opportunity-awareness': exploring and exploiting options, to learn and develop. Students analyse the extent of fit between their identified profile and the requirements of various options, occupations, organizations, industry sectors and alternative opportunities that are realistically available to them (Chapter 8). In a broader global sense students need to understand the demands of the changing world in which they will be implementing their aspirations (Chapter 9).

The formation of realistic and achievable Aspirations (the A of SOAR) in Chapter 10 puts the spotlight on decision-learning, making choices in learning and in work that are based on sound information about Self matched with Opportunity. The processes of decision making, problem solving, researching and action planning are shown to be intimately connected and capable of improvement.

The SOAR process is punctuated by means-goals or Results (the R of SOAR) and culminates with end-goals at the transition stage for life beyond university. At that point results gained through the SOAR process need to be demonstrated – through self-promotion on applications and self-presentation in person (at interviews and assessment centres). This stage draws together all the previous elements (Chapter 11).

Finally, Chapter 12 is about transfer skills, review and further development. As 'self' looks back to look forward and measure results (the 'distance travelled' or 'value added' by SOAR) we tutors also need to seek feedback and evaluate the impact of our interventions.

Style, content and pedagogy

This book draws upon a wide range of concepts and examples to show how curricula can accommodate practical activities with an evidence base. Due to the encompassing nature of the SOAR framework, I adopt a broad-brush approach with references to more in-depth reading if you want more information. Each chapter contains exemplar material, making connections between theory and its applications, suggesting practical activities and reflective exercises that are based on skills audits, survey findings, case studies, readings and Internet material – linked to constructively aligned outcomes and pedagogy. I encourage you – and students – to take a critical stance to theory, to test it against real-life experience.

Facilitating students through a SOAR process of reflective and experiential inquiries provides a way of scaffolding student development (Vygotsky, 1978) investing in 'self as hero in the journey of life' thereby developing self-efficacy (Bandura, 1997), self-regulation (Zimmerman, 2001) and intentionality (Bereiter and Scardamalia, 1989). These are essentially social and personal constructionist approaches to learning, where subjective realities and opinions are constructed through and within encounters with others in different social contexts (Berger and Luckman, 1966). The pedagogy lends itself to action research, and has been used and evaluated with different groups of individuals, in both real and virtual learning environments (VLEs). The methods may be innovative for some, but are not extreme or difficult to incorporate. They are offered in the spirit of AI as indicative and flexible inquiries: as you and your students apply them the results 'appreciate in value' through the SOAR process and ideally achieve balance or congruence between elements.

I use many external reference points to inform individuals' SOAR reflective processes – bringing together perspectives from employers, students and tutors. I have found that my careers colleagues have the necessary dual focus to mediate between perspectives, especially between students and their futures, between HE experience and employers' requirements – and I am grateful to many who have shared their knowledge and stories generously with me. To illustrate the points I make I have occasionally used examples from my own life-career pathway. As such this book represents the place I currently occupy in my thinking and I hope this corresponds with the 'state of the art'. I encourage you also to use your career trajectory as a reference point, and of course get students to use theirs.

As PDP requires students to write about themselves in reflective accounts, I sometimes model a more personal, conversational and informal style of writing here than may be usual in academic publications. As a result there are different voices and viewpoints in the book, and a change of voice is signalled by icons that act as navigational beacons. The voice can change from autobiographical to descriptive to analytical to pragmatic and to speculative, depending on the material and its purpose. I hope this variety will generate ideas rather than prove disconcerting.

The following icons are used to alert you to exercises directly addressed to students, and to signal what that type of exercise might require.

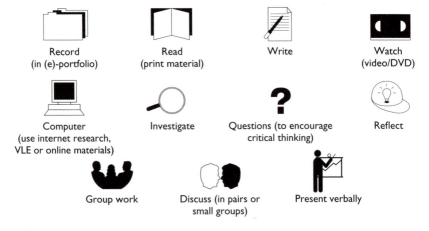

Record (in (e)-portfolio)   Read (print material)   Write   Watch (video/DVD)

Computer (use internet research, VLE or online materials)   Investigate   Questions (to encourage critical thinking)   Reflect

Group work   Discuss (in pairs or small groups)   Present verbally

The book also has a companion website, www.routledge.com/professional/ 978041542360-1, where you will find some sample worksheets that you can download as pdfs and use with students, figures in colour you may wish to project in order to support, illustrate and develop ideas or exercises, and live links to relevant websites and online resources mentioned in this text.

SOAR can bridge the divide in conceptual terms between disciplines, and between terms such as academic, vocational, personal and professional – and integrating between bipolar positions is a key success factor in implementing the model. The development of skills in all these areas can be those of a higher order, as you will see throughout this book. We can apply quality standards and pedagogical principles to personal and career development as to any other subject.

Chapter 1: Summary of main points

- SOAR is a process model for holistic, integrated and personalized learner development.
- SOAR is related to a range of concepts – chief of which are the DOTS framework, widely used for careers education, and Appreciative Inquiry.
- The model can provide solutions for many issues facing HE today, and has been developed, tried and evaluated over the past few years as a response to requirements in the UK for HEIs to deliver the Progress File/PDP agenda.
- This book is for you if you are interested or involved in designing, delivering or formulating policy for HE curricula – anywhere in the world where pedagogy needs to be enhanced to deliver personal development, career management skills and employability.

You will find in this book:

- (re)-definitions of key terms and concepts in the context of our times, with a focus on contemporary working conditions;
- an inclusive conceptual framework for personalized development, under-pinned by theories that give your work an intellectual evidence base;
- practical applications of the model, as it gives rise to both content and process that can be integrated into course and programme design;
- a reconciliation of skills development with pedagogical issues in HE;
- a practical resource, with ideas and activities you can adopt or adapt and use with students;
- examples of teaching, learning and assessment methods that engage students in developmental processes, enhance employability and self-efficacy;
- suggestions for further reading and references to useful, freely accessible web-based materials.

Chapter 2

Defining key concepts and principles

Are we speaking the same language?

My main aim in this chapter is to foster a shared understanding of the language, rationale and framework within which SOAR can be used to design or enhance curriculum approaches to integrated development. In conversation with others I have usually assumed we are talking about the same thing when we use familiar terms such as 'career', 'career development learning', 'work' or 'vocational guidance' – until I realized with something of a shock that we need to explicitly redefine such terms to reflect the complexity of the context in which individuals now have to choose and proactively manage their work, life, study and leisure activities.

Carry out a 'thought experiment' for yourself, or discuss and try this with a colleague. Try this in introductory sessions with students, too. What do each of the words in Table 2.1 mean to you? Write this in the left-hand column. Return and write revised definitions in the right-hand column when you have read the next section – see if your perspectives have changed.

Table 2.1 Key concepts and meanings

What do these concepts mean to me? Here's my definition:	*An agreed definition after discussion and reading the sections below:*
Career:	
Work:	
Personal development:	
Career development learning:	
Employability:	

The shift in concepts of 'career'

When clarifying this for students I ask them to discuss some assertions one might make about 'career', e.g. a career is:

a   an occupation or profession I will enter when I graduate;
b   a job for the young and upwardly mobile;
c   a pathway or progress through life or history, involving a sequence of life and work experiences;
d   a lifelong process of developing skills and personal qualities that I can transfer between a range of work and project tasks, study and leisure activities.

They score points with me if they choose c and/or d: both these perspectives fit with the labour market realities of our times. They reflect significant differences from earlier definitions that narrowly equate 'career' with the terms job, vocation, profession or occupation – i.e. paid employment. Career is now increasingly being viewed very broadly as a 'lifelong and life-wide career' in which paid work may be central, but is just one of many roles played out in the course of an individual's progress through life.

Super, a major theorist of occupational choice, began to formulate ideas of life-span, life-space career development from the 1950s onwards, so this perspective is not new. However, we continue to use the same words for 'career', 'work', etc. – although the concepts have changed. Super usefully placed the role of 'worker' in perspective (Super, 1990), by viewing a career as a sequence of nine life roles or positions occupied by a person (child, student, leisurite, citizen, spouse, home-maker, parent, worker and annuitant/pensioner) in the course of five life stages (growth, exploration, establishment, maintenance and decline) in four

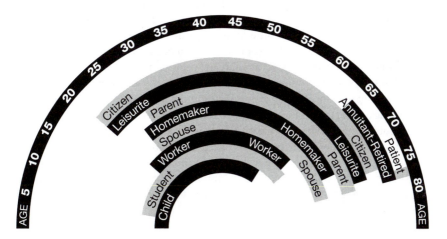

Figure 2.1 Super's life-span, life-space approach to 'career'.

principal theatres of life (home, community, educational institution and workplace). These are graphically represented in the Life-Career Rainbow (LCR) (Watts *et al.*, 1981: 28)

? While Super's ideas are consistent with the broader definition of career, do you agree with his LCR representation of the rigidity and predictability of life stages in relation to life roles? For each age band you have passed through, do you find any correlation between the ages suggested and your own activities at that life stage?

Super later revised his delineations of life stages and life roles to accommodate the repeated transitions between work and other life roles that are now common across the lifespan. He also recognized that a major career decision consists of several mini-decisions; and individuals recycle through several mini-cycles of tasks and stages as a result of changes – some planned and some forced on them. You may wish to compare his theory with others I outline later.

In fact it is possible to look at 'life-career' concepts through the lens of many different philosophical and historical perspectives. For example, if you are teaching English literature, ask your students to find out and compare the LCR with the seven ages of man Shakespeare speaks of in *As You Like It* (2. 7. 139–67):

> All the world's a stage,
> And all the men and women merely players:
> They have their exits and their entrances;
> And one man in his time plays many parts,
> His acts being seven ages.

Super's correlations do not fit my experience and that of many others in contemporary life, especially women. In my early twenties I found myself switching from full- to part-time jobs, paid to unpaid work, as I had three boys to raise by my third wedding anniversary. I had previously worked in India as a magazine journalist, and then for an international airline as a stewardess, but moving from India to the UK meant I had little knowledge of the local labour market, little confidence in returning to it after some years of domesticity, and my qualifications from India were not recognized at equivalent levels in the UK. So I went back to my books when my youngest son started school. My experience of HE in the UK opened many doors for me. Being a late entrant to stable work (and something of a late developer), here I am working harder than ever when I could be retired.

Students too may choose to prioritize any of these roles at different life stages, against a backdrop of changing needs and circumstances. You can use the LCR as a tool to raise discussion about their career planning needs at their particular life stage. For example, if they are young adults they are probably still at the 'exploration' stage. This is fine, but they will soon need to develop clarity and focus in order to establish an aspiration they can implement by the time they graduate. They are faced with often complex and dynamic relationships between personal roles, choices and values: between employment (of various types), training, organizational change and government policy. For mature students HE may be an element of life rather than a distinct life stage. Concepts about age have also been radically reconstructed in our times, especially due to the demography of many developed countries that have an aging population.

Some international perspectives on 'career' and CDL

I was delighted to discover lucid affirmation of my broad perspective on 'career' and CDL when I came across papers written to make the case for 'a lifespan career development framework or blueprint' in Canada, and more recently in Australia. Thousands of people in these countries have been involved over 14 years in developing, piloting, evaluating, revising and implementing nationally agreed standards for modern career competencies and frameworks. *National Career Development Guidelines* (NOICC, 2001, 2004) for the US began to be formulated in 1986 and were later adapted for Canada's *Blueprint for Life/Work Designs* (NLWC, 1998, http://blueprint4life.ca/).

To complement and extend the success of the Canadian Blueprint, the Australian Blueprint for Career Development (ABCD) subsequently provided a means of mapping, unifying and coordinating the CDL efforts of different education sectors and the provision of careers services across Australia. Significantly the ABCD concludes:

> Lifelong career development learning is a key global strategy for economic success this century [and] . . . Investment in the development of the ABCD will reap the rewards of economic growth as a result of a population well-equipped with appropriate skills and competencies to be successful life/career managers.
>
> (Miles Morgan Australia, 2003: 14)

Modern conceptions are convincingly explained by Straby, for example:

> Work is now defined not by occupational titles or categories, but by skills and values. Effective career builders know how to shape and build their careers, project by project. This is a new competency, still largely unrecognized by most adults in the workforce.
>
> (Straby, 2002: 6)

If 'career' is more inclusive of skills, values and experiences from different life roles and life stages, this has implications for provision in HE for careers education, career development learning or career management skills – terms often used interchangeably by careers professionals. In your thought experiment above did you define CDL as 'learning to manage one's life, learning and work over the lifespan'? Recent researchers have redefined career development as involving 'one's whole life, not just occupation. . . . It concerns him or her in the ever-changing contexts of his or her life . . . self and circumstances – evolving, changing, unfolding in mutual interaction' (Wolf and Kolb, 1980, cited in McMahon *et al.*, 2003: 4).

The changed definition of 'career' makes it the unique possession of the individual, not as a job – such as a job in the legal profession or financial services sector, that can be objectively defined and measured – but as a subjectively experienced life-career which is increasingly likely to include many jobs in relation to other roles. Such a perspective implies that HE is an important developmental phase in students' life-careers. In terms of inclusion and diversity, this conception of the CDL process in HE can be meaningful for all students because *everyone* has a life-career, regardless of age, ability, disability, social and cultural background, aspiration or employment status.

Jarvis (2002) similarly explains the shift in meanings:

> The career management paradigm is not so much about making *the* right occupational choice as it is about equipping people with the skills to make the *myriad* choices necessary throughout their lives to become healthy, self-reliant citizens, able to cope with constant change in rapidly changing labour markets and maintain balance between life and work roles.

Jarvis goes on to outline the new High Five principles of contemporary CDL (ibid: 3) – see Table 2.2. Alongside I have listed some questions that arise from the principles.

Table 2.2 'High five principles' of CDL . . . and some questions

The new 'high five principles' of CDL	Some questions about HE practices
Know yourself, believe in yourself and follow your heart.	Do you 'teach' self-awareness, self-assessment, self-belief and self-efficacy? To what extent?
Focus on the journey, not the destination. Become a good traveller.	Do you emphasize engagement and positive participation in a developmental process, given that HE is an important phase in students' life-career journeys?
You're not alone. Access your allies, and be a good ally.	Do your students demonstrate good interpersonal behaviours, build effective relationships and create productive workplace contacts?
Change is constant, and brings with it new opportunities.	Do you enable students to assess and manage 'change as opportunity rather than threat', and to grasp suitable developmental opportunities in the light of their needs?
Learning is life-long. We are inquisitive by nature, and most alive when we're learning.	Do you see why HE should be a foundation for lifelong learning, and encourage a positive response to learning from a range of experiences?

SOAR has the potential to bring Jarvis's High Five principles to life in HE. The model is also consistent with the knowledge-age career competencies formulated in the North American and Australian Blueprints, which are attempting national coordination of quality approaches based on lifespan notions of self-managed CDL for all their citizens. However, since my interpretation of SOAR was essentially developed to fit with the PDP national government agenda for UK HEIs, it is time to take a closer look at the main tenets of PDP.

The PDP agenda for HEIs in the UK

A clear adoption of redefined career concepts is not explicitly present in work undertaken in the UK, as in the North American and Australian Blueprints. The implied emphasis of PDP is on *personal* development, although career planning and the enhancement of academic learning are also clear expectations. Partnerships between academic and central support services are recommended but not pre-scribed. To address the need for clarity and coherence and to 'benchmark' careers education in UK HEIs, in 2002 I initiated a robust national process of consultation, working with the Association of Graduate Careers Advisory Services (AGCAS) Careers Education Task Group in order to develop an agreed Careers Education Benchmark Statement (AGCAS, 2005). It became clear through this exercise that in practice some careers services had been brought centre-stage within PDP-related initiatives, while others were struggling to carve out a niche in relation to the currently dominant PDP agenda, which was being interpreted and implemented in many different ways.

The UK Progress File and PDP initiative is based on ideas that emerged from the National Committee of Inquiry in Higher Education (Dearing, 1997) and subsequently gained definitions, policy intentions and recommendations for phased implementation within a set timescale (2001–6), with sector-wide consultation and agreement.

In essence the relevant recommendations were:

* to make the outcomes and value of student learning more explicit;
* to support the principles of lifelong learning.

The Progress File Implementation Group (PFIG) devised guidelines (QAA, 2001b) to support HE practitioners in developing and implementing their own related policies and practices. Although the generic term 'Progress File' suggests that it is a document charting an individual's development, the overall concept is much more complex and contains three interrelated definitions and expectations:

1 **The transcript** is a formal, comprehensive and verifiable certificate or record of the student's achievements, to be provided and accredited by the HEI (by 2002/3); a means by which students can monitor, build and reflect upon their personal development.

2 An individual's **personal record** of learning and achievements, progress reviews and plans – which can be used as source material for self-promotion, e.g. for applications to employers, admissions tutors and others. It is the student's responsibility to maintain this as part of a holistic formative process, to plan for self-development and monitor progress towards achieving goals. The expectation is that HEIs will provide e-learning tools for students to create e-portfolios.

3 **PDP** is defined as 'a structured and supported process undertaken by an individual to reflect upon their own learning, performance and achievement, and to plan for their personal, educational and career development.' The idea is to enable learners to identify, articulate and evidence their skills, knowledge and personal attributes, to enhance their progression through learning and work, and to provide other stakeholders (e.g. employers) with the information they require. The provision of a system for delivering PDP was to be developed and defined by individual HEIs, and 'the policy objectives should be operational across the whole HE system, and for all HE awards by 2005/06'.

The **primary objective** for PDP is to improve the capacity of individuals to understand what and how they are learning, and to review, plan and take responsibility for their own performance, helping students to:

- become more effective, independent and confident self-directed learners;
- understand how they are learning and relate their learning to a wider context;
- improve their general skills for study and career management;
- articulate personal goals and evaluate progress towards their achievement;
- develop a positive attitude to learning throughout life.

There are considerable parallel benefits for both staff and students, because PDP can:

- assist with widening participation, retention, progression on course and beyond university;
- achieve goals in relation to employability;
- reinforce the value of the subject discipline in a wider context;
- explain the concept of transferable skills and develop them practically;
- encourage teamwork and group cohesion;
- produce more self-reliant and motivated students;
- enable staff to discharge their 'duty of care' and record the support provided;
- help to 'market' the subject department.

The relationships between PDP, CDL and employability

When PDP requirements were formulated in 2000, I welcomed them because I subscribed to all those principles before they became a government agenda and a bandwagon. It has not been easy to implement them, however, because the common ground and conceptual relationships between PDP and other related initiatives are not explicitly defined in PDP documentation. Key players still need to create a common conceptual map that will encompass PDP, CDL and employability outcomes, and most HEIs need to agree an infrastructure where accountability is shared for developing, updating or enhancing programmes and resources.

By now you may know what I am going to advocate – yes, we can do this within the SOAR framework! To build conceptually towards this model let's bring 'employability' into the picture.

? Take a look at Table 2.3. What relationships and common intentions can you tease out from comparing these official definitions?

Intentions and implications

If you are attempting to integrate and deliver the intended benefits implied in the definitions in Table 2.3, teasing out the relationships and commonalities between

Table 2.3 A comparison of definitions and intentions: CDL, PDP and employability

Career development learning/careers education/career management skills:	Personal development planning is . . .	Employability is . . .
'. . . formal processes that empower individuals to identify, develop and articulate the skills, qualifications, experiences, attributes and knowledge that will enable them to make effective transition into their chosen futures, and manage their careers as lifelong learners, with a realistic and positive attitude.'	'a structured and supported process undertaken by an individual to reflect upon their own learning, performance and achievement, and to plan for their personal, educational and career development' (as defined by national UK *Guidelines for Progress Files*, QAA, 2001b).	'a set of achievements – skills, understandings and personal attributes – that make graduates more likely to gain employment and be successful in their chosen occupations, which benefits themselves, the workforce, the community and the economy' (Yorke, 2004).
Definition agreed by UK careers professionals in HE during a consultative process of benchmarking careers education, and published in the Careers Education Benchmark Statement (AGCAS, 2005: 2).		'a journey with staged outcomes, requiring knowledge, skills, attitudes, experience and the ability to network.' (Peter Forbes, Vice President, Association of Graduate Recruiters, UK, workshop definition.)
		The Skills*Plus* project's USEM account (see Chapter 2, Section 3).

them becomes essential. Attempting to unpack the concepts raises questions for practitioners such as: What skills and attributes need to be developed? How should we structure formal interventions in HE that will enable each student to develop those they need? How can we ensure we provide at least a consistent, minimum level or standard of development for all?

The concept of a *structured journey* or *formal developmental process* is typical and common across all definitions given above. Formal delivery of PDP requires 'a structured process', but a widely understood structure has not been specified and agreed. I am aware through interaction with colleagues that the lack of clarity has created many ongoing tensions and confusion: a split between process and content, fragmentation between programme levels, sectors and contexts. PDP is also intended to be 'a *supported* process', but lack of shared understanding about structure has resulted in potential key supporters often asking: 'Where do I fit with PDP as a structured process? How can I contribute?' Or worse still, 'Why are my (potential) contributions not recognized/incorporated/rewarded . . .?'

Another feature of our times is that the boundaries between 'work', 'training', 'education' and 'time out' are becoming increasingly blurred. In our ever-changing environment the ability to learn from different experiences becomes increasingly important. Students must become more discerning in evaluating their skills and abilities as portable benefits that they can apply and develop through a range of opportunities. They must seize suitable options, and take personal responsibility for making the most of them. Moreover one must assume that if students' activities are more planned than random, benefits and skills-development can be identified in every phase and area of life, and be promoted more readily by them. For immediate practical purposes this is especially important at the point of transition beyond university.

Graduate recruiters, especially in the UK, value generic, transferable skills developed through a variety of curricular and extra-curricular activities. Applicants are expected to give examples of competencies acquired from different types of experiences, to demonstrate they are balanced individuals. During HE the onus is on each student to exploit opportunities within and outside the curriculum to develop skills according to his or her interests and capacity. The view from a large retail employer, for example, is 'I believe that given all the opportunities that university life provides, responsibility for employability lies squarely with the individual.' Students do, however, need to be made aware from induction onwards of the range of opportunities available, and why and how they should use them to build their extended curriculum vitae (CV).

Our practices still often give students the impression that it is sufficient to get a good degree; or, going further, to choose an occupation and gain the qualifications required for entry to it. Although these still remain important goals for careers guidance and for HE in general, the really important end-game is equally to 'teach skills and attributes' in the broader life-career context, because this will largely determine success and progress in individual life-careers. 'The key in the workplace as in life is not just finding the right job, friend or life partner: it's *becoming* the right worker, friend or life partner' (Jarvis, 2002: 7). This is very closely aligned to be(com)ing a good learner in HE. I commend Harvey's (2003) emphasis in approaching employability 'as a range of experiences and attributes developed through higher level learning'.

Practitioners in the UK are often concerned that CDL and the type of support for employability offered in HE may not be appropriate for international students. However, research findings reported by Harvey and Bowers-Brown (2004) indicate that expectations of graduates the world over are very similar due to increased mobility in a global knowledge economy. In some countries qualifications by themselves are viewed as sufficient evidence of employability; in others, where graduate attributes other than academic ability are also explicitly sought, 'skills' have been integrated into the curriculum in various ways. Cross-country comparisons show that concepts and measures of employability may differ but there is much common ground in approaches, and 'a growing need for a model of generic skills that is recognized internationally' (Cranmer, 2006: 170).

SOAR and skills terminology: core, key, transferable, generic, hard, soft?

The skills vocabulary has grown in volume and complexity to the point where agreeing a single model seems difficult if not impossible. In every such survey it is apparent that there remains a lack of common language on skills between HE and employers (Bennett *et al.*, 2000). An analysis of skill requirements for graduate entrants to financial and related business services (FRBS) reports that:

> There is currently a wide disparity in interpretation and use of the 'language of skills' by different stakeholders, and a general lack of consensus on defini-tions for skills terminology. . . . This lack of clarity confuses the messages being sent to potential graduate employees and to HEIs and makes it difficult to identify exactly what employers want. . . . The result is that, despite appearing to utilize a common language of skills in dialogue, FRBS employers and UK HEIs, and even employers among themselves, are often speaking at cross-purposes on the topic.
>
> (FSSC, 2006)

Some recruiters, particularly the Civil Service and Armed Forces, are very clear on the attributes they are seeking, while others use vague or subjective words such as 'hardworking' or 'common sense'. Even a cursory look at recruitment litera-ture will show that employers use 'skills' as shorthand for a range of behaviours and attitudes, and this is a feature of their 'competency-based approach to recruitment'.

So what can you do in a situation of such ambiguity? For the purpose of providing a skills-rich curriculum I believe it is unnecessary to get pedantic about skills and hung up on buzzwords, jargon or precise employer-specific definitions.

The point about jargon is that it is gobbledygook to some and an in-language to others. The field of personal and career development is not jargon-free either, and there may be abbreviations and words used in this book you need to look up in 'Acronyms and Terms Explained', despite my attempt to use plain English. I do not avoid these words altogether though, because it is important for us and for students to understand the language employers speak (often perceived as business buzzwords). Students will then be at a distinct advantage when they start job-hunting.

There is no reason to be put off by a skill label as long as you give students ways of identifying what type of capability you (and employers) are talking about, *what it looks like in actions and behaviours*, and how they can map their competencies to jobs, occupations and employer organizations. There is a sense in which 'employability' is the unique possession and requirement of an individual – and SOAR emphasizes each student's responsibility for defining this at a personal level. At various points throughout this book I have included self-audits that link the competencies expected in ideal learning with the typical competencies required for employability, and these provide important external reference points against which students can assess their current attributes and develop their potential.

I think it is perfectly valid to think of grouping similar skills for the sake of showing how they appear in contextualized skilful practices. For example, students must discern that they are developing information literacy, written communication, problem solving, critical thinking, analysis and evaluation skills (to name but a few) when they research and write essays and reports at university. They must also discern that any given 'skill label' can look very different within a specific occupation, employer organization or industry sector. For example, negotiation, assertiveness, influencing, written and oral presentation, etc. may all be subsumed under the umbrella term 'communication skills' – and these are required in various ways in different jobs. To deal with this complexity, it is far better to make students proactive and enable them to analyse in depth exactly what *they* will need, but not to spoon-feed them with precise information. It would then simply be your job to facilitate and support the process of their investigations – referring them to relevant resources, etc.

My attempt to list skill-sets from different sources is presented in Table 2.4, with the aim of unravelling these skills through the chapters that follow.

Relationships between different skill-sets

You will see that the skill-sets in the columns of Table 2.4 represent academic, career-related and employer points of view. It is not difficult, however, to bridge the conceptual gaps between these skill-sets, or at least to show how they are mutually supportive and not diametrically opposed. I have been in groups where subject tutors brainstormed the attributes they desired in an ideal learner, and they were almost identical to those that employers seek in an ideal employee. In a

Table 2.4 Skill-sets

1 Traditional intellectual skills developed in HE *Curriculum Authority (QCA) UK*	2 Key Skills recommended by the Qualifications careers education	3 Career Development Learning/Career Management Skills/	4 Skills and attributes graduate recruiters say they want (AGR, 2006)
• Critical evaluation of evidence • Research and information literacy • Ability to argue logically • Apply theory to practice • Model problems quantitatively and qualitatively + other degree-specific and/or occupation-specific skills relevant to the subject field. These are contained in Subject Benchmark statements (QAA, 2001a) and Employability Profiles (HEA, 2006) developed by UK Subject Networks. Many HEIs accept it is their responsibility to develop not only intellectual skills but also a range of 'soft skills' for transfer to work and future life N.B. In fact even academic activities develop many generic key skills.	• Improving own learning and performance • Communication • Application of number • Problem solving • Working with others • Information and communication technology (N.B. These skills were initially defined by the QCA and applied to UK secondary schools, but they can be equally further defined at HE and postgraduate levels.)	**'Self-awareness'** Self-assessment Self-esteem Self-efficacy Self-management **'Opportunity awareness'** Critical awareness of options, occupations and other opportunities related to one's degree, skills, abilities, interests and personal preferences; an understanding of the changing world **Aspirations** Forming and implementing aspirations, making decisions, setting realistic goals, action planning **Results** Demonstrating results through self-promotion and self-presentation – on paper and in person (communication and presentation skills). (N.B. CMS key skills in bold follow the SOAR sequence)	• A good degree: often specify 2.1 or above for graduate schemes • Commitment and drive • Self-management and motivation • Team effectiveness • Communication and self-presentation skills • Customer focus • Problem solving • Managing own learning and career • Commercial awareness • Planning and organization • Leadership • Numeracy • Cultural sensitivity • Computer literacy • Project management • Report writing • Risk taking/enterprise

separate exercise, we looked at the skills that can be developed by traditional academic teaching and assessment methods – and discovered their close relationship with generic key skills. I will return to these in later chapters and show how to make these links explicit for students. This is important because most students and graduates do not perceive or promote them convincingly during the competitive selection process for graduate jobs.

Principles and features of SOAR

In the third column of Table 2.4 you will see the SOAR model expressed as CDL competencies. The themes that emerge from this column enable students to assess the extent to which they possess the skills in the other columns, and to understand how they might transfer from one context to another. These are overarching, generic 'meta-skills', as they are not in themselves subject-specific, or occupation- or industry-related. Extending this last point leads me to explain an important principle of the SOAR model.

SOAR Principle One: expressing SOAR elements as enabling 'meta-skills'

'**Self-awareness**' skills are an important means by which students 'can reflect, identify, analyse, personalize and make better use of any other particular skill. If you are a careers professional reading this, you will be accustomed to working at the interface between different skill-sets, explaining them and getting students to make connections between their personal abilities and those required by various chosen 'opportunities'. This ability to think laterally and make connections is central to job choice, job search and employability. It is the 'connective glue' between different perspectives (self, peer, tutor, employer) as well.

Analysing and rating the level of ability one has in various skills such as communication, IT, etc., is a key feature of planning for self-development, and in managing effective relationships with learning and with work. This addresses the subjective question for each individual: What are my strengths and what am I capable of achieving? Through realistic self-appraisal, learners can identify and capitalize on their strengths, interests, priorities and preferences. They can also capture and value attributes developed from extra-curricular experience, and understand the extent to which these might transfer into different options and occupations. Self-awareness can enhance self-efficacy and self-management – essential attributes in the less supported environments of our times, both in HE and in work.

Developing students' academic and vocational skills is not sufficient without CDL, as students then do not necessarily name and claim their strengths and limitations, and do not (by extension) engage in self-development to address their limitations. These meta-skills are by their trans-disciplinary nature transferable across a whole spectrum of life, study and work settings. Moreover, the transferability of other skills from one context to another is more readily understood when CDL processes complement and reinforce the development of the skill-sets in columns 1, 2 and 4 of Table 2.4.

The Skills *Plus* project[1] discusses four influences in employability (USEM[2]), summarized here and followed by my comments. USEM is the acronym for:

- Understanding (deeper than 'knowledge', relates to whatever subject is being studied).

Students also need to understand where their subject can lead them in future. Although subject knowledge is very important, many graduates enter unrelated areas of work and are likely to use the skills developed by their studies rather than the discipline content. Sixty per cent of UK graduate employers advertise vacancies open to graduates of any discipline (Graduate Prospects 2005–6, 2006, 2007). Due to the pace of change, knowledge becomes redundant ever faster, and the willingness and ability to learn, re-skill and up-skill are increasingly highly valued.

- Skilful practices (a term considered more appropriate than 'skills' as it avoids narrow notions and reductionist approaches to skills).

There is also a need to express these as behaviours and actions, so that they become observable and assessable in the same way that employers define the competencies they are seeking during selection, and at assessment centre activities.

- Efficacy beliefs (self-theories and personal attributes) are of critical importance: 'the extent to which students feel that they might be able to make a difference.'

SOAR, with its positive investment in 'self' typically enhances self-esteem, confidence and motivation, through its formative, supported methods of development.

- Metacognition (synonymous with 'self-awareness'): defined as 'the capacity to reflect on, in and for action.'

You will see that the SOAR model is entirely consistent with USEM principles, as you read on and apply it practically. Part 2 of this book in particular expands on concepts related to self-awareness, and provides exemplar material you can use to enhance self-assessment, self-esteem and self-efficacy.

'Opportunity-awareness' engages 'self' with the world of opportunity, which provides external reference points for self-appraisal. Learners become aware of the similarity between tutors' and employers' requirements, and are encouraged to explore the full range of options and occupations realistically available to them, in the context of the contemporary labour market. The importance of other sources of influence, help and information in their lives is acknowledged. This can result in enriching extracurricular experience, leading to new opportunities. It addresses their real-life concerns: Where will I suitably fit into the world out there? Do I understand how life and work are changing, and what new demands will be placed on me? How do I match up to these demands?

As mentioned earlier, a life-career may include education and training, any type of work, leisure activities and 'time out', so you should promote the value of engaging in a range of academic and extracurricular experiences (placements, part- or full-time paid or unpaid work, leisure activities) to develop competence in a planned manner. By adopting a holistic approach, you can enable students to identify and express the full value of their learning, from a broader range of opportunities. This is important because graduate recruiters often favour a well-rounded applicant with evidence of attributes derived from different areas of life.

Part 3 of this book focuses on 'Opportunity' and connects 'self' with 'opportunity' at the three levels students need to understand the term: (1) an ability to access immediate, short-term opportunities to strengthen skills and gain experience; (2) a more analytical assessment of the extent of 'fit' between their identified profile and a chosen occupation or alternative opportunity; and (3) a macro-level awareness of the demands made by our changing world.

'Aspirations': The process of forming achievable aspirations and making decisions should interconnect 'self-awareness' with 'opportunity-awareness' and lead to appropriate choices and actions. It addresses questions such as: Am I aspiring to enter work (or alternative option) that will use my strengths, hold my interest, meet my needs and allow me to express my preferences? Can I meet the entry requirements now or do I need to strengthen my chances? Can I manage my time to meet critical deadlines? The information needed to make complex decisions in our times is readily available, so deciding what is relevant and how to apply it is a key skill, and one that is needed time and again in a changing labour market. Decisions have therefore become more fluid and short term. It is useful for students to experience a rational, planned and complex decision-making process, but also to explore how people may actually adopt intuitive, opportunistic aspirations.

In its practical form decision learning typically appears in topics related to:

- identification of the personal factors that affect an individual's aspirations, and an understanding of strategies for making sound, informed choices – and that sound strategies should be progressively developed for future re-use;
- understanding connections between the process of decision making, problem solving and action planning;
- producing action plans that are personally relevant, achievable within a set time frame and capable of appropriate adaptation as circumstances change.

Part 4 of this book focuses on decision making, problem solving and action planning.

'**Results**' in the context of the SOAR process depend on the ability to learn from implementing aspirations and gain access to chosen opportunities. This stage in effect draws on all the previous elements, and also the student's understanding of how his or her 'profile' might transfer from one context to another. In some fields it is imperative to generate opportunities through building professional portfolios, networking and nurturing contacts. A range of job-search skills are required to justify and implement one's choices – often through a demanding selection process that can involve designing targeted CVs and covering letters, completing online or paper-based application forms, coping with telephone and face-to-face interviews and a range of assessment centre tests and activities. For those who intend to start their own business it involves market research, the ability to formulate a business idea and a plan, generate finance and create a network of business contacts.

Topics that address the transition concerns of students are:

- A critical appreciation of the recruitment and selection methods and media used by graduate employers (from both applicant and employer perspectives).
- Understanding and demonstrating the techniques required to present oneself with impact (in writing and in person). Demanding selection processes require high level communication skills, written and verbal.
- Effective approaches to seeking appropriate employment or learning opportunities.
- Coping with and managing change. Destinations of Leavers from Higher Education findings (Graduate Prospects, various years) and more longitudinal research studies (Elias and Purcell, 2004) show that aspirations take longer to implement, require perseverance and resilience.

Note that information of various types is integral to all the SOAR elements in different ways. For example, information about 'Self' is personally and socially constructed, through psychometric questionnaires and reflection, linked with feedback from others and real-life evidence. 'Opportunity-awareness' directly develops research skills, as learners retrieve and analyse information on jobs, occupations, employer organizations and industry sectors. Analysis and synthesis of information takes on paramount importance as part of the fact-finding and decision-making stage, taken one step further at the point of transition, when further research is required into employers and the work roles they offer. Information is complemented by support (e.g. careers guidance, personal tutorials, learning resources, learning support, counselling and diagnostic assessment, etc.).

SOAR Principle Two: theoretical and applied

SOAR is underpinned by a variety of discipline-based concepts and theoretical models. Parts of the process can be covered via one-off guidance interviews or partial coverage in the subject curricula, but the benefits of the whole process can best be delivered by inter-linking the two dimensions:

1 a knowledge-based, intellectually rigorous framework (using theories);
2 personal, applied skills – providing mechanisms for individuals to reflect, take ownership of the learning and apply it to manage their own unique life-careers, and to develop employability attributes.

These two dimensions together can satisfy the pedagogical requirements and quality standards of learning in any HE programme, including postgraduate level.

Career theory (and accordingly contemporary CDL) covers a lot of ground. However, there is little contradiction between the theories – they supplement each other – and the latest formulations (e.g. Career Learning theories by Law from 1997 to 2002) are mid-range or composite theories which indicate what career management entails: its psychological *and* sociological *structure*; and of how this can be changed – its *dynamics*. My approach to theory (as you will have noticed with Super's LCR above) is to take a critical and historical stance to its main tenets, and get students to consider its real-life applications. I will return to theories where relevant in the following chapters.

Returning to the earlier comparisons between PDP, CMS and employability, I would like to pick up on the concept of a journey or process that is common across the definitions. In this respect, I offer you SOAR as an inclusive process model that accommodates the needs of all students – see Figure 2.2 and SOAR Principle Three.

Reflection and action are in-built within SOAR

Figure 2.2 'Self' as hero in the journey of life.

SOAR Principle Three: a universal and personal process or journey

A defining feature of SOAR is that it functions at both a universal and personal level. In particular the relational dynamic between 'self' and 'opportunity', between the internal and external worlds experienced by individuals, offers timeless, generic and universally applicable themes. These can be presented as a collective process in diverse classrooms, and at the same time can be personalized by individuals. It is flexible enough for you to choose or emphasize subject- or occupation-specific topics and skills, as you judge necessary. Appropriate teaching, learning and assessment methods should accommodate the needs of diverse student or client groups, whether differentiated by age, gender, level of ability or ambition, background or subject discipline. Promoting equality of opportunity and valuing diversity are implicit values.

The journey to develop skills and attributes may be collective and generic (in group or classroom situations), but personal journeys are undertaken uniquely by each individual. This ownership by 'Self' is critical for success. It is imperative to give students a generic map and signposts to create personally meaningful routes through the journey. This requires a different approach from 'teaching a subject', where the starting point is a syllabus and the methods can rely on a one-way flow of telling and instructing. It also differs from 'training', which starts with professional or employer needs. PDP and CDL start with and focus on the individual 'self'. It follows then that interactive student-centred techniques should provide mechanisms for self-assessment, facilitating activities, giving feedback, motivating and effective questioning. Students will need to act, reflect, plan and personalize their learning, adapting it to their needs and aspirations. The responsibility is theirs to participate and derive the intended benefits.

Any choice students make in the journey through life (and HE is a phase along that pathway) is technically a 'career choice'. *They* should choose their goals in the knowledge that this will be a recurrent but dynamic process in a world where change is fast-paced and far-reaching. Your role is to facilitate ways in which students can develop high-level skills and attributes to map against 'graduate level opportunities'. It is valid for students to form their own idea of success – I would recommend you withhold value judgements about their aspirations and choices. At the same time you are in a uniquely influential position to empower them in making and implementing positive, ethical choices that reflect their level of ability and interest.

Undertaking the journey requires and develops a range of specific skills, awareness and attitudes, which can be defined at different levels and stages. We need to identify and foster these in classroom activities, encourage and model positive thinking, and create environments where learners can feel that 'there is no failure, only feedback'. We should accept that realistic self-assessment is complex and often challenging for students. Helping them to map their profile against employability and life skills creates a rationale that most students find motivating because they see the practical relevance. Self-, peer- and tutor-assessment, formative and constructive feedback all take on added significance and help to stretch students out of their comfort zones into a 'safe risk zone' where they can learn and grow.

A structured process

Next I would like to pick up on the need for 'a structured process', flagged up by the definitions in Table 2.3. SOAR gives us a linear structure, starting with 'Self' and going through a sequence which ties together both process and content. This is covered in depth in Chapter 3. For now, it gives rise to a different way of representing the sequence – see Figure 2.3 and Principle Four below.

SOAR Principle Four: Linear, Lateral and Cyclical: a structured process

The sequence in which SOAR elements structure programmes is based on the assumption that 'Self' engaged with 'Opportunity' leads to realistic 'Aspirations'

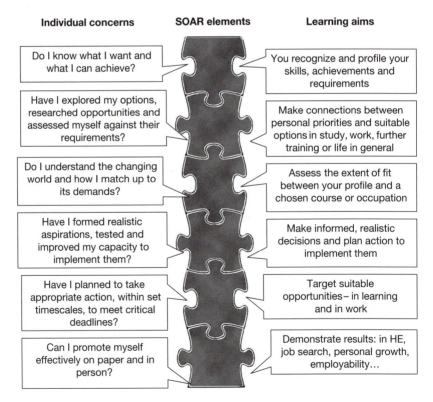

Figure 2.3 A linear structure for formal programmes or modules.

and effective 'Results', facilitated by specific information and support. The jigsaw graphic indicates that each piece is part of a wider picture.

In practice these components are highly interrelated, and one should not deal with each in isolation. It is the dynamic interplay and synergy between them that enables learners to apply the generic process and coverage to their personal life experience and circumstances. Making these connections is like putting jigsaw pieces together to take one's career-planning puzzle to a 'whole' new dimension. But the whole picture is not complete or static for long. SOAR may be linear and sequential for the purpose of structuring programmes, but 'self' develops, opportunities change, aspirations have to be reviewed for new results and transitions. SOAR is therefore cyclical for developmental purposes (see Figure 2.4).

SOAR Principle Five: present and future focus

SOAR processes connect the past to the future through a reflection-action dynamic. It can be a success spiral in action, bridging access to HE, success through levels of study, and progress beyond HE. Some students will have prior experience of compiling portfolios of evidence at work or in apprenticeships, or Records of Achievement (RoA) at school or college. This experience may or may not be perceived as useful but the potential of RoA is similar to PDP and the SOAR process. Much depends on how this potential is realized, how it is promoted and implemented. SOAR can make an immediate positive and holistic investment in

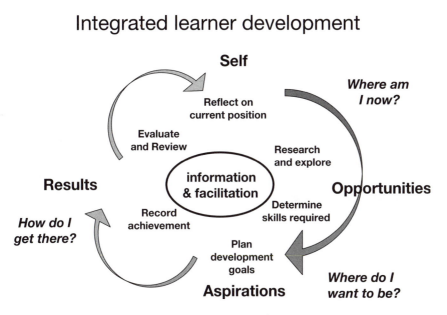

Figure 2.4 SOAR as a cyclical, developmental process.[3]

learner development, and its future focus provides a rationale and a trigger for students to engage in developing skills for life and work roles outside and beyond the immediate curriculum.

When evaluating results at the transition stage, the skills of reviewing and improving enrich self-awareness by reflecting on the experience of implementing career plans. This helps learners to refine and adapt their plans. It closes the loop and takes learners into the future – but also back to taking stock of 'self' once again (Where am I *now*?), presumably at a higher self-awareness level (even though their external 'career progress' may have stalled or declined).

We could view the SOAR elements or jigsaw pieces as parts of a whole picture but the picture is never complete and static and it will only ever be a snapshot in time. It will need frequent re-evaluation over a changing life-career, giving this process an iterative application, where individuals progressively revisit their plans and use the same process to manage their lifelong learning, career reviews, performance appraisals and CPD (see Figure 2.5).

Practical examples

It is important to avoid the risk of being trapped by models without any deep translation of them into meaningful interventions for students. The rest of this book develops SOAR themes and gives many examples to indicate how you might

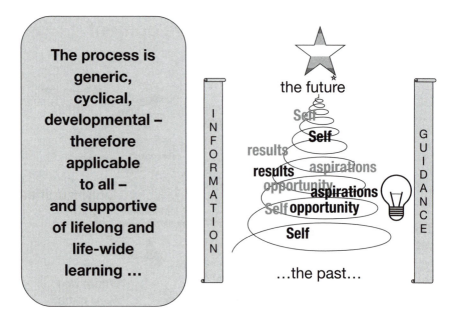

Figure 2.5 SOAR as an upward spiral of lifelong development.[4]

engage students. Here I have taken the generative potential of SOAR and turned it into a self-audit questionnaire (see 'It's *My* Journey through Life: Am I in the Driving Seat?'(pp. 36–41)). You will find a few different self-audits scattered as learning tools throughout this book. You can use them in various ways, with groups or individuals, as paper-based or computer-based exercises. Remember, however, that students' ratings represent their self-perceptions, and may also be influenced by what they perceive as being socially desirable and 'cool' in the eyes of their peers. The following essential points should therefore guide your own interpretation and your briefing to students:

Learning from self-audits

- Each statement represents an *ideal* end position, making your expectations explicit and clearly setting out end-goals as check-points. Each is therefore implicitly a learning objective.
- The statements alert students to what they need to do and develop in order to achieve the goal. They can be used to start discussion and reflection.
- Students should ask for clarification if they do not understand any of the words.
- Audits may be supplemented with case studies to illustrate the points further. These case examples may be built up and shared by students themselves as they progress, to show 'distance travelled' between start and end points.
- Self-audits serve a diagnostic purpose and are intended to be formative rather than summative self-assessments. The purpose for students is not simply to come up with a score. They should rate themselves honestly in order to derive a personal action plan to drive change towards improving their ratings.
- Students should know that we (they) are looking for potential and not perfection (arguably there is no such thing). In becoming competent, low ratings are to be expected and should be considered the raw material for development.
- You can reassure them their ratings will not be seen by you, it is for them to measure their own progress. You will try to provide (or refer them to) the means by which they can make that progress.

Debriefing and follow-up

- Audits can initiate useful reflection and discussion. Ask students to connect their ratings with real-life examples to substantiate their claims. Can they identify patterns of strengths from high ratings linked with evidence from their experiences? Can they similarly identify development needs from low ratings? Get them to discuss and plan exactly what they will need to learn and do in order to improve their ratings.
- Discuss the importance of particular behaviours and attributes. What would be the benefits of demonstrating these behaviours? What would be the consequences of not engaging?

- Negotiate or make clear the range of activities that may be involved. Create 'buy in' from students to participate in these, emphasizing the real-life relevance.
- Ask them how they would expect to engage in these activities during their module/course/HE experience, and gain their agreement and commitment to 'travel towards the intended destination' and the learning outcomes they need.
- Identify what stands in the way of full participation. Who and what can help, and how?
- You can get them to return to the questionnaire half-way through or at the end of your module or course to evaluate the extent to which they have progressed. This also helps you to evaluate your module, to measure the extent of its effectiveness. The audit then acts like a diagnostic, self-developmental and evaluative tool.

'It's *My* Journey through Life: Am I in the Driving Seat?' is adapted from the Self-Audit of Me plc,[5] based on the attitude of working with complete responsibility for yourself (very apt for today's less supported environments in HE and the workplace).

> When I was conducting training I would ask the audience who they worked for. After they told me the name of their employer I suggested that they may want to work for 'Me Incorporated'. After all, if I can no longer hold a manager or someone else responsible for my results, then I pretty much have to become totally accountable myself. Once we are in that place of accepting responsibility for our own results, we become very POWERFUL! This stuff really works! . . . Now that you own and control your own company, you are free to do whatever it takes in order to succeed. . . . The positive, mental decision to run your own life like a company has been the turning point for many top people. Make it!
>
> (Andrew Wood, author, and sales and
> marketing expert at Legendary Marketing)

It is congruent with the earlier reframing of career concepts too:

> emerging definitions of career and career development are reflective of a proactive, individual centred, lifespan, life/career management process where individuals are active in responding and adapting to change and in creating, constructing, designing and identifying paid employment opportunities, life and learning experiences that will enable them to create satisfying lives.
>
> (ABCD – Miles Morgan Australia, 2003: 4)

You will see that the items in the audit are framed within the SOAR model: the audit statements can guide the way in which you structure or develop your modules, courses or programmes. It can help to identify existing good practice,

It's *My* Journey through Life: Am I in the Driving Seat?

(Adapted from *The Windmills Programme*, Dr Peter Hawkins, Liverpool University Graduate into Employment Unit)

Rate yourself for each statement, along a scale from 0 to 4:

0 = not considered   1 = poorly   2 = partially   3 = adequately   4 = optimally

1) Self-Awareness/Self-Assessment/   **Ratings 0–4**
Self-Efficacy/Self-Management

A I can express the full value of my learning: the
   benefits I gain through my personal, academic and
   extracurricular experience (including part-time
   jobs, voluntary work, etc.)   _____

B I can explain how my interests and values relate
   to possible career ideas/intentions   _____

C I am aware of the strengths and limitations
   associated with my personality (styles, attributes)   _____

D I have an accurate, complete picture of my career
   profile – my unique mix of skills, experience,
   interests, knowledge and attributes – that makes
   me stand out in the employment marketplace.   _____

E I maintain comprehensive evidence which
   convincingly demonstrates my strengths and
   interests (e.g. a record of achievement, an updated
   CV, portfolio, examples of major achievements)   _____

F I can build and maintain a positive self-image, and
   realize how this influences my life and work   _____

G I have high-level self-management skills (I can
   effectively organize my time and workload)   _____

H I am able to accept and learn from both success
   and failure in a positive manner   _____

2) Opportunity

A I am aware of how my degree and subject
   knowledge are perceived in the graduate job-market   _____

B I have examined how my current mix of knowledge,
   skills, priorities and experience could be applied to
   different options after university   _____

C   I understand how my essential skills can transfer and develop from one situation to another   _____

D   I am building up a clear picture of the type of work I am likely to enter when I graduate   _____

E   I know what level of skills and knowledge will be required to progress and grow in my area of interest/expertise   _____

F   I can explore and take advantage of opportunities on offer – at work, within the community, socially and through my current higher education experience   _____

G   I recognize the benefits and limitations of pursuing particular career paths (e.g. that there are diminishing jobs in certain industry sectors)   _____

H   I understand the changing world of work   _____

I   I have assessed my response to the demands made by the changing world of work   _____

3)   Information and Support

A   I regularly seek and use feedback from people at all levels regarding my performance – e.g. my peers and tutors have given me objective feedback on my strengths and areas for development   _____

B   I can retrieve, evaluate and make effective use of careers information from a range of print and internet sources – e.g. I know where to look for my chosen job vacancies and employers, and can analyse occupational/course descriptions, job advertisements, person specifications, etc.   _____

C   I make the most of my support network – people who can inform, advise and help me achieve my objectives   _____

4)   Aspirations (Decisions and Plans)

A   I can make informed decisions for the short and longer term, based on a realistic assessment of my core strengths, motivations, experiences, assets and constraints   _____

B I am aware of internal and external factors that
can help or hinder me (e.g. my own limitations or
funding decisions out of my control) _____

C I continually set myself practical, specific career
development objectives with measurable outcomes
and defined timescales. These are broken into
manageable steps and written down, but are flexible
and reviewed regularly _____

D I am able to adjust my goals and timescales in the
light of changing circumstances _____

**5) Results (Implementation, Transition Skills,
Review and Improvement)**

A I understand the methods different employers
use during a typical recruitment process _____

B I can make clear connections between my
'career profile' and the requirements of various
options and opportunities realistically available
to me _____

C I can clearly express my strengths and motivations
through written or visual communication (e.g.
targeted CVs, letters, applications, project
proposals, a portfolio of work) _____

D I am confident at orally promoting the benefits I
can bring to a situation (i.e. good interview and
self-presentation skills) _____

E I have undertaken work experience in my chosen
occupation, or in a related area _____

F I am prepared for the demands that can be made
by assessment centre activities _____

G I continually seek to develop my skills and
expertise to enhance my employability _____

YOUR RATINGS

If you scored mostly 4s: you're very focused, aware of your strengths and opportunities, flexible in a changing world and a self-starter, with all the hallmarks of a true lifelong learner.

Action: Keep going – what you're doing is not a static process, so you will still need to maintain your ratings and focus on continual improvement in your journey through life.

Mostly 3s: You're well on your way to effectively managing your career and lifelong learning.

Action: Take another look at your ratings. Ensure you understand where the gaps are and develop a plan of action to address areas that need development.

Mostly 2s: You're doing well, but are you making the most of the opportunities to manage your learning and career?

Action: You may wish to consider: How can I be more proactive? Where are my real obstacles? Do they revolve around time, ability, resources or motivation? Can someone help me develop an action plan?

Mostly 1s: You may be good in certain areas, but you need to think carefully about how you can be more proactive, confident and motivated.

Action: Like many people you have capability but you need to work on the consistency of your approach. Positive steps to improve may include: taking time out for reflection, finding a mentor, building your network and researching future opportunities available to you.

Mostly 0s: You have a long way to go, but you have the opportunity to benefit greatly from the PDP and CMS learning opportunities provided for you.
Take action as suggested for 'Mostly 1s', see above.

where these needs are already being met, and pinpoint elements that are missing or inadequately covered.

It is important to brief and debrief students, as above, when you administer self-audits. This particular audit alerts students to what they need to achieve in order to take control of their life-career direction, and to prepare for transition beyond HE (items focus on capacity to enter graduate-level positions).

This self-audit alerts you to the skills and actions needed to control the direction of your life-career. Add up your ratings in each section separately and pay attention to low ratings. These indicate the areas in which you need to concentrate your efforts to become more self-reliant and pro-active in managing your career.

You should be looking for potential rather than perfection – participating in development opportunities will improve your ratings. You can return to this questionnaire at a later date and use it as a checklist against which to measure your progress. You can also add up ratings in total to get a general idea of how well you are currently doing.

Follow-up exercise for 'It's My Journey through Life' (20 minutes)

Ask students to Name Those Skills!

1 Ask students to take a look at the audit individually and get a feel for the skills that will be needed to navigate through this process successfully. A variety of skills are implicit at different stages in the SOAR process. If you are offering a module that covers this content, point out that the knowledge, skills and attributes will be learning outcomes from the module. For example, information flows are required at every stage – and information retrieval and analysis are important skills developed when you participate actively in this process.

2 Brainstorm in small groups of three or four as many skills as you can spot in this audit, and that you need to develop in order to improve your scores.

3 What tasks and activities will you need to participate in, to develop these skills?

4 How do these relate to the skills you are developing on your degree? What connections do you see between CMS and personal transferable skills, or key employability skills required by graduate recruiters today? (To help students see the relationships, refer them to the Employability Profile for their subject area – available from Higher Education Academy, 2006)

5 Feedback results of discussions to the whole group – a scribe should list skills on whiteboard or flipchart paper, and you could also use a labour market quiz to make the links between skills required and changing conditions of work. This will be covered in more detail in Chapter 9 on 'Understanding the Changing World'.

Card Sort Developing Career Skills: What Do I Need to Do and When?

Another way in which you can alert students to activities involved in career management or planning is to give them a set of cards that are printed with each activity. Make up a set from the example below. Ask students to work in pairs or groups of three. Start by putting the pile of cards face down in the middle of the table. Each student in turn takes the top card from the pile and leads a discussion on the suggested activity. Next, sequence the activities in an order that represents the steps they might follow to achieve their career-planning outcomes.

I usually present some preliminary material and explanations of SOAR before this exercise, and in my experience some students sequence the cards following a linear SOAR structure, whereas others see more relationships between the activities and have difficulty deciding which comes first. Arriving at a strict order doesn't really matter, but you can point out that the card printed with 'design a CV that reflects my strengths in relation to my chosen job' should be placed towards the end of the process as this is all but impossible if you haven't identified your strengths first and matched them to a chosen option or opportunity. The main aim is to use this activity as a starting point for reflection and discussion, so that individuals can make sense of a SOAR sequence and derive a personal plan of action from this. If appropriate, you can explain that the plan of your module or session follows a similar linear but relational structure.

The box opposite lists some of the things you will need to do in the process of developing and planning your career. What will you need to know and be able to do in order to undertake these tasks? They are presented here in no particular order. Please sequence them in order, as steps you might take in implementing a plan of action, either as a flowchart or a list.

Chapter 2: Summary of main points

- Personal and career development (major contributors to 'employability') are rising in importance the world over due to the demands of a complex global knowledge economy.
- Concepts of 'career' need to be explicitly redefined to reflect contemporary conditions and create shared understanding and values among staff. I define career broadly as 'an individual's pathway through life'. See Canada's *Blueprint for Life* (NLWC, 1998), and the *Australian Blueprint for Career Development* (Miles Morgan Australia, 2003.)
- CDL is the process of managing learning, work and other life roles over an individual's lifespan, and the boundaries between roles is less distinct.
- In HE this boils down to the need to develop each student as a whole person rather than to just teach subject knowledge: graduate attributes, skills and experience are increasingly important and required at a competitive level.
- The national Progress File and PDP agenda for all HEIs in the UK is intended as a vehicle for students to reflect and plan for their current and future personal, educational and career development.
- Staff in UK HEIs are faced with many agendas – PDP, CMS, employability, skills transcripts, entrepreneurship, work-related learning – and implementation of PDP is proving problematic for many reasons.
- The terminology used to describe graduate attributes is not commonly under-stood by all involved. Staff and students principally need to understand what 'skills' look like in behavioural terms, how they transfer into different opportunities, and how they are assessed by recruiters.
- Bearing these issues in mind, I advocate the SOAR model as the common denominator needed to integrate skills and to enable students to progressively

Identify tasks and requirements to do the job	Design a CV that reflects my strengths in relation to my chosen job
Be clear about what motivates and inspires me	Research career areas and industrial sectors
Undertake a realistic assessment of my skills and personal attributes	Prepare a targeted application for my chosen job
Weigh up the pros and cons of future options available to me	Regularly record and review my skills and achievements to use as evidence in the selection process
Prioritize what is important to me in life/career	See what people with my type of qualification have gone on to do
Decide which employer organizations match my criteria	Prepare for interviews and assessment centres
Check out an organization's website	Have a plan of action
Talk to someone who is doing the type of work in which I am interested	Identify sources of vacancies in my chosen field
Recognize my decision-making style and develop my own model for career planning	Relate my strengths and priorities to a job description and person specification
Understand how employers recruit	Decide which skills and attributes I will need to develop
Find and use opportunities to develop the skills I will need for my future career	Anything else . . . ?

build a composite personal 'graduate identity'. This acronym transforms into four relational, dynamic elements: 'Self', 'Opportunity', 'Aspirations' and 'Results'. The themes that emerge from these elements are underpinned by theories and are mutually supportive and developmental for real-life outcomes.

- SOAR functions as a universal, generic, timeless *and* personal process that gives rise to content with inbuilt requirements for reflection, personalization and self-management of lifelong and life-wide CDL. The process can be used to structure sequential curriculum approaches, but is cyclical for developmental purposes, connecting past experience with current learning and future success.

Chapter 3

Realizing the potential of SOAR

At the present time in UK HEIs, PDP concepts and intentions are being slowly but increasingly accepted: more independent and responsible academic learning, career planning and employability skills are meant to be the outcomes for students and graduates. Although these *values* are no longer generally contested, fundamental questions still relate to *provision* in this area – for example, should PDP be delivered within or outside the curriculum? Should it be a core, compulsory part of the student experience or an extracurricular option? Who should lead, support and deliver such interventions? What learning, teaching and assessment methods will achieve the desired outcomes?

Against the background of such debates and their implications for the SOAR model, I offer in this chapter:

- a brief evaluation of some different approaches that are being tried in the UK;
- how the integrated benefits of PDP, CDL and employability can be realized through the SOAR model, whatever the subject you teach or the circumstances in which you work;
- a case example of a customizable module framed within SOAR principles, and its associated teaching, learning and assessment methods;
- how SOAR elements can be translated specifically into process and content at different levels of degree programmes.

The main point is that the SOAR model, as defined earlier, has the potential power to integrate and achieve the aims of PDP: it can ensure students go through 'a structured and supported process' to reflect on and plan for their educational, personal and career development. It can do this through its focus on 'meta-learning': fostering an over-arching reflective habit enabling students to learn about learning, to assess their own learning in and through multiple contexts and identities. But it doesn't have to stop with reflection – SOAR is not simply a *means* for recording achievement, it can *foster* achievement through its processes. You will see through the examples provided in this chapter that it engages students in a reflective-active learning dynamic between 'self' and 'opportunity', which develops many skills and attributes. I will show how SOAR can give rise to the design and delivery of discrete modules, and offer some suggestions and examples that I have used to engage students through interactive teaching, learning and assessment methods.

There are also ways of dispersing SOAR elements throughout a programme of study. This is only effective, however, if you adopt the principles that are consistent with the model of learning that SOAR is intended to promote. John Wilson, from University College Lancaster, made the useful analogy that 'while the subject modules are the bricks of our wall of provision, PDP is the mortar which runs through and holds them together'. True, but if you have been concentrating on building 'bricks', how should you now mix and apply the 'mortar'? In other words, if you have a mindset aligned with teaching a subject discipline, how can you now engage students in a trans-disciplinary process for the linked purposes of personal growth, intellectual ability and preparation for future careers of rapid change and lifelong learning?

Recent research suggests that there are no agreed or easy answers (Bennett *et al.*, 2000; Harvey *et al.*, 2002; Yorke, 2004). There are many reasons for this: the complexity inherent in the PDP agenda, lack of consensus on what 'graduate-ness' is or should be, who should take responsibility for developing the requisite attributes, opposition to a perceived 'employment-led curriculum', and a paucity of evidence to prove the longer-term benefits.

SOAR solutions for provision

The SOAR model can be applied in different ways in HEIs to suit different needs, levels of study and contexts. My own experience and preference is for SOAR elements to be delivered within a coherent, structured process via discrete credit-bearing, assessed modules. These can either be generic modules open to students from any discipline (as SOAR is capable of being personalized according to the individual's needs and aspirations), or the model can be tailored and adapted, for example:

- to meet more subject-specific or occupation-specific needs in different disciplines;
- by putting more emphasis on 'opportunity': learning from non-academic and extracurricular opportunities such as work experience, placements, voluntary work, leisure activities;
- by developing a range of specific skills, e.g. enterprise and business awareness;
- to meet the needs of particular student groups – e.g. international or mature students.

To be effective however, it must be clear that any such programme is essentially based on a trans-disciplinary generic process that retains the centrality of 'self' and includes all four SOAR elements as a minimum entitlement. Having outlined the defining principles in Chapter 2, I give indicative examples here, starting with the template of a generic, customizable module (Table 3.1) and the content that arises from it (Table 3.2). Far from being a constraint, in practice at local level this model allows much flexibility. Seeing SOAR as a whole system requires you to move from:

- seeing parts to seeing the whole, understanding and integrating it;
- seeing students as passive recipients of programmed learning to seeing them as active agents in the construction of their own realities, learning and development;
- reacting to the present to simultaneously creating the future;
- being concerned purely with assessing students for competence, to being more concerned with enabling them to enhance confidence, motivation and self-efficacy – all essential attributes for success in HE and beyond.

This type of designated module within a competency-based curriculum approach is particularly effective because it ensures systematic delivery of learning opportunities aligned with learning outcomes that are therefore explicitly recognized by students and experienced as a coherent process of development. If these are a core, accredited part of degree programmes, students perceive they are valued by the HEI, and assessment ensures they are taken seriously. It is easier to monitor quality standards and ensure equality of opportunity so that all students have access to consistent levels of personal and career development. An exemplar is given in Table 3.1 for a successful accredited and assessed module that I have delivered in the penultimate year of different degrees, both in generic and subject-specific modes.

The development of complex skills, however, takes more time than is available on a single module, so the ideal would be to *also* adopt active pedagogy wherever possible in the broader curriculum to enhance these. If the skills outcomes are explicitly identified and made visible to students in all modules at all levels of study, SOAR can then be a means for students to name and claim their personal skills and attributes wherever they are being developed. Recording their achievements in personal (e-)portfolios of evidence will satisfy the Progress File requirements for HEIs in the UK, and serve as a flexible 'extended CV' from which they can select and develop self-promotion documents for employers and other selectors at transition points beyond HE.

Some writers, staff and students in HEIs favour a wholly embedded approach that disperses skills development across the whole curriculum. I think this is excellent but insufficient on its own. My experience of this approach and empirical data gleaned from students and graduates suggests that they have more difficulty in identifying these skills, and the nature of their transferability, if there are no separate CDL opportunities to make them explicit. It also fragments their experience and fails to provide a coherent framework, rationale and end goals to motivate and direct skills development (Evans, 2006). Individuals are accordingly at a disadvantage in making and justifying their choices at the point of transition beyond university. In such cases, where some but not all SOAR elements are contained in isolated efforts and activities, the benefits are only partially derived.

Alternatively, in some HEIs personal and career development is delivered wholly outside the curriculum, through a series of workshops, events and careers guidance interventions, usually supported by online learning. Some universities (e.g. York) offer excellent short certificated courses delivered by Careers Services or Employment Units, but the main disadvantage of optional learning opportunities is that many students who really need these benefits will not opt for extracurricular approaches.

Personal tutorials and/or individual careers guidance can make specific skills and attributes explicit for students and provide both academic and 'employability incentives' for them to evidence their profile in a learning log or (e)-portfolio. In the final analysis we need not see PDP and CDL skills development as two ends of a spectrum – either wholly embedded within courses or 'stand-alone, bolt-on' approaches. This does not have to be an 'either/or' forced dichotomy – rather a 'both/and' ideal might lie in composite approaches where skills are explicitly integrated and made visible in the context of the subject and also brought together in designated units or modules that are separately accredited and assessed. Skills outcomes and their transferability should be transparent and explicitly recognized by students, both horizontally across all modules and vertically in all levels of programmes.

The SOAR model in itself has multiple uses – you may use it as a template to:

- audit the existing curriculum, discover the different ways in which these elements are already being facilitated, and pinpoint those competencies that are missing from the student experience (e.g. use the learning outcomes from Table 3.1, or the questions arising from the 'High Five Principles', or the self-audit questionnaire 'It's *My* Journey through Life' – see Chapter 2);
- review, evaluate, develop or redesign existing programmes within this framework;
- plan and design new course or module content and process, aligning learning opportunities with learning outcomes, ensuring all SOAR elements are covered;
- review resources and materials, to determine which of the SOAR learning opportunities they provide;
- produce new material related to specific SOAR competencies;
- organize information resources and support according to the template;
- evaluate and assess a student's level of competence in this area so that they may take action to improve.

I will end this short discussion of provision within the curriculum by arguing for an ideal: that SOAR processes and their associated teaching, learning and assessment methods need to be integrated not as a mechanistic 'bolt-on' or piecemeal attempt, but implemented with a clear vision of how they can promote both higher and deeper levels of learning within a transformative SOAR-as-culture-change model.

SOAR applied to accredited modules

The generic process of personal and career development is expressed through the four inter-related stages of Self, Opportunity, Aspirations and Results (SOAR) in the exemplar summarized in Table 3.1. Information is implicit in all elements, and especially prominent in exploring and researching 'Opportunity'. Each stage has its own learning outcomes, which may be achieved through varying modes of delivery and assessment. Content that may be customized is indicated in **bold** font.

The SOAR framework in Table 3.1 gave rise to the content and assessment of the generic module outlined in Table 3.2. This has been delivered in the second year of degree programmes, and also customized to different subject disciplines.

Features of an accredited SOAR module, as in Tables 3.1 and 3.2

Real-life relevance and timing

There are advantages to focusing on CDL in the penultimate year of degrees: it is topical and timely, as students need to realize that many deadlines for applications (for employment, postgraduate courses and 'time out' or 'gap year' opportunities) come up before Christmas in their final year. This external driver dictates that they need to have made their choices by then, and acquired the skills to implement their aspirations. Once they get job-search out of the way, they can focus more on final year study, but continue to develop requisite skills and prepare to manage their transition beyond university effectively.

The real-life relevance of the module motivates students to 'kill two birds with one stone': gain credits *and* prepare for future life beyond the boundaries of the classroom. This can engender intrinsic motivation, as students both want and need this type of curriculum approach, as evidenced by the positive feedback comments students make in module evaluation wherever similar programmes are offered (see quotes, Chapter 12, p. 278). Sometimes it is not until graduation that the value is recognized or the lack of preparation is keenly felt (*If Only I'd Known*, Hawkins and Gilleard 2002). Again this comment from an unemployed graduate in a focus group is typical: 'I think when you are in college it's a fantasy world isn't it, but when you've finished with your degree and you're in the real world and it's really hard, you don't know what to do.'

Table 3.1 An example of a flexible 'SOAR module'

SOAR Process	Tasks (addressed to students)	Learning outcomes	Assignment
1) Self-awareness' What am I interested in and capable of achieving? (Self-assessment)	Identify and profile your interests, values, abilities and personal styles as 'your unique profile'; also external assets, influences and experiences relevant to your interests and intentions. These will include **subject-specific and occupation-specific** knowledge, skills, experience and interests, using recommended resources, e.g. **Employability Profiles or subject benchmark statements** and also skills and attributes developed through extracurricular work and leisure activities. Identify and assess your profile by using psychometric measures, questionnaires, reflective exercises, group tasks, feedback and discussion, and relevant theories. Visit your HEI's Careers Service, relevant websites and support services to access appropriate information, support and guidance.	Self-awareness skills. Realistic self-assessment. Enhanced understanding of one's 'self-concept', appreciation of one's current position and what one needs to do/ develop to achieve goals. Reflective skills. Applying theory to personal experience. Using feedback from peers and tutors as formative learning opportunities.	Specify and present your 'personal profile' – that you have identified via systematic, guided, personalized self-assessment and peer-assessment, using the conceptual and reflective tools given.
2) Opportunity-awareness What options are actually available to and suitable for me? (Short term choices for the present, and longer term choices for the future.)	Explore range of options and occupations **realistically available to graduates from your discipline** – both as short-term opportunities (part-time paid or unpaid work experience while studying, vacation work, industrial placements) and as longer-term possibilities. Look at actual destinations of graduates from previous year. Understand how conditions of life and work are changing, and the new demands placed on workers. **Labour market can be looked at through subject- or occupation-specific lens** – e.g. in Geography, the global spread of occupations or the globalization of the economy.	Imagination. Autonomy. Information retrieval and research skills, using people, paper and computer-based formats. Informational interviewing skills. Critical understanding of the labour market and of particular options.	Undertake an in-depth, analytical Personalized Occupational Study of your choice (making connections between your personal profile and various aspects of the job in the context of the labour market and changing world of work).

Do I understand the changing labour market?	Choose and study an occupation, preferably one you are interested in and can enter as a new graduate. Use a variety of information sources, compare and analyse to gain an in-depth understanding of your chosen option and how you match up to its requirements. *The option chosen may or may not be related to your programme of study*	occupations, and the implications for employees. Lateral thinking: making connections between personal priorities and how these transfer into further opportunities, whether in employment, study or life in general.	Present your findings and interpretation in report format **(or in pictures for Art and Design, or acted out in Drama . . .)**
3) Aspirations (Decision learning, action planning.)	Make informed decisions and plan action to implement your aspirations and achieve goals within set time-scales and critical deadlines. Transition goals may relate to further study or training, gaining work experience or planning a 'year out'. Career decision making can be supported via individual interviews with careers advisers and personal tutors – seek advice.	Report writing. Decision-making skills for implementing informed and realistic aspirations, preferably based on relevant experience. Action planning and problem-solving skills.	This element may be assessed formatively or an action plan may be part of a summative assessment.
4) Results (Transition skills) Review and further development	Research intended choices further and seek information as appropriate, e.g. on employer and vacancies **(these choices may relate to the subject area and may be an end goal or a stepping stone to achieve eventual aspirations).** Develop a critical understanding of employers' recruitment practices that should **take account of differences in occupational sectors, entry levels to employment and size of company.** Design effective CVs and CLs **tailored to the job or opportunity you decide to enter.** Complete a graduate-level job application. Practise interview and assessment centre skills.	Ability to interpret, extend and utilize information contained in job advertisements and job descriptions. Ability to identify specific sources of employer and vacancy information in a chosen field, targeting suitable vacancies and using appropriate job-search sources and techniques. Self-promotion and self-presentation skills on paper and in person reflecting self-assessment and job research.	Design and present a targeted CV and cover letter (CL) and a completed application form. Demonstrate the skills and attributes of self-promotion and employability you will need in interviews and Assessment Centre exercises.

Table 3.2 An example of scheduled in-class and homework topics, based on the SOAR framework as shown in Table 3.1.[1]

There will be continuous peer-assessment of verbal presentations based on homework topics, as outlined below (an assignment brief and standard marking criteria will be agreed with you and used in small groups). Absences will therefore affect grades.

1 Introduction: What is 'Career Development'? How does it relate to 'employability'? Complete the questionnaire 'It's *My Journey through Life'*. View the *Assessment Centres* DVD. How will you learn and be assessed? Formation of groups.
   Homework: Complete questionnaires and read relevant web pages on *Interests and Values* – to be found online. Prepare a 4-minute presentation on the topic: 'Having identified my interests and values from doing the questionnaires, the ones most important to me are . . . I know this because I am most motivated by these in my real-life experience and achievements, as evidenced by: . . .' (fill in the blanks). This will be your first practice presentation next week.

2 Practise presentations and giving feedback. Working in groups: roles, leadership and dynamics. Self-awareness topic: 'Personality types' and the Myers Briggs Type Indicator (MBTI).
   Hand out assignment brief for the *Personalized Job Study*.
   Homework: Research and interpret your MBTI results, using books such as *Do What You Are* and websites such as www.personalitytype.com or www.personalitypathways.com and www.teamtechnology.co.uk
   Prepare to present the topic: 'What strengths and blind spots are associated with my personal preferences? How does this manifest itself in my actual experience? To what extent is my personality aligned with my aspirations?'

3 How do people form aspirations and make career decisions? Career theories. The Lifeline exercise.
   Homework: Complete your 'lifeline'. Read about career theories in (recommended text). Write a paragraph relating the theories to your personal circumstances. Prepare to present on the topic: 'What relationships or groups have most influenced me – in both positive and negative ways? How might this affect my career choice(s) for the future?'
   (Use the community interaction theory and grid to help you think about this, in conjunction with the 'lifeline exercise'.)

4 Understanding jobs and transferable skills. Choosing appropriate job hunting methods.
   Homework: Familiarize yourself thoroughly with the Personalized Job Study assessment brief and marking scheme. Complete the Skills questionnaires online. Use *Prospects-Planner*[2] to help you prepare for a presentation on the topic: 'What are my aspirations (or what job ideas have I generated), and to what extent do they match with my abilities, strengths and interests?'

5 Researching your options and specific occupations. Making sense of different sources of careers information. Lies, damn lies and statistics!? Homework: Identify sources of information for investigating your chosen occupation, think about and write down questions you could ask when you interview someone actually doing that type of job. Prepare to present the topic: 'How can my information sources help me to write an analytical report on my chosen job area (and not just a descriptive essay)?'

6 The changing world of work. How to find out about trends and developments in the UK and global graduate labour market. Homework: Find job adverts and descriptions from sources of vacancy information (use the Internet and recommended websites, employer directories, newspapers, and *Prospects* publications, for example. Interview international students to add a 'global dimension' to your enquiry.) Prepare to present on the topic: 'What I have discovered about different employer organizations and industry sectors in which my chosen job occurs.' (Include – or focus on – self-employment possibilities if you wish.)

7 How do employers recruit? Equal opportunities issues. Hand-in date for Personalized Job Study assignment (enter date). Homework: Read case examples and materials in our Resource Centre which raise the debate on Equal Opportunities and Diversity in the Workplace. Prepare a presentation on the topic: 'What I think about the barriers I might face in securing a graduate job, and what I could do to overcome such issues.'

8 Designing a winning CV: what do employers look for? How can you stand out from the crowd? Hand out assignment brief for CV, CL and application form.
   Homework: Do the 'CV Preparation Exercise' (online). Produce your draft CV tailored to the job of your choice, and prepare a presentation justifying how its layout, format and content relate to your chosen job, explaining what specific problems you are having with designing a targeted CV and CL. (We will expect to see you referring to your draft CV when you present.)

9 Completing Application Forms effectively. An interactive exercise.
   Homework: Complete an application in draft format and bring to class. Prepare a presentation explaining how your answers reflect your skills and experience in relation to your chosen job. Also discuss any parts of the form you have found difficult to complete.

10 Preparing for and getting through Interviews and Assessment Centres.
    Homework: Think through 'Tough Questions' and practise your answers out loud. Familiarize yourself with the criteria employers use to assess good candidates at interviews and assessment centres. Prepare to role play and assess a mock interview at the following session.

11 Planning action to meet critical deadlines. Time management. Hand-in date for CV and CL and application assignment (enter date).
    Homework: Produce a personal action plan that reflects your circumstances and career goals – one you can use to implement your aspirations and manage your transition beyond university.

12 Come prepared to talk through your plan of action. Evaluation of results achieved: reviewing and further development for the future, closing the loop. Course evaluation.

---

1 Note that this is written for and addressed to students. Material for homework was available online – on web pages and in Blackboard, the university's adopted virtual learning environment (VLE).
2 Prospects Planner is freely available via www.prospects.ac.uk

Individual choice, personalization and customization

You will see from the tasks outlined in Tables 3.1 and 3.2 that mechanisms for constructing a personal profile encourage students to find their unique strengths and capitalize on them. They get to choose an occupation or alternative opportunity to analyse – preferably one they want to enter when they graduate – and apply for this through convincing self-promotion techniques. Reflective exercises ensure they take individual responsibility for making personal decisions and achieving results.

You get to choose suitable teaching and assessment methods when you design subject-related SOAR modules. Your methods can present material in modes students will relate to, as long as all SOAR elements are adequately covered. You can be flexible in delivery and assessment – e.g. art and design students may graphically illustrate their career concept and job study, computing students may want to use more Internet-based sources of information, drama students may want to enact an occupational project. Bear in mind, however, that all students need to develop good written and oral communication skills, as employers in every sector want professional CVs and professional conduct, whatever the job – and effective communication and interpersonal skills are central to this.

Position learners at the heart of their learning

SOAR by its very nature requires students to become active, independent and responsible learners. One way of clarifying this expectation is to project Figure 3.1 at the start of a programme, module or session, to encourage more 'buy-in' to the learning objectives, more enthusiastic engagement with the learning opportunities, methods and materials. Let students decide for themselves (wherever possible) that the intended learning outcomes are needed in order to do or develop some essential real-life task. Discuss the end goals and negotiate the interactions you expect between learners and learning enablers in order to achieve these. In Figure 3.1, the middle segment where the circles overlap is the place where synergy is created and transformation can occur. For this to happen effectively though, you need to ensure the 'constructive alignment' of learning opportunities, methods, objectives and outcomes.

Constructive alignment

It is pragmatically evident in classrooms that students are motivated when they experience the type of coherent model summarized in Tables 3.1 and 3.2, where learning activities, teaching methods and assessments are harmoniously aligned to produce learning outcomes they see as beneficial and necessary in real life. When your teaching goals are congruent with students' learning goals you can set up challenges and help students achieve at their best (hopefully!). This is not to deny that there will always be sceptics and 'horses who refuse to drink', no

3–way interaction:
learners at the heart of their learning

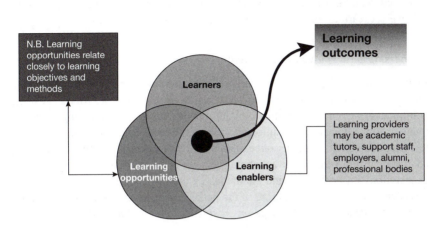

Figure 3.1 Learners central to the 3-way interaction in their learning.

matter how you try to make 'the water' good for them and show that it is clearly needed. I have found that those who are thirsty will not only drink deep, but also go looking for it elsewhere – and this is the whole idea.

Constructive alignment in the SOAR module:

1   Students are expected to specify their personal profile in depth. Teaching tasks enable them to discover and build this, with guidance and support. Assessment judges how convincingly and analytically they justify their claims, aspirations and results.

2   Students are expected to make connections between their profile and an occupation of their choice. Teaching enables them to explore, research, generate and clarify aspirations. They must assess the extent to which their profile matches the occupation they aspire to, locating it in the wider context of the graduate labour market. Assessment criteria are based on the quality of realistic self-analysis and job-analysis demonstrated in this matching process.

3   Students are expected to appreciate employers' recruitment practices and promote themselves in relation to their aspirations for transition beyond HE. Teaching focuses on developing skills in self-promotion and self-presentation, on paper and in person. Assessment relates to outcomes: students' results are to be demonstrated in writing application documents, and in interview and assessment centre activities.

Learning enablers: who should be involved?

Learning enablers should include a variety of people who can influence, design, deliver and/or assess this curriculum. Their contributions should be planned, coordinated and introduced to students so that their relative strengths are used to achieve set learning objectives within a coherent SOAR programme.

Partnership between you and students

PDP is intended to be 'a *supported* process'. In supporting and facilitating students on their journey, do you wish to be a guide, coach, mentor, friend, teacher, coordinator, resources investigator, monitor-evaluator (or something else – a judge, critic, advocate, companion traveller . . .)? Your role is critical and needs to be negotiated with students and explained to them. It helps to draw up a learning charter or group contract in collaboration with learners, that explicitly clarifies expectations on both sides and encompasses the principles of becoming 'good travellers', mutually participating in the pedagogy that enables students to reach appropriate destinations (see *Tips on making the most of the module* p. 59).

Partnerships within university-wide collaboration

Support should be convened on a university-wide basis: the responsibility for PDP has usually been given to subject staff, but the agenda has also raised the profile and status of central support services as possible key players. Careers staff are key contributors to CDL and employability, through the provision of information resources and access to opportunities such as work experience, expertise in developing CMS and contact with employers. Careers educators have the dual focus to mediate integrated approaches between staff who teach and assess and employers who assess and recruit. Learning resources staff can often not only teach vital library skills and research methods but also train students to make best use of the Internet and cope with information overload.

Counselling, Learning Support / Learning Development units, employer-facing units such as business development or employer liaison staff have much to offer too. Most HEIs have adopted VLEs, and education technology support is needed with the e-portfolio or recording element of Progress Files. In addition, class-based activities can usefully be complemented by online or e-learning, as there is a good deal of relevant web-based material that supports personal and career development.

Partnerships with external professionals

Another important role for PDP and CDL is to facilitate transitions within and between sectors – from school, college, HE and on into employment and CPD. PDP processes can act as an integrating force, providing continuity over the sometimes fragmented experience of 'learning' between different sectors, and also in different contexts. If students are to experience learning as a seamless continuum, pre-entry advisers should facilitate access to HE, staff within the HEI should ensure smooth transitions between different programme levels, and employers, alumni or professional bodies can help to facilitate transition at the exit end. External contributors often reinforce messages with more credibility – for example, employers bring a welcome 'straight from the horse's mouth' real-world element into the classroom that carries weight with students.

Although collaboration on this scale can generate much synergy, coordinating such effort is proving problematic in most HEIs. In view of the broad, trans-disciplinary nature of the SOAR process, and the different perspectives of learning-enablers that can enrich the experience, a course team approach works well. Academic and central support staff, researchers, employers and education technologists should come together to share ideas and good practice, knowledge and expertise that is integral to good scholarship as well as employability.

The learner's journey and destination

You could use 'Self as Hero in the Journey of Life' (Figure 2.1) as a metaphor for individual stories in personal and career development. I use some elements (but not a pure form) of Enquiry-based Learning (EBL) to set students off optimistically on their 'journey of self-discovery' and 'learning from opportunity', in order to gain clarity and focus on the fundamental questions: What do I want, what do I *need*, what am I capable of achieving, and how will I achieve it? Each student should be encouraged to tell his or her unique story, record it as a private diary, reflective journal or extended CV, and to select and compile from it documents that can be presented for assessment to tutors, employers and other selectors.

EBL requires prompts to fast-track students into the future, so that 'Self' engages with Opportunity to generate (or clarify) Aspirations and achieve Results. 'Be proactive' and 'start with the end in mind' are the first two habits in Stephen Covey's book *The Seven Habits of Highly Effective People*, where he says that:

> to begin with the end in mind means to start with a clear understanding of your destination . . . so that you can better understand where you are now, and so that the steps you take are always in the right direction. In business . . . the extent to which you start with the end in mind often determines whether or not you are able to create a successful enterprise.
>
> (Covey, 1989: 98, 99)

This does not mean that students need to have definite aspirations or clear expectations of results in order to benefit from a SOAR process. There are basically two sorts of travellers: one sort think that *if you don't know where you're going, how will you get there?* They feel more motivated and settled when they have specified a destination and can work steadily towards it. The other sort would agree with Lao Tzu: '*A good traveller has no fixed plans and is not intent on arriving.*' They want to keep options open for as long as possible, so give them freedom to set off and explore flexibly some opportunities that tickle their fancy.

Neither way is more or less effective; there are pros and cons of being focused on end goals, and equally so of being focused on means goals. The main point is that both sorts need to learn, improve, achieve results and realize their unique potential. That is both an end goal and a means goal, depending on how you look at it – but it is what all students need to commit to in HE generally.

To engage students in this process, give them some glimpses of their future needs (which may simply be the learning outcomes of the module) and ask: What skills and knowledge will you need to achieve the best possible results? Or to implement your aspirations successfully? What specific learning tasks and activities will help you prepare? Think individually, discuss in pairs, share with the whole group. (Think, pair, share is generally an effective technique.)

Here are some EBL prompts good for introducing SOAR:

- Administer the self-audit and follow-up exercises for 'It's *My* Journey through Life: Am I in the Driving Seat?' This alerts students to what they will need to do/develop in order to take control of their career.
- Show clips from the *Assessment Centres* DVD (AGCAS, 2000) and ask students to take note of the skills they see being observed and assessed. This is very effective as it brings to life the behaviours considered effective in group work, interviews, presentations, and social situations.
- Show examples of winning CVs and ineffective CVs (your Careers Service is likely to have these). Alternatively, role-play with a colleague or student a good selection interview and a poor one. Ask students to spot the differences. Ask: How could you ensure you end up with the skills and attributes needed to enter and perform successfully in graduate employment?

In this way you can build negotiation of the curriculum into your module so that you involve students in decision making and gain their agreement and commitment to 'getting there' – because they see not just what you want, but what they need. This is closely aligned to the module planned for them anyway, so you do not have to worry about changing it to suit students' stated needs – you just say 'Here's one I prepared earlier – will this meet your needs?' If it follows SOAR, as set out in this book, it will go a long way towards meeting their needs!

Developing the requisite skills will take some students well out of their comfort zones, so it is important to acknowledge this, support and empower them. These needs are implicitly borne in mind in this book, but you can also explicitly agree ground rules with students: to go with the journey, to do things a little differently, to push the boundaries, to have fun, to participate as required. Negotiate a learning contract that clearly sets out everyone's expectations, and that everyone agrees to abide by.

Tips on making the most of the module (a learning contract)

1 **Play the game!** This is not a module where you simply sit and take notes. Ask questions. Share your views. Contribute wholeheartedly in the discussions and activities – many of these are in small groups and in pairs. At the same time, show respect for other members of the group and listen to their viewpoints. The real advantage of this module is that you can take control of **your** learning and develop useful skills. Therefore, consider each session to be a training opportunity where it is all right to run, fall and get up again. You will benefit so much more by playing the game than by sitting on the sidelines – and you can also make it more fun.

2 **Attend the sessions.** Because of the interactive nature of these sessions, you are required to attend. The discussion that takes place around topics in the classroom will help you complete your assignments and develop important skills. You cannot hope to do well if you simply rely on reading and writing.

3 **Be there for a prompt start!** To some extent the course replicates the world of work, where punctuality and reliability are important qualities. For instance, BBC *News at 10* goes out precisely at 10, not at 10.05.

4 **Meet and mingle.** This programme will provide opportunities for getting to know others. In classes where you have a diverse mix of students, you have ideal opportunities to learn to value diversity, build effective relationships with people from different backgrounds, learn about other cultures and countries, make constructive use of differences in teamwork – to develop personal, interpersonal and workplace skills. You are encouraged to form self-help and peer-support groups – work together as well as individually. Research for your assignments should take you out into the world of work, where you can meet employers and expand your network of contacts.

5 **Relate what you learn to yourself.** Do not settle for 'abstract knowledge'. Keep your current goals in mind, together with a future focus. As you gain new insights and skills, ask yourself: How does this apply to me, my life, my future goals? Use the resources available to retrieve relevant information from paper and multimedia formats, and analyse the usefulness of different sources in relation to your personal needs. The tips and information provided will have relevance far beyond the boundaries of the classroom, for use in career planning and job-hunting, both now and in the future.

6 **Don't get left behind!** Undertake the activities suggested, make reflective notes to keep on track, and you should have no problems with the content and assessments. Plan towards assessments as you go along (rather than in a mad rush

just before deadlines). This means you will produce better work and get more from your studies.

7 **Tell us what you think!** If there are aspects of the course and the assessments that you do not like, tell us – either during the course (so we can consider changes to benefit you), or in the evaluation at the end (so we can consider changes to benefit future students). We will welcome your views, suggestions and constructive criticism.

Fostering autonomy in learners and dealing with complexity

One of the reasons that 'employability' is usually a problematic concept is that its components and skills are perceived as complex, difficult to define, measure, develop and transfer. In broad generalities, this need not be the case – because every survey seeking to discover 'what graduate recruiters want' reveals more similarity than diversity, no matter which occupation or industry sector is under scrutiny. (See Table 2.4: Skill-sets.)

> Employability skills are not job specific, but are those skills that cut horizontally across all industries and vertically across all jobs from entry level to chief executive officer. They are the attributes of employees, other than technical competence, that make them an asset to the employer.
>
> (Toby Loskove, quoted by Chabon-Berger, 2006)

The specific requirements are, however, difficult to pin down, except when they are contextualized within a particular job, occupation or employer-organization. Many new PDP practitioners feel overwhelmed because they wonder if it is their (daunting!) responsibility to learn about this as a whole new and complex 'subject'. My response to this is that you cannot possibly become an expert in every career under the sun (and in outer space!) or even every career option that is potentially available to students from your subject area. Students are not a homogenous group, and even if they were you certainly could not expect to become an expert on each student's specific employability needs.

One way of dealing with this in mass HE situations is to motivate each student to become proactive in exploring and researching his or her options and opportunities, and developing requisite skills. This is not a ploy to abdicate your responsibility, it is consistent with the need to foster autonomy in students (a key aim of HE). The onus is on them to identify and develop the skills, knowledge and expertise they will need. Your role is to ensure provision of learning opportunities, resources, tools and techniques – and engage them with these.

Pedagogy for the SOAR process

Many PDP practitioners are starting to include in the HE experience for students an integrated or parallel process of planning, doing, reviewing, reflecting, evaluating and recording outcomes, and translating the new knowledge and skills into changes in behaviours. They are developing such offerings as skills audits and skills development, opportunities for reflection, goal setting and action planning, diagnostic testing, self-assessment, extended induction, CV building – ideally starting in the first year with a focus on study skills, and concentrating in later years on career development and progression. Such practices are having the effect of blurring the perception of 'academic' and 'employability' skills as distinct and separate skill-sets, and are in some cases beginning to transform teaching, learning and assessment methods within a more imaginative curriculum.

Traditional HE assessment typically rewards student achievement and performance in subject-specific knowledge and skills through summative grades. The methods used to convey knowledge are generally teacher-centred. SOAR requires a shift from achievement-orientation to a *development* focus that recognizes the personal 'distance travelled' or 'value added' by the individual, and emphasizes that development involves taking risks and experimenting with concepts and practical skills. Early failure is therefore not only acceptable, it is to be expected. It should be viewed as the raw material for learning.

A development model is process-driven, generic and student-centred, supported by active learning, formative assessment and constructive feedback. In summary, the shift looks something like that shown in Table 3.3.

How can we better motivate students to undertake the tasks and participate in the learning opportunities we might set to foster their holistic development? I have referred to many methods that are apt for our purposes here, but in general these are best delivered in groups no larger than 25. You can use tutor input followed by student activity, reflection, discussion, business games, audio-visual and multimedia resources, quizzes and questionnaires. These may be supplemented by online learning and discussion groups, peer support, individual guidance, tutorials and information materials.

Table 3.3 Traditional learning methods vs PDP and CDL requirements

Traditional HE favours:	Personal and career development requires:
Book learning	Active learning in different contexts
Vicarious experience	Real-life, direct experience
Achievement orientation	Development focus
Subject-specific knowledge	Generic practical and intellectual skills
Theories and concepts	Practical applications and relevance
Teacher-centred methods	Student-centred methods, self-assessment
Summative assessments	Formative assessment with feedback

The sheer variety of activities that are now encompassed by the terms 'teaching', 'learning' and 'assessment' have made the boundaries between these more fuzzy, and some aspects have much in common with research. I think the transgression of boundaries is breaking across what are unnatural divisions in any case. Greater trans- or multi-disciplinarity mirrors the world of work, and can enrich learner development, exciting the intellectual imagination of students in a knowledge-age society. Innovative examples now abound – where students are working in small groups on authentic projects, collaborating with students in other faculties to achieve results, or with employers or community organizations.

For example, survey findings represented in 'The Learning Pyramid' (McKay and Cabrales, 1996) reproduced in Figure 3.2 show a variety of methods, suggesting that the most effective retention comes from teaching others. An effective way of keeping bright students engaged in classes of mixed ability is to build in methods where their learning is stretched by getting them to teach their peers who need extra support. This is of mutual benefit, but the students involved in helping or teaching often don't perceive its value to themselves unless they are given examples and required to reflect/tease out the benefits. In any event, if students have opportunities to hear, see, read, discuss, experience and practise whatever they are meant to master, they are likely to shift from surface learning to taking a deep approach.

The Learning Pyramid

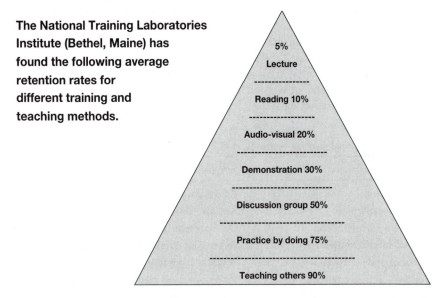

The National Training Laboratories Institute (Bethel, Maine) has found the following average retention rates for different training and teaching methods.

5%
Lecture

Reading 10%

Audio-visual 20%

Demonstration 30%

Discussion group 50%

Practice by doing 75%

Teaching others 90%

Figure 3.2 Effective teaching methods in 'The Learning Pyramid'.

Blended learning

An effective SOAR programme will combine formative, ipsative and summative assessments and draw on a wide range of theoretical, academic, empirical and applied perspectives. I advocate a variety of supported online and blended teaching and assessment methods that will accommodate different preferences for learning and suit full- and part-time students studying across multiple and dispersed locations. Online tutorial material should almost stand alone if necessary, supporting those learners who are on remote sites and overseas in being able to learn flexibly, any time, any place. Such material needs to be learning-focused, not technology-driven (Kumar, 2005). I have seen examples where staff are seduced by exciting technological possibilities and have completely lost sight of their objectives!

The most successful examples use a blend of:

- class-based learning with e-learning, using a VLE or web-based material;
- interactive exercises in class with homework topics that use online learning, require reflection and personal research;
- theories and concepts linked with their practical applications in real-life situations;
- formal input interspersed with small group discussion and individual reflection;
- learning from different information sources – paper and Internet-based formats, multimedia and talking to people;
- learning derived from a range of experiences: formal study, informal and leisure activities, work experience and placements, vacation or voluntary work.

The SOAR structure provides the 'connective glue' that will prevent students from experiencing these as disjointed and meaningless activities, and a CV can draw them together selectively for specific applications.

Tailoring SOAR to a subject – e.g. Accounting for Your Future

What follows is a more detailed example of a specific attempt we made at University of Bedfordshire to tailor the generic SOAR model to accommodate the needs of students on the second year of a degree in Accounting and Finance. 'We' in this context refers to collaboration between the principal lecturer – Rob[1] – and myself. This was a standard 15-credit rated, assessed, core module that all students on this programme were required to take. It consisted of 13 contact weeks, and was offered in the first semester (for logistical reasons). There were 64 students in total, divided into two groups so that interactive skills development could be more easily managed. Rob and I met initially to design the module and at weekly intervals to plan each two-hour session, which we then co-delivered twice each week.

The curriculum was designed in three parts. First, students were required to identify and articulate their own strengths and development needs in terms of skills, interests, abilities and personal priorities, and appreciate the transferability of their attributes. Models for analysis, such as Belbin's team-roles (1981, 2003) and the MBTI®[2], were used to encourage students to adopt a structured approach to self-analysis. There were also questionnaires online and inbuilt requirements for reflection to ensure a social and personal constructionist approach to building a personal profile.

Second, two presentations were organized from The Association of Chartered Certified Accountants (ACCA) and The Chartered Institute of Management Accountants (CIMA) to encourage students to understand careers needs within the accounting profession. Following these two sessions, two more followed to reinforce the ability to research and analyse the Accounting and Finance industry and the career opportunities within it, and to understand further study and training needs as new recruits to the industry.

Finally, students were presented with techniques for personal presentation for employment through CVs, cover letters, application forms and interviews. At the start of study and again at the end students were presented with examples to enable appreciation of employers' needs and the recruitment processes they use. A key aim was to enable students to develop actionable plans for skills improvement and the transition beyond university.

Assessment

Student assessment was in three parts. First, a weekly presentation was done on a peer-assessed basis. Students were organized into groups of four at the start of the semester. These groups were formed such that each group, as far as possible, reflected the diversity of the cohort. As the semester wore on, and some students did not always attend, the groups of four evolved from their original mix. Students had a pre-instructed task that they had to present in turn within their groups, for assessment by their peers. They were given time to feedback orally and informally to each other, using the guidance given (see pp. 67–70).

Students quickly realized that peer-assessment meant they could grade with freedom, and thus most groups decided to give A grades for the presentations. This element of assessment therefore effectively became a grade for attendance and participation. Rob and I opted not to interfere with this interpretation as independent student activity was involved and thus engagement was encouraged. Feedback from students indicated that they valued the opportunity to make prepared presentations in a relatively unthreatening situation.

The second assessment was a summation of the semester's work involving a job analysis and the personal suitability for it. The conclusion was a personal plan to develop skills beyond the end of the semester. Students were required to append a summary log of week by week semester development in support. Most students who had engaged with the semester performed quite well in this assessment, although they were a little unsure about how to maintain their momentum beyond the semester.

The final assessment was an Applications Pack consisting of a personal CV targeted to a graduate position, an accompanying cover letter, and a Standard Application Form (available online). Once again, students who had engaged effectively produced good work. A common failing was the inability to link real examples to assertions about their capabilities. Some overseas students seemed to have very few life and work experiences to present in support of applications.

One of the problems for us was the need to give effective feedback in a relatively short period of time and this was overcome to a degree by using a standard feedback sheet and summary comment. However the feeling persisted that some students needed extensive individual counselling in order to maximize their career potential.

Assessment doing triple duty

A number of educators (Brown *et al.*, 1997; Ramsden, 2003) make the point that students perceive assessments as being the defining points of the curriculum: whatever is assessed assumes greatest importance in their eyes and directs the amount of effort they put in. I would like to draw your attention to the assessment regime for the module outlined in Table 3.1 (p. 50). The column on the right indicates three assignments, which are all fairly traditional pieces of written work that were handed in to be tutor-marked. I will return to these in later chapters, but for now I want to expand on the 'continuous assessment of mini-verbal presentations' referred to in Table 3.2. This represents the new assessment strategy Rob and I introduced for the following reasons:

- to develop practical skills outcomes for employability and career management, which was not achieved if students relied heavily on reading and passive learning methods;
- to encourage them to attend and engage in every session;
- to involve students in establishing an environment where they would feel obliged to prepare and think about class and homework topics (every week, in advance) – on a continuous basis – thereby creating their personal realities through both social constructionist and psychometric approaches;
- to introduce elements of discovery learning and EBL, for tangible real-life goals;
- to improve their potential as active participants in class and increase levels of self-confidence in interactions and presentations, become comfortable and natural in practising talking about themselves (and the topics), as they would have to do in real-life selection interviews and contacts with employers;
- to put forward their experiences and opinions against specific presentation criteria, have them challenged and assessed;

- to learn reciprocally from the experiences and opinions of others, appreciate other points of view and develop interpersonal skills;
- to learn to give and receive feedback in order to improve;
- to provide a richer experience of more holistic assessment: they were undertaking self-assessment through homework, peer-assessment in class, and simultaneously preparing for a tutor-assessed piece of written work to be handed in as a learning log and job report at the end of the module;
- to encompass formative assessment for self-development *and* summative grading for certification;
- to focus on immediate tasks *and* build capacity for coping with uncertain future life-careers;
- to engage in the process of PDP *and* attend to the knowledge content domain of CDL.

I felt it was important to assign value to these endeavours by awarding grades. Peer-assessment has potential for encouraging affiliation and support within the small groups, but it may conversely also provoke antagonism and/or inhibitions in some members. This can be exacerbated by diverse groups where there are younger and more mature students, home and international students, etc. It is a moot point as to whether you allow students to self-select themselves into 'friendship groups' or allocate groups with a view to positively valuing diversity. I strongly advocate the latter, but this needs careful initial briefing, and monitoring.

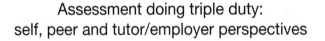

Assessment doing triple duty:
self, peer and tutor/employer perspectives

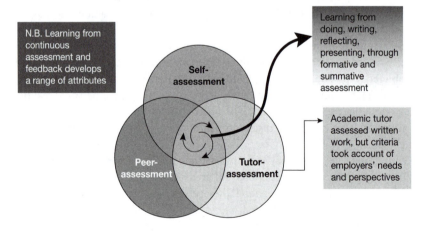

Figure 3.3 Assessment doing triple duty.

We emphasized that everyone has learning points to contribute and receive, that diverse groups afford richer learning experiences which can transfer to diverse workplaces. In any event, it is important to negotiate and define explicitly and clearly the protocols of good group work and communication, and gain agreement from all students that they will abide by these (see Chapter 7).

We introduced the assessment regime carefully at the outset. The grading system was explained and students were involved in devising the criteria by which the mini-verbal presentations were to be assessed. This was done through a visual presentation and subsequent discussion about what makes for effective oral communication and formal presentations, and what to avoid. I made comparisons with the type of verbal communication required in formal situations such as interviews and assessment centres.

Student brief for the continuous assessment of mini-verbal presentations (note that this is addressed to students)

Assignment 1 briefing   **Weighting: 30%**

Assignment 1 involves continuous assessment of how you engage and participate in module sessions. A total of 10 sessions (out of 12) will be assessed through three types of evidence:

1 **Attendance**: you cannot expect to develop practical and interactive employability skills if you do not attend. Treat your class as a training ground replicating the workplace – use it to practise professional conduct. Employers will expect you not only to turn up for work but to be punctual, take responsibility for organizing yourself, and demonstrate enthusiasm.

Please make sure you sign the register towards the end of each session. If you cannot attend at times, this will have to be for valid reasons justifiable in light of the university's mitigating circumstances policy, e.g. a sickness certificate presented to your academic adviser.

2 **Evidence of preparation**: each week you will have a set homework topic to prepare between sessions, as outlined in your Module Handbook. In-class exercises, materials and guidance will lead up to these topics, which may require you to complete online or paper-based questionnaires, undertaking some activity or reading. Details and web links will also be posted online, under Course Documents week by week. What is important here is that you reflect on the outcomes of each exercise, evaluate what they mean for you, and link them to appropriate evidence from real life to support your claims. It is this personalized learning that you should write up briefly to present in class at each session. Your weekly learning log will also form the basis for the written reflective account you will present as part of your Job Study and Report assignment at the end of this module.

3 **4-minute verbal presentations in class**, peer-assessed in small groups (see separate briefing for this). The first half-hour of each weekly session will be devoted to these, so you need to arrive punctually and manage your time effectively. Each student will present in turn, while others listen carefully. Grades should be awarded using given marker sheets (p. 69), based on three basic criteria that we will together develop and agree in class.

After each presentation, give brief feedback to the presenter in order to encourage and help him or her to improve. See separate guidance about giving helpful feedback.

Skills and qualities you can develop through this type of self- and peer-assessment

- Organizing yourselves (into small groups at the start of each session, and generally, too).
- Time management (keeping on track with workload in general, and specifically managing the rota of four-minute individual presentations plus feedback, so as to finish within the first half hour).
- Communicating, listening and presenting (these are complex skill-sets, which we will cover in more detail separately, too).
- Peer-assessment skills, discerning 'good' from 'bad' presentations. (Important! We want to see you make distinctions – see your marking criteria on the grading sheets.)
- Giving feedback with sensitivity and consideration (see handout, and practise this).
- Receiving feedback without getting defensive (you will only improve if you can use feedback to change for the better).
- Interpersonal skills (use this opportunity to build productive relationships with others).
- CMS (skills related to the SOAR process model will be developed through the topics we will cover together week by week).
- Confidence (feedback from previous students indicates that most of them felt that this assessment – and the overall module – developed their confidence in various ways).

Instructions for peer-assessment in small groups

- You will work in groups of four (or three if four is not possible).
- Enter your name at the top of the marker sheet.
- Enter the name of the presenter in the left-hand box.
- Understand the criteria for grading – what are you looking for? How will you grade?
- Understand the grades – what do they mean?
- Decide how you will keep time: each presentation should be four minutes.

- Give encouragement to the presenter – be aware of eye contact and body language.
- After each presentation, spend a couple of minutes grading each criterion by putting a ring round the appropriate grade (you can use the space in between to write + or – if you want to).
- Aggregate the final grade, based on your overall impression, and enter it in the end box.
- When all presentations are done give formative feedback to each other, bearing in mind the tips given.
- Think of any questions to ask or comments to make about:
  - The topic in relation to career planning;
  - The group dynamics and how things are working out.

Proforma for peer-assessment of mini-verbal presentations

Module title: .... Date:..................................

Name of assessor:..

Name of student being assessed	Addressing the topic – being specific and personal	Evidence of preparation – e.g. notes or scripts for presentations, print-outs of online questionnaires	Presentation – Clarity, Coherence, Time-keeping	Aggregated grade A – F
	A B C D E F	A B C D E F	A B C D E F	
	A B C D E F	A B C D E F	A B C D E F	
	A B C D E F	A B C D E F	A B C D E F	

A = Excellent   B = Very Good   C = Good   D = Satisfactory   E = Fail

F = Nothing of Merit

Giving constructive feedback

Giving and receiving feedback should be explained as an important (but often difficult) interpersonal skill that everyone has to use at times in real life and at work. The aim should be to provide constructive and advisory feedback, with sensitivity and consideration for the recipient. It is essential that students learn to do this in such a way that the person they are speaking to understands what they are saying, accepts it, and can do something about it.

The following guidelines for **giving helpful feedback** were discussed and agreed with students:

- Feedback can take the form of comments, questions, replies, clarification, challenges etc. – but this is a two-way discussion where both parties need to listen and attend carefully.
- Ask the recipient first: 'What do you think was effective or not effective about your performance today?' (People are sometimes unduly self-critical and need encouragement to see their strengths, or they may have a hard time accepting their development needs).
- Balance positive and negative points if you can – e.g. you could say 'one good thing was . . .', 'one thing to improve is . . .', 'one further question that arises is . . .' Avoid being purely complimentary (unless there is genuinely no room for improvement) or condemning the performance outright.
- Make honest and direct comments, but be sensitive and frame your suggestions as steps towards improvement, e.g. 'I think this could be an excellent presentation if you speak with more enthusiasm.'
- It is important to refer to specific examples of behaviours you have observed, to demonstrate the points you are making, e.g. 'When you were speaking about your interest in dolphin training you twirled your pen continually and looked nervous. I was not convinced – where does that interest come from?' Giving superficial or evasive feedback does not help people to know what they should stop doing and what comes across well.
- Be aware of your tone of voice and body language – often the way you say something is more important than what you say.

A simple formula for receiving feedback

- If you are receiving feedback, don't be defensive or take it personally. Remember this is a learning experience for all concerned. Be open to the message, however it is given. It is better to be saved by criticism than ruined by praise!
- Try to put the feedback into your own words to check you have understood exactly what has been said.
- Ask the 'observer' to clarify or give an example if a point is not clear, or to suggest how your performance could be more effective.
- You may or may not wish to try out suggestions that have been made, but think about what has been said and give yourself time to absorb it.
- The observers should be talking about your behaviour and not about you personally. If they are causing you discomfort, explain the reasons for this and discuss what might be done.

PDP and CDL at different levels/years of degree programmes

When delivering structured programmes it becomes necessary to define outcomes at different levels (roughly equated with the different years of delivery). Table 3.4 is an example of how the SOAR process builds from the first year to the final year of a typical degree. Examples of activities at different levels of challenge and skill-development are scattered through this book, and for these it will be your decision as to what best meets the needs and abilities of your students.

Scaling down to year one

One of the aims of PDP is to bridge back to the student's prior experience and smooth the transition into HE. A SOAR process can form part of induction and continue through the first year in various ways. At the University of Bedfordshire a range of such approaches have been developed and are now being evaluated and improved. In HEIs that have widened access to non-traditional students it is particularly essential to build the capacity of those students for studying the conventions of their subject at higher level. With this in mind we developed integrated core modules for PPAD that are now compulsory in most subject fields. In others the philosophy is currently permeating the entire first year curriculum, transforming it into a series of supported project-based topics for students to investigate, report on and present, reflecting on their learning. The main aim in year one is to induct students on an extended basis to engage with their subject disciplines, to develop study skills and learning strategies for HE, and to take more personal responsibility for their holistic development.

Raising the game for the final year

I have described a fairly flat regime for assessed verbal presentations in the section of this chapter titled 'Tailoring SOAR to a subject' (p. 63), but you might challenge students by raising standards and varying the pattern as you proceed. For example, get them to prepare as usual, but pick students at random to present from up front to the whole class. Agree an overall grade and provide feedback; discuss the difference between formal presentation skills and the small-group ones, the use of visual aids, etc. You should expect more discerning judgements relative to the ability to build coherent, clear and concise arguments. If the group is small enough, set up a formal debate between two halves of the class. If possible, monitor the written work they do to prepare their presentations, and provide instant feedback that will help to close the gap between their expectations and yours. Also raise standards in group work to the professional level expected in assessment centres for graduate recruitment (see Chapter 7).

The SOAR process in my experience has been equally successful and needed by postgraduate students. More ideas follow, and indeed all these themes are developed through the rest of this book.

Table 3.4 Skill levels related to the SOAR process

SOAR in years 1, 2 and 3 of degrees	Evidence must show you can
Year 1:	
Develop a strategy for planning and implementing your choice(s) in learning and work experience, based on: • realistic self-assessment; • awareness of opportunities; • decision-making skills using reliable information; • career-planning skills for short-term actions, against background awareness of the labour market and longer-term action planning.	• Identify, assess and articulate your skills, abilities, personal attributes, interests, values, experiences and circumstances, and relate these to different opportunities • Establish opportunities for developing a range of skills and attributes, and clearly identify the outcomes you hope to achieve • Identify relevant sources and research the information needed for planning purposes.
Year 2:	
Monitor, progress and adapt your strategy, as necessary, to implement your plan. This will involve: • A CV and cover letter reflecting your self-assessment in relation to the requirements of a chosen occupation or opportunity; • A focused job application form; • Self-presentation skills to cope with interviews and assessment centres.	• Identify what employers are seeking in terms of academic, personal and professional achievement • Promote yourself effectively on paper and in person, emphasizing strengths and experiences relevant to a particular job or alternative opportunity • Monitor and critically reflect on your use of skills, adapting your strategy as necessary to produce the quality of outcomes required.
Year 3:	
Enhance and demonstrate skills to cope successfully with transition beyond university. Evaluate your overall strategy and present a plan that will effect a smooth transition to your chosen future destination, and further career development.	• Demonstrate a realistic match between career aspirations and personal characteristics, knowledge and experience • Plan for the further development of skills, knowledge and experience to meet career aspirations; • Assess the effectiveness of your strategy, including factors that had an impact on the results you achieved, and identify ways of further extending your skills.

Chapter 3: Summary of main points

- I evaluate briefly some different forms of provision for PDP and CDL in UK HEIs and advocate both accredited 'SOAR modules' and skills embedded in the wider curriculum.
- SOAR provides solutions for the challenges of integrated curriculum provision.
- Exemplar material is given for a customizable SOAR framework (Table 3.1) and a generic module in year 2 (Table 3.2).
- Features of the generic module are discussed, indicating congruent and constructively aligned pedagogy.
- An example of tailoring SOAR to the needs of Accounting students is described, and detail given of the revised assessment regime, together with supporting guidance documents.
- SOAR is a flexible and scaleable process model that can be adapted for different levels of study.

Part 2

'Self' in the SOAR process

Building a MAP for the journey through life

Building a 'Self-MAP'

Who am I?

Why focus on 'self'?

'Know yourself, know your future' is an inscription above an ancient Greek monument. My version of this is 'Know yourself, create your future'. You will recall from Part 1 that 'Self' is the S in the acronym SOAR, and I suggest you engage 'self as hero' at the heart of the personal life-career journey. 'Self-awareness skills' are central to CDL – but also to general success. Careers professionals generally accept this as 'an awareness of the distinctive characteristics that define the kind of person one is and the kind of person one wishes to become' (NICEC, 1992). This definition suggests the uniqueness of each person, and that current self-awareness has potential for future aspirations and identity formation. It is also synonymous with the term Metacognition – the M in the USEM formula that is advocated as an essential component of employability (see Chapter 2, p. 27).

As a facilitator of enhanced 'self-awareness' I believe you can make a big difference in students' lives, and of course apply the same insights in your own life. This example, taken from a second-year student's reflective account, is typical of those who have experienced a SOAR module:

> I feel I am in a much stronger position than I was only 3 months ago when I began this module. I have realized that managing my career is an ongoing process that requires constant reflection, something I was ignorant of before . . . I have made great progress in understanding my character, what skills I possess, and which I need to work at. I feel this opportunity for self-reflection and the skills of self-analysis I learned have given me a great advantage over my peers who have not completed this module.

What is self-awareness – and its associated skill-set?

The ability to observe oneself objectively is uniquely human. Try closing your eyes for a moment, take your imagination up to a spot high above you, think of yourself as an 'eye in the sky' on this particular day of the week/month/year, and describe what you are feeling and doing in the third person. I am sure you will easily be able to do this. Animals can be observers and actors in their own dramas, but they cannot be self-observers (as far as I know). As humans we have imagination, conscience, independent will – and we are therefore responsible ('response-able' or able to choose our response to suit different situations). Without this capacity, all our efforts to educate for choosing an appropriate response, or for changing behaviours, would be fruitless.

Your task within the SOAR process is to get students to exercise this responsibility progressively for enhanced self-awareness, self-assessment, self-esteem, self-efficacy, self-promotion and self-management. I treat these here as a 'self-awareness skill-set', while recognizing that these terms encompass more than skills: they extend to personal beliefs, feelings, experiences and behaviours. Identifying and enhancing these aspects of self can in turn develop interpersonal effectiveness. Given that they are interrelated (see Figure 4.1), crucially important, and in need of constant development, it is probably surprising that our reflective capacities for self-awareness are usually 'under-educated'. Yet students will need in-depth, analytical and realistic self-awareness as the key to creating their futures in a proactive and positive manner. In the UK the Centre for Recording Achievement (CRA)[1] strongly affirms the value of PDP as a tool to promote reflection and develop student self-identity – 'arguably the original academic purpose of HE' in the words of its director, Rob Ward.

Self-awareness skills are vital because they enable students to:

- identify and assess their current and potential level and type of skills, strengths and development needs;
- identify and prioritize what is of interest and importance to them in forming aspirations and making balanced choices;

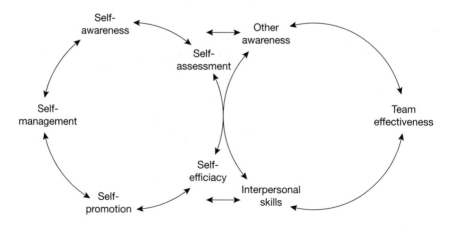

Figure 4.1 'Self-awareness' and 'other-awareness' skills in a success cycle.

- generate ideas and interest in grasping suitable developmental opportunities, both short and longer term;
- understand their relationships with learning, work and leisure;
- defend these choices when the need for self-promotion arises, especially at transition points, e.g. during competitive selection procedures in graduate recruitment;
- understand others and build more effective relationships with them;
- take control and manage the direction of their life-career more effectively;
- construct and develop their identities positively and proactively.

There is a good deal of evidence from surveys that self-awareness is at the heart of success in graduate jobs. For example, in 2004 Strategis conducted research for a number of major recruiters into factors contributing to the ongoing success of graduates three to seven years into their career, and found that habits of self-awareness, reflection and pro-active learning were central to career development. This emphasis on the ability to drive change, both for oneself and for the organization, is increasingly shared by all major employers and is also highly valued by the small and medium-sized enterprise (SME) sector.

Mark Armitage of Exeter University also conducted similar research in which he asked a number of pertinent questions, including one on 'what makes certain applicants exceptional – e.g. those who obtain several job offers'. His findings, reported in *Phoenix* 117 (AGCAS, 2006: 10–11), show that:

> successful graduates demonstrated a high level of awareness of the skills and abilities sought by their current employer. . . . Graduates realised how the application process had tested their potential [and] there were high levels of confidence, maturity, self-efficacy and 'can do' attitudes, linked to a strong acceptance of the work and organization.

Self-efficacy beliefs and 'can-do' attitudes

What can we learn from recent research on self-efficacy and goal-setting theories? Bandura (1995a in Bandura, 1995b: 2) tells us that 'Perceived self-efficacy refers to beliefs in one's capabilities to organize and execute the courses of action required to manage prospective situations. Efficacy beliefs influence how people think, feel, motivate themselves, and act.' Many researchers (e.g. Lent *et al.*, 1994, 1996) have shown that self-efficacy beliefs play a critical role in determining academic goals and paths, career choices and subsequent success.

What people subjectively believe about themselves is a key determinant rather than what is objectively the case. Individuals construct their own realities from person-environment interactions and feedback, so self-theories are malleable. My own action research tells me that SOAR interventions can have positive effects on self-esteem and self-efficacy beliefs – something for you to put to the test. The concepts and examples given in this book implicitly apply the lessons learned from psychological approaches (Jarvis, 2005) and social cognitive research findings (Dweck, 2000).

Research (see Chapter 5) also shows that achievement drives the success of entrepreneurs: they set challenging goals for themselves and strive optimistically to continually improve their performance, driven by intrinsic motivation. Within these behaviours, goal setting is thought to be important; it is also a major career-planning skill:

> Much human behaviour, being purposive, is regulated by fore-thought, embodying valued goals. Personal goal-setting is influenced by self-appraisal of capabilities. The stronger the perceived self-efficacy, the higher the goal challenges people set for themselves and the firmer is their commitment to them.
>
> (Locke and Latham, 1990)

Goal-setting theory indicates that setting difficult goals leads to better performance. I make no apology for my self-audits in that case! These audits set out ideal end-goals in the form of challenging expectations, mirroring what graduate recruiters say they want for competitive positions – but these goals are also made personally meaningful and relevant for all students, which in itself can motivate. It is equally important, however, to break these end-goals down into manageable sub-goals that act like navigational beacons along the journey towards those ends.

We also know from experience that many students lack intrinsic motivation for a variety of reasons. You need to accept that developing the 'self- and other-awareness success cycle' (Figure 4.1) is going to be part of a slow and challenging process, and to share these concerns with students. Fostering self-reflection is a crucial part of that process, but many people believe that reflection is alien to the 'digital natives' of the current generation; some argue that modern life pushes them towards extraversion and kinaesthetic preferences for learning. I am not sure this is generally true – if reflection is tied in or implicit in activities that link 'self' with relevant benefits, it is my experience that most young learners participate with interest.

What do students need to assess about themselves?

Self-awareness is not a warm and fuzzy introspection that takes place in isolation, but a hard-edged education and business need. Students need external reference points from the 'world of opportunity' against which to assess themselves. These can come from a variety of sources. The main social constructs for our purposes here come from tutor expectations and HE regulations, to enable 'self' to be(come) an effective learner; and from employer requirements, so that 'self' can be(come) an effective worker. Students who are aware of their relative strengths, interests and priorities in relation to such external requirements can then detect opportunities in study and work that will:

a   allow them to express their interests and values;
b   use and develop their skills and assets;
c   work with like-minded people, employment organizations and sectors that
    accommodate their personal styles and preferences.

Although this is important for students and job seekers alike, the same features
are also important for tutors and recruiters. For example, nearly every question
on application forms and in interviews falls into the same three categories:

1   Will you like the job/course – are you motivated to achieve results here?
2   Can you do the job/course – do you have the ability: skills, qualifications,
    experience, attributes and knowledge?
3   Will you fit into the team/organization – is your personality compatible with
    others, and with company culture?

Self-mapping: who am I?

I call these three aspects of 'self' **M**otivation, **A**bility and **P**ersonality for the
purposes of this book. They may be referred to by different terminology elsewhere, but are generally accepted as making up an individual's 'career profile'.
They together provide a composite personal **MAP** (see Figure 4.2) that defines
individuals at their stage of life – a map that can be used to navigate a particular
stage of the life-career journey. MAP interacts with the individual's external
circumstances (assets and constraints) to determine his or her aspirations, results,
life-chances and choices. We can require learners to become critically aware of
the relative strengths that come from all three of their MAP facets. As Raymond
Chandler puts it, 'Ability is what you're capable of doing. Motivation determines
what you do. Attitude determines how well you do it.' (Chandler, undated)

Students should think of their personal MAP as a guide along their pathway
through life. It's important to remember that the map is not the territory: it is a
guide for them to make sense of the territory through which they are travelling at any given time. This is a map that each learner will have to construct,
de-construct and re-construct as 'self' engages with different opportunities
and is faced with recurrent decisions and transitions through life. In addition to
being an aid to navigation, it is also a blueprint each student will use to create
his or her life. The formation of an identity changes through different ages and
stages of life. For the time that students spend in HE, they need to discover – and
proactively construct – their MAP identity through the mechanisms and techniques
you provide.

Having introduced self-awareness broadly in Part 1, in this chapter I continue
the general theme linked with associated activities before going on to cover each
of the MAP aspects more specifically in the next three chapters, each dealing
more specifically with Motivation, Ability and Personality. Self-assessment is part

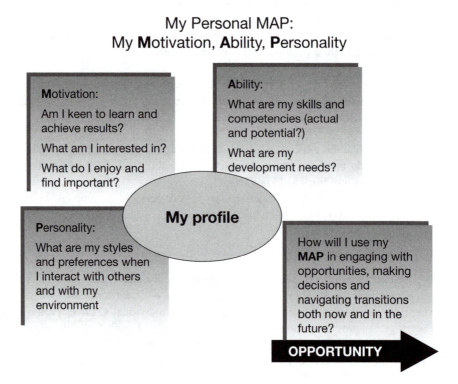

Figure 4.2 A personal **MAP**: **M**otivation, **A**bility, **P**ersonality.

of a mix of strategies in my earlier assessment example (Chapter 3), but an alternative is to set a piece of written work asking students to identify their personal profiles, and to write their reflective accounts in an (e)-portfolio. This assignment can act as a mechanism for pulling together the learning that occurs over a single module, or over the entire three years of a degree. In effect it reveals the thinking which leads students to make certain claims about their MAP. In doing this they are generating useful documentation – a sort of extended CV – from which they can select relevant material when needed. This goes a long way towards fulfilling the requirements of the Progress File agenda for UK HEIs.

Finding my Profile: a self-assessment example and tutor-marked assignment

At the outset it is worth giving students an idea of the composite MAP profile they should end up with and be able to demonstrate through working with the material and exercises given here. The following student brief and marker sheet provide guidelines you may adapt.

Finding My Profile (please aim for about 1,500 words) (Note that this is addressed to students)

Weighting: 30%   **Deadline date: (enter)**

Purpose and Learning Outcomes: This assignment should enable you to:

- specify a composite personal career profile which reflects systematic self-analysis based on the outcomes of a range of activities, questionnaires and career theories;
- discover and use resources for self-assessment and career choice;
- highlight specific examples from any area of your life (study, training, work, leisure activities) which convincingly demonstrate you possess the attributes you claim;
- make career-related choices based on your profile;
- build on strengths, and address your development needs.

In particular, it will enable you to articulate four different aspects of your 'career profile':

- Motivation: the interests and values most important to you, and your type and level of motivation in learning, developing and achieving results;
- Ability: skills and abilities, strengths and development needs;
- Personality: your preferences and styles in how you interact with the environment and with others;
- External influences on your career choices up to now, any circumstances, constraints or assets which may influence your career choices.

Now take this one step further: reflect on all four aspects and create a composite picture by examining the relationships between the different aspects of your profile. Each aspect of your MAP is partially insightful in isolation (and many of the self-assessment exercises and questionnaires you undertake will elicit just part of the picture), but pulling them together to see if a theme or pattern is emerging is most beneficial.

How can this help you choose suitable options in work and further learning? Try working this out through an analogy: imagine you are going shopping for a dinner party. What factors would you need to consider? Probably:

- the number of friends you've invited;
- their tastes and any special dietary or physical requirements;
- whether your party is to be formal or casual;
- how much time you have for shopping and cooking;
- your level of culinary expertise;
- the amount of money you want to spend.

Having a shopping list gives you a clear idea of what to buy, and some idea of what you can compromise on, how far you can be flexible. To go shopping with your profile list, prioritize – for example, 'I want to:

- use my language, communication and interpersonal strengths;
- work with people, preferably face-to-face and one-to-one;
- work in a caring capacity – healthcare or education;
- find a job that offers relative security rather than high wages – preferably in the public sector.'

And so you may decide to investigate congruent possibilities such as speech or occupational therapy, teaching English, perhaps as a second or foreign language, careers guidance, health or education psychology, counselling . . .

So, returning to your own profile, do you see a coherent picture emerging, patterns in your responses to people and events, or patterns of feedback from others? For example, you may find that your thinking and feeling come together with a certain integrity: that you enjoy what you are good at, and have relevant experience and positive feedback from others to give evidence of your predominant interests, abilities and personality.

On the other hand, you may discover apparent contradictions and inconsistencies. For example, you may be a Sociology graduate with the interest and ability to teach in secondary schools, but without the necessary subject qualifications and/or experience required to gain admission to the teacher training qualification. Or you may feel that particular personality traits (such as confidence or leadership qualities) do not reach the level at which you will need them, perhaps for entry to a graduate management position.

Are you unable to reconcile such conflicting elements? This assignment should help you to identify any discrepancies and deficits. You can then indicate the steps you will take to address such issues. This will allow you to further determine what you may need to do and develop in order to implement your aspiration(s) successfully.

Having a clear idea of who you are and what you can achieve is central to the career decision-making process. However, a couple of words of warning:

- Please contact one of the module team if you have any difficulties accessing any of the resources recommended for this assignment. Activities in class are essential, and audio-visual, web and print-based resources will be used and recommended as we progress.
- A range of tools, in the form of questionnaires and psychometric tests, is given online for self-assessment. Please give yourself plenty of time to use a reasonable range to analyse and build up your profile. Remember, however, that these are simply instruments to aid your own reflection and self-analysis. Any test results you report must be supported by evidence from real life and feedback from others. Avoid describing the tests and resources you have used – we know what they are. We are interested only in your personal interpretation of the results. Avoid saying 'the test told me I am . . . and so I must be . . .' This assignment requires you to link test results with specific personal examples to demonstrate the attributes you claim, just as you will have to do when applying for jobs or courses.

- Evidence should be drawn from any area of your life – education, employment, leisure, domestic and life experiences. Choose specific, pertinent examples and explain how they are appropriate and relevant. Do not generalize or repeat yourself – write concisely about specific examples that are convincing to the assessor or selector (see marking criteria). Given the word limit, write clearly, concisely and analytically.

- Only you can detect how the various aspects of your MAP fit together to provide the synergy that captures the rich complexity which is your unique career profile. Discussions with careers advisers and others can help, but you are the ultimate decision-maker in charge of your life-career. You could think and write about how your MAP might affect:

  - your future career-related choices;
  - your choice of employer and industry sector;
  - your impact in a team;
  - how you relate to others;
  - your aspirations;
  - your style of working;
  - the problems you might encounter;
  - the situations you should avoid;
  - what you need to work on.

- Self-knowledge is essentially fluid and dynamic, so the picture you construct now will hold good for just this stage of your life, and relate particularly to your transition beyond university. The attributes you define are not static – skills can be developed, values can change. Given that both 'self' and 'jobs' are subject to continuous change, review is an important part of the career-development process. Self-knowledge is not easy for yet another reason: we can never completely know ourselves. Even though the information you are working with is changing and partial, the attempt to assess yourself honestly will pay dividends in all areas of your life.

Assessment criteria:

We will look for evidence that you have:

- understood your brief and met the aims outlined above;
- undertaken systematic self-assessment using the range of learning opportunities and resources recommended and provided;
- reflected on outcomes of such exercises to identify and realistically profile your competence, motivation and personality factors;
- appreciated the concepts that have been presented – e.g. MBTI, Holland's self-concept theory, etc.;
- interpreted such factors in relation to specific real-life evidence, giving pertinent examples (achievements, experiences, activities from any area of

your life) that demonstrate you actually possess the ability, interest or attribute in question;

* identified any special external circumstances – assets or constraints – you might have;
* constructed a composite picture and prioritized which attributes you are likely to use in making your career choice(s);
* indicated possible choices which may fit your profile and priorities.

Please follow the format provided below for your assignment, and also use the marker sheet on p. 88 to understand what we expect and how you will be graded. Use this as a checklist and, before you submit, grade your own performance. Later you can compare your self-grading with tutor-awarded marks.

Format for assignment: Finding My Profile

Copy out the headings and sub-headings given in bold, to structure your Profile. Pay particular attention to the instructions given in brackets.

Motivation

---

1) I have used 'It's *My* Journey through Life: Am I in the Driving Seat?' and other activities to discover that . . .
   (To what extent overall do you feel you possess the motivation and skills you will need in order to take control of your career direction? What do your separate ratings in the sub-sections and your experience indicate about you?)

2) My strongest interests are . . .
   (Visit this page to identify your interests: http://hrnt.jhu.edu/cmp/Holland Types.cfm)

3) The values most important for me are . . .
   (Use the work from Chapter 4.)

4) Evidence: I know this because . . .
   (Think of real-life examples where you have felt motivated to do or achieve something.)

Ability

---

5) My strongest skills and abilities are . . .

6) My preferred learning styles are . . .
   (Use work from Chapter 6 and your studies generally to identify the knowledge and competencies you are developing and are best at.)

7) Evidence: I have achieved . . .
(Demonstrate your abilities through examples of achievements, experiences and activities – from education, work or leisure.)

Personality and attitudes

---

8) My personality type according to MBTI or Kiersey . . .
(What are the main characteristics of your type?)
The Kiersey Character Sorter is on http://kiersey.com/cgi-bin/kiersey/kcs.cgi.
Also see www.personalitytype.com (MBTI-based).

9) The team role(s) I tend to adopt . . .
(from the MBTI and Belbin exercises in class, online, audits and real-life evidence).
Useful web-sites: www.belbin.com;
www.teamtechnology.co.uk/belbin.html (also has MBTI explanations);
www.mtr-i.com (makes a comparison between Belbin and 'MTR team roles').

10) Evidence: I know this because . . .
(Demonstrate main personality traits through pertinent, brief real-life examples.)

Circumstances – assets and/or constraints

---

11) Other *external* influences and circumstances that may affect my career choice . . .
(Use career theories and the 'lifeline exercise' to reflect on your career history to date.)
This section refers to **external circumstances** rather than innate abilities or disabilities, values, etc. This gives you a chance to identify assets such as family support, the freedom to move and accept a job anywhere in the country or world, or barriers such as being tied to a particular geographical area, mounting student debt and so on – anything external that will affect your career choices.

12) Patterns emerging from 'pulling the pieces together' . . .

13) Possible implications for future career plans, e.g. skills I need to develop/ stepping stones I may need to consider in order to achieve my goal, such as further study, work experience, etc. . . .

Marker Sheet for Assignment: Finding my Profile (can be used for both self-assessment and tutor awarded grades and feedback comments).

Name of student: ....

A: Outstanding   B: Very Good   C: Good   D: Satisfactory
E: Further work needed   F: Unsatisfactory/weak

Realistic and authentic	A	B	C	D	E	F	Inadequate attempt
Shows excellent appreciation of relative strengths and limitations							Unrealistically high or low perception of capabilities and development needs
Self-assessment undertaken thoroughly, covering MAP							Patchy coverage of topics
Material drawn from a range of sources							Material drawn from one or two sources only
Claims are supported with convincing evidence							Unsupported claims
Substantial critical comment and independent judgement							Little or no analysis; no independent viewpoints
Valid conceptual understanding							Many/major errors in interpreting concepts
No waffle/irrelevant material							Rambling; irrelevant material included
Conclusions appear authentic							Conclusions do not follow from arguments
Clearly and accurately identifies areas requiring development							Does not identify key areas for development
Specifies an achievable, timed approach to address the need							Does not outline how the need will be addressed
No errors in grammar/ syntax, spelling and typing							Poor written communication skills

COMMENTS

MARKS

Self-concept, self-assessment and feedback from others

Having an open mind and willingness to learn are crucial attitudes in navigating the 'voyage of self-discovery'. In the words of Marcel Proust:

> A pair of wings, a different respiratory system, which might enable us to travel through space, would in no way help us, for if we visited Mars or Venus while keeping the same senses, they would clothe everything that we saw in the same aspect as the things of Earth. **The only true voyage of discovery, the only really rejuvenating experience, would be not to visit strange lands but to possess other eyes** . . . [emphasis in bold is mine].
>
> (Proust, 1982, vol. 3: 260)

To 'see with other eyes', however, is not easy. It's important to evoke interest and set this up as a purposeful and adventurous exploration of 'self' rather than mere obedience to any authority you might impose.

Alert students to the crucial and interrelated nature of four perspectives that influence self- and other-awareness as listed in the following box:

---

1) your subjective perception (or self-concept) of your strengths, interests, personal qualities, styles and preferences when you think about and attempt to explain your behaviours and approaches. This will determine your responses to all self-assessment questions and to the real-life choices you make.

2) your perception of the above characteristics in others, which will determine the judgements you make about them, and influence your relationships;

3) others' perceptions of who you are, which adds up broadly to 'your reputation' and obviously has an impact in every area of life. For example, the judgements that 'significant others' make about you are evidenced in teachers' reports, school certificates and employers' references – documents that may be presented as evidence of your MAP.

4) a third party perception of interactions between two or more people – for example, employers train observers to objectively assess candidates' interactions in assessment centre activities, and score them against set criteria.

Switching perspectives and looking 'with other eyes' at a problem in a task, or a conflict in a relationship, can help students to be more objective and to resolve the situation. Accessing different states or 'modes' through dissociating from an event or memory, and switching between viewpoints, is used as part of the learning process in some of my practical examples.

Most people develop their sense of self from feedback from others. This develops from the impressionable years of childhood onwards. Feedback can be positive or it can be damaging. Kissing a frog and turning it into a prince is not just a fairy story, and you do not have to be a beauty to tame a beast. The power to empower others resides in all of us. So am I suggesting you go out and kiss a frog today? Well seriously, stop now and ask yourself: 'Am I using my feedback powers wisely?' (Not just a frivolous question – this is closely connected to a valuable leadership style or skill.) And it's worth remembering that the more you give away this power the more it 'comes home to roost'.

The road to maturity is about progressively developing one's own identity and possibly breaking away from any negative perceptions and expectations others may have imposed (though even in adulthood this is not easy). A mature approach to feedback is to invite constructive criticism from people you trust, people who can help you see your strengths and limitations more clearly. The technique of 360° feedback is used frequently in leadership training, where peers or subordinates are asked (anonymously) to complete a questionnaire that reveals various aspects of the management style under review.

The more congruent these perspectives are with each other the greater will be your level of comfort in your person-environment interactions and your chances of success. However, these interactions are highly complicated and subjective.

**What matters most
is how you see yourself**

- Roles (study vs other roles)
- Responsibilities
- Strengths
- Opportunities
- Aspirations
- Results
- Resources
- Needs

(a miaow or a roar?)

Figure 4.3 Self-perception and self-esteem.

Even staying for the moment with (1) in the box on p. 89, self-concept has different strands and levels, and is subject to blind spots.

Conscious and subconscious aspects of 'self'

Freud is reported to have said 'The mind is like an iceberg, it floats with one-seventh of its bulk above water.' You can use the iceberg (Figure 4.4) as a rough analogy for the human psyche, simply to point out that 'self' has conscious and subconscious layers and strands that are inextricably linked. Thoughts, emotions, ideas, values and beliefs that may be buried in the subconscious – below the waterline – drive the actions and behaviours we observe in different environments, above the waterline in this analogy. It seems self-evident that even capabilities and interests are only reportable but not directly observable until they turn into performance and behaviours.

Robert Dilts, a neuro-linguistic programming (NLP) practitioner, explains these relationships:

> values operate together with beliefs to create meaning and motivation in our lives. They relate to why we think what we think and do what we do. Values and beliefs support the identity and mission of an individual or organization,

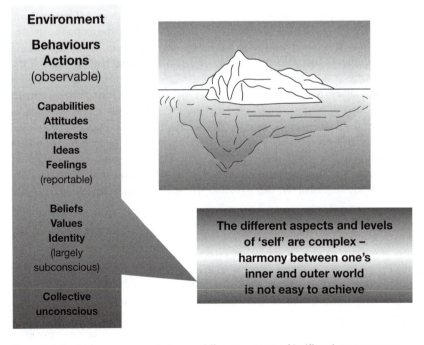

Environment

Behaviours
Actions
(observable)

Capabilities
Attitudes
Interests
Ideas
Feelings
(reportable)

Beliefs
Values
Identity
(largely
subconscious)

Collective
unconscious

The different aspects and levels
of 'self' are complex –
harmony between one's
inner and outer world
is not easy to achieve

Figure 4.4 Seeking congruence between different aspects of 'self' and environment.

and provide the reinforcement (motivation and permission) that promotes or inhibits particular capabilities and behaviours. A particular identity or role, for instance, will be associated with several core values and beliefs. These, in turn, are supported by a range of skills and capabilities, which are required to manifest particular values and beliefs as actions in a particular environment or context.

(Dilts, undated)

Breaking the ice of unproductive mental maps

Learning about 'self' can and does take place anywhere at any time, in unplanned ways and unstructured situations, all the time and over a period of time. Students will have developed subjective mental models from their experiences, maps they use to navigate through life – but this is likely to have been an unconscious process. That's fine if their map is working productively for them, but many students come to university with self-limiting beliefs that are more damaging than any lack of ability. Many do not realize and accept that they have the ability to engender the results they desire, and they tend to blame circumstances or other people. In these cases personal growth must go beyond adaptive changes to the existing mental map – it must generate a new map that allows for new self-efficacy beliefs and empowering behaviours.

> As people grow up and find various ways their map does not serve them, those who are more conscious seek to change or improve the map. The unconscious just blame the world for not being like their map, without realizing that the map is just something made up as an aid to navigating through the real world.
>
> Approaches to personal change that are effective, then, bring about changes in this map of reality. And here is where the trouble starts for those of us seeking personal growth. In order for a new and better map to replace the one that isn't serving you very well, there has to be an interim period where the old map goes into temporary chaos, breaks down, and then is replaced by a new one that more accurately reflects reality and more resourcefully allows you to be happy, creative, and spiritually connected to other people.
>
> (Harris, n.d.)

'As a man thinks, so is he' is an accepted law of cause and effect. The causal arrow, however, points in the other direction too, because experiences often reinforce thinking. Changing students' thinking and negative self-talk is the first step in motivating those who have little or no drive for achievement. We as teachers may similarly need to realize that inappropriate beliefs and reactions to events and people can cause us needless stress – e.g. if I believe that I should be totally competent, liked and respected by every student and colleague, and achieving in every aspect of my work, I am likely to become stressed if I make even a small mistake. On the other hand, if I accept that mistakes are inevitable and are only the raw material for development, I can invite feedback from colleagues and make progress.

Typically, traditional education identifies and attempts to teach learners to solve problems at the top of the iceberg, in the external environment. This is based on the well-known 'experiential learning cycle' defined by Kolb (1984: 68–9): learning is a continuum that moves through a single feedback loop between concrete experience, reflective observation, abstract conceptualization and active experimentation. To put this simply, doing something and thinking about the experience allows a learner to relate the experience to what is already known, sifting and deciding on its relevance and usefulness for solving the problem or dealing with the issue at hand. Learners experiment with the new knowledge and then add to or adjust it through further experiences.

This type of learning is adaptive – it corrects errors in an immediate, short-term way; and it is incremental – developing skills and knowledge, producing movement, *but in the same direction* – reinforcing or amplifying the same subconscious mental map. Problem solving in this way is important, but it does not question the problem itself or change the mental map where needed. 'Double-loop learning' is about going deeper and reflecting critically on the beliefs and values of the individual, or indeed of the organization. Argyris and Schon (1974) coined the terms 'single-loop' and 'double-loop' learning to describe the difference between this type of surface learning and deeper learning for development. The latter enables one to keep an open mind, objectively comparing and adjusting one's mental maps where necessary, to allow for personal growth through congruence and integrity between different layers of the psyche.

Bringing subconscious beliefs to conscious awareness through reflection is an important stage in converting random experiences into insights that enable students to identify and change the beliefs that subconsciously condition their actions. Inciting such insight is the first step in bringing about a change in behaviour. HE students are in developmental mode and usually also at an impressionable age, but it is still difficult for us (and them) to reach those parts under the waterline. I have met staff who say 'don't go there, it's very tricky' or 'how could we do this with our 1001 students?' I think we need to try, because their (and our) blind spots can cause all sorts of failures and problems. When identified and used constructively, however, they can be the source of much undiscovered personal energy.

Constraints may of course genuinely arise from students' circumstances, but they may equally arise from their *response* to what they consider obstacles. They sometimes report life-changing insights through reflective exercises – for example 'I realized that my partner was not actually holding me back in my career, it was just me believing that I needed to be home with him every evening. Actually deep down I felt I wasn't good enough to become a teacher. I've decided now I am going to give it a go.'

Creating the conditions for 'self' to flourish

Finding personal congruence

A parallel process is at work here: as a reflective practitioner in HE you also need to create curricula (and your own future) in an integrated frame of mind. Everything you share with students can equally be applied to yourself. It will be apparent to you that success depends on the extent to which your beliefs, interests and capabilities are congruent with your behaviours. So in a thought experiment here, ask yourself: *Do you believe self-awareness skills are central in preparing students for future transitions in a world of super-complexity? Is it your job to do this? Are you excited and confident about empowering them?* Your thoughts are charged with the power to succeed or fail as they will translate themselves into the attitudes and actions that will make the difference. 'Meaningful reconstructing first takes place within the minds of teachers and their beliefs about the nature and possibilities of their students. From there, all else follows' (Campbell and Campbell, 1999).

At the same time as we might seek greater balance and congruence between our feelings, values, beliefs, interests and capabilities in relation to what is expected of us in any particular environment, we must accept that such congruence is rare, and we learn a great deal from simply attempting to balance our mental states in different environments. What might you do to achieve greater congruence in 'walking your talk' if you discover discrepancies? For example, you may believe in SOAR aims but identify that you would like to build your capacity to engage students in the process. What support and resources are available to you? You may want to discuss your responses to these questions with others, or reflect and take action for yourself.

Fostering self-efficacy

I have attempted to incorporate the extended 'self-awareness skills-set' and principles throughout in designing and delivering my SOAR model, so they are already enshrined in my previous chapters. Some that relate in particular to fostering self-efficacy are emphasized here.

EBL and end-goals: As a self-efficacy intervention, I want to refer again to the power of EBL (not a pure but a partial EBL approach) – i.e. make the gains visible and relevant, for both current study and longer-term life-career purposes. Get students to see why the goals are important and relevant, and then allow as much personal freedom as possible for them to achieve results in ways suited to their styles and preferences. In reality the demands of accreditation and assessment may curtail the amount of freedom you can allow, but credits and accountability are in themselves powerful external drivers for students.

Plan and align: Planning and organizing any programme for success is about setting out the long-term aims and desired results, then breaking them down into learning objectives and learning opportunities that are interesting, relevant and manageable for students. It is equally important to provide tools, techniques, resources and feedback in support of progress towards these goals. Be clear about the learning, teaching and assessment methods you will be using, and make the criteria explicit as to how students will be judged. Set up peer support and self-help resources that will stimulate interest and commitment. Remember all those principles of constructive alignment! Many students see the empowerment that results from investing in 'self' and choose to undertake their personal developmental journeys in creative ways.

Provide constructive feedback: If you are to provide feedback that will enhance self-esteem and self-efficacy, assigning grades for a piece of work is insufficient and unhelpful. All that I have said about teaching students to provide formative feedback to each other in peer-assessment (Chapter 3) should equally apply to the feedback you give, both informally in class and more formally for assignments. A main SOAR aim is to encourage reflection and self-assessment, so it is in keeping with this aim to ask the learner: What worked well? (identify strengths and good points to do more of in future). What was less effective? (identify points for improvement). How else could the topic/activity be tackled? (this can give both the provider and recipient of feedback insight into their pre-conceptions and strategies, and greater flexibility in tackling the topic or task next time).

Students are more likely to understand and accept your feedback if you provide it against the learning goals and criteria you have explicitly stated earlier. Shifting the goalposts can lead to immense frustration and to loss of credibility because students may feel unjustly judged in ways they were not prepared for. Be specific and communicate clearly.

Students will accept feedback in different ways, depending on the type of achievement motivation they have. For instance, if they are seeking deep learning, constructive feedback will be perceived as guidance to improve learning; if they are surface learners they may just want feedback to check and confirm how they are doing in order to regulate and direct minimum effort to get by. Students who lack confidence may feel threatened by feedback, even if you give it tactfully. They persist in seeing it as a judgement of their capability. Try to counter this in your general briefing by pointing out that in your eyes there is no failure – that feedback is the raw material for learning and development.

Reduce anxiety: As a facilitator of learning, there are several ways in which you can reduce students' concerns about the threat of failure. You may wish to acknowledge that most goals worth striving for stretch people out of their comfort zones, pose dilemmas and present obstacles. Discuss the perceived obstacles that stop students from achieving. I sometimes ask them to write anonymously on scraps of paper any expectations or issues they may have about a learning task (e.g. breaking out in a nervous sweat at interviews or presentations!) and put their 'fears in a hat' at the start of a session. I pass the hat round again, we pick out notes at random and deal with each other's fears in small groups, so in effect we are sharing and helping to resolve each others' problems.

You might assure them you will not put anyone on the spot. In fact it is sometimes advisable to allow them to set up an activity, and go off-stage or monitor from the sidelines. Allow them freedom to take active responsibility, to develop at their own pace and choose just what they consider to be a 'safe risk zone' where it is fine to fall, pick themselves up and try, try again. Research shows that giving individuals some control over their environment helps them to see it as benign rather than threatening. In assessing performance you can invoke the desire to 'travel optimistically' from their starting point to an improved level of competence. Ipsative assessment approaches are most in tune with this, as they primarily measure the 'distance travelled' or the 'value added' by the individual rather than awarding summative grades.

Try 'flooding': This is a technique that induces anxiety, but can be very effective. Put students in a fearful situation without any preparation, as early as possible in your course or module – so they learn that the situation does not kill them and they can cope. For example, when I was in training to become a careers adviser, the group was taken (without prior warning) into a very large auditorium, and each of us in turn was required to go on stage and speak to our peers (who were lined up in the far top row of seats) for a couple of minutes on a given topic. I was terrified of making presentations to large audiences, but having done this once I knew I could do it again, and do it better with the training and preparation that followed on our course.

Creating the right environment

Students are likely to see that worthwhile skills development requires effort and courage, and they will be given support and resources while being stretched out of their comfort zones. Everyone in the group must take responsibility for respecting and helping others along the journey to self-discovery and personal growth.

This type of tolerance and acceptance cannot always be taken for granted – you will have to work at creating the right environment for students to undertake honest self-appraisal. You could ask your group to agree some basic ground rules. I usually say that 'self-awareness exercises are somewhat different from other areas of the curriculum, so you will learn best if you are in an environment that encourages sharing, trust and reflection. How shall we together create such an environment?'

The ideal is to end up with an agreement that everyone will abide by principles such as these:

- We agree to participate actively and gain insights from each exercise.
- We will allow for the different pace of learning and the different preferences of others.
- We agree that learning is both an individual and a group process and responsibility.

- We can learn best from each other if we trust and respect each other's opinions, values and experience.
- We will share only that personal information we feel comfortable about revealing, and will treat each other's personal information as confidential.
- We will work hard but we will have fun.

Exercises to enhance self-awareness skills

'I am . . .' statements and suggested extensions

Sometimes it's easier for us to 'see' other people's personality than to be objective about our own. You can start a simple self-assessment exercise by asking students to write a few statements beginning with the stem 'I am . . .' as if they were Superman (or any hero they know of). Most people, including international students, know Christopher Reeve in his Superman role, and many also know about his inspirational personal story. Discuss this briefly, then ask them to write (confidentially) up to ten true statements about themselves, beginning with 'I am . . .'

You can put most items of this sort roughly under four headings:

- Social or socio-economic roles – e.g.
  I am the youngest of three brothers.
  I am studying History and working part-time as a museum assistant.

- Physical characteristics – e.g.
  I am the spitting image of Brad Pitt.
  I am older than I look.

- Personality descriptors – e.g.
  I am guilty of watching too much TV and indulging in chocolate.
  I am described by my classmates as a stand-up comedian.

- Declarations of capability or interest – e.g.
  I am interested in using my affinity with power tools in my choice of dentistry as a career.
  I am good at inventing harebrained schemes.

Such descriptors reveal self-concept, which may or may not correspond with objective truth (what is the latter anyway?). Whether that image is predominantly positive or negative will have much to do with one's own and others' expectations – and will have an impact on self-esteem and self-efficacy beliefs. If a student looks in the mirror expecting to see Superman and sees Danny instead, his self-esteem is likely to descend into his socks (not that there's anything wrong with being Danny!). Self-esteem may be defined as '. . . the disposition to experience oneself as being competent to cope with the basic challenges of life and being worthy of happiness' (Branden, 2001).

Attitude statements are often evaluative rather than just descriptive, such as 'I am better at basketball than tennis'. Ask students to examine their statements: 'Are your perceptions realistic or unnecessarily self-deprecating? What do they say about you?' You could deliberately focus on positive descriptors by asking students to write with the stems 'I am good at . . .' 'I am at my best when . . .' and 'I am interested in . . .' These stems relate more directly to the philosophy of AI and the MAP components of a career profile.

You can extend 'I am . . .' statements in many different ways. I have used it as an ice breaker for 'knowing me, knowing you'. If the group is small enough, ask each student to read out one of their statements (one they feel comfortable about sharing), and get others who identify with it to stand up and say their names. Through this the group get to know and learn something about each other.

Identifying similarities and differences may be used effectively as an introduction to a session on cultural awareness, but equally as an introduction to self-awareness and self-promotion. Use it as a starting point for discussion and further exercises through which they will progressively deepen their understanding of themselves so that their descriptors will look increasingly more analytical. To illustrate this point, show them examples from good profile statements in CVs or letters of application so that they see what convincing self-promotion looks like at the point of transition. The Careers Service at your HEI should be able to give you examples related to applications for different types of occupations and industry sectors.

A variant which I like is the 30-second CV. Students use their 'I am . . .' statements to write a short thumbnail sketch of themselves, including only positive features and something memorable so that they make an impact. Give them five minutes to do this and then practise saying it out loud to each other in pairs.

Alternatively the 'elevator pitch' exercise enables students to create favourable first impressions, especially in formal situations. The concept is taken from the world of business where entrepreneurs have to turn a business idea into a clear and captivating pitch that can be given in 30–60 seconds – the time it takes for an elevator to ride up or down a typical high-rise building. In that brief span of time they need to communicate the value they can bring to a potential investor or client.

Ask your students to 'imagine getting into an elevator in an employer's office building after a job interview. There is just one other person riding in the elevator – a senior manager in the firm – and, as you start descending, he turns to you and says: "I noticed you were in an interview with Angela today. What's your background?" The clock has started ticking. You now have between 30–60 seconds to make that all-important first impression.'

Points to make:

1) The Elevator Pitch is something students should practise and be able to adapt and use appropriately in formal settings, whenever they need to introduce themselves effectively to potential employers or business contacts. Examples include:

- going to a recruitment fair;
- employer presentations;
- in selection interviews (as the foundation of your answer when you are asked that tricky question: 'Tell me about yourself.');
- on the telephone;
- in teamwork activities or group discussions at assessment centres.

2) They never get a second chance to make a first impression – and first impressions are based on body language, posture, appearance, as well as how people speak: pitch, pace, tone of voice and words used.

3) Practice makes perfect – nobody has a great answer first time round. Ask students to develop a personal representation of their best features, but this shouldn't sound like a rehearsed textbook answer. They need to become comfortable delivering this with ease so that they can adapt it as necessary for different situations.

4) Give feedback, or let students work in pairs and give each other feedback. They need to come across as friendly, respectful, intelligent and ambitious individuals with integrity and good self-esteem.

Using psychometrics and computers for (self)-assessment and development

Graduate recruiters often use sophisticated psychometric measures during the selection process to understand a potential employee better, to screen out inappropriate recruits, or to positively try and find someone with particular qualities that are missing in their existing team – e.g. someone with strategic vision, or an eye for detail, or . . . whatever. Dorothy Spry,[2] a business psychologist, comments:

> Psychometric assessments, questionnaires, inventories or the dreaded word 'tests' – as they are referred to – are becoming more important than ever when recruiting graduates into the workplace. Employers are consistently finding that the calibre of the graduate, whilst adequate on the knowledge and intelligence front, falls short on the following attributes: the ability to show initiative and solve problems, being a flexible member of an organization, being a team player and having the right attitude with fellow workers, clients or customers. To quote a psychology colleague, *'We hire people for their specific skills and competencies in the job and we fire them for personality clashes.'*
>
> (Dr Cripps, 2003 in Spry and Cripps, 2007)

Students should practise taking aptitude tests (some are available online and some careers services offer workshops) as ways of brushing up and familiarizing themselves with numerical, verbal or abstract reasoning tests. Personality 'tests' are different however – in fact they are not tests with right or wrong answers as such, but rather questionnaires or inventories which seek to elicit certain characteristics, and it is difficult to second-guess what the employer is looking for. Applicants are best advised to answer honestly. After all there would be no point in getting a job where you couldn't 'be yourself' and end up getting stressed. Students can get a head start though, by thinking about the type of personal approaches that are needed for good job-fit and company-fit.

Before students or graduates encounter psychometrics as 'something done to them', we can introduce them to such measures as tools for self-development. I do not believe they should accept without question the results of psychometrics (or indeed passively accept programmed knowledge of any kind). The ways in which they build self-knowledge should be based on a process of doing something, thinking about or questioning it, adjusting, experimenting, evaluating, recording, taking further action and modifying – and there is no reason why the trigger for learning should not be a psychometric measure combined with a personal constructionist approach.

This approach is advocated by some occupational psychologists who have devised psychometric measures that are available online – e.g. TeamFocus[3] provide a university licence (at a cost) for unlimited use of a web-based battery of aptitude tests (verbal, numerical and abstract reasoning), a Learning Styles Indicator (LSI) and a Type Dynamics Indicator (TDI) that generates a detailed career report. All these can be built into the curriculum, or taken as stand-alone instruments that provide immediate personalized feedback to the 'test-taker' via email.

Computerized support for personal and career development comes in various forms. The main package widely used in UK HEIs is Prospects Planner.[4] There are four entry routes and it is possible to start with any one of them. The first route invites users to input information on their interests and skills, which is then matched against occupational information held in its database. Users can compare the resulting matches on-screen for best-fit, or print out the list of occupations to explore further, either still online or in print format. The process can enhance self-awareness linked to opportunity-awareness, decision making and transition skills. Adult Directions[5] is similar – both packages are intended to 'teach CMS' rather than prescribe best-fit occupations.

Theories of career choice: do we need them?[6]

Many people believe that they fell into brilliant careers by accident or luck – just happened to be in the right place at the right time, having met the right person. Another variant of this belief is that the answer lies in the stars – not the stars in your eyes, but in astrology. Life is of course full of chance encounters and coincidences – but is it sufficient to use these as explanations of the factors that determine our lives? The accident hypothesis fails to recognize that it is not so much the chance event that is important but the individual's response to that chance. 'The *meeting of preparation with opportunity generates the offspring we call luck*', says Anthony Robbins in *Unlimited Power* (1986).

The background

The policy and practice of careers education and guidance has a theoretical and historical basis. Career theories are not, however, proven scientific theories in an academic sense, they are social science attempts to describe, explain and predict the process of occupational choice. Adopting a critical stance to them can give you new insights into your own decision-making process. Attempt a critique as you read: Where do you think these theories are lacking? Do you identify with them in any sense? Are they applicable to the conditions that prevail today?

The first theories of this type were just common sense psychological approaches, formulated in the US some 100 years ago. They imply that a large element of individual choice is possible, and that people exercise a great degree of control over their decisions. Such beliefs are a modern phenomenon. Previous generations had no choice but to grow their own food/work in textile mills/go down coal mines – or starve to death. Then the industrial revolution from about 1850 onwards brought about three main trends: a great increase in and diversification of jobs, population expansion and mobility, and education reform.

The two world wars subsequently gave a major impetus to the evolution of organized career counselling. Choice has always been differentially available to people, but suddenly there seemed to be a new range and greater impact of influences on where people worked and what work they could do, right across the social structure. Theories evolved as attempts were made to analyze these new influences, tending to emphasize either internal or external influences as primary determinants of career choice. The main psychological theories are outlined here, and theories that stress external factors, using sociological explanations, are described in Chapter 8.

Psychological theories of career identity are broadly of two kinds:

a) Trait and factor theories (e.g. Parsons, 1909) put an emphasis on what people can be shown to be like – in their abilities, attainments and personality – and gave rise to the use of psychometric aptitude tests and standardized inventories in careers guidance, until the work of Carl Rogers (1965) led towards a counselling bias.

b) Self-concept theories emphasize the importance of how people see themselves in ability and motivation, and how self-concept changes over the lifespan. (I have already introduced Super's LCR in Chapter 2.) By the late 1960s the developmental concepts introduced in the US (e.g. Super, 1953; Holland, 1966) began to cross the Atlantic and to be 'translated' into British terms (Hayes et al., 1972). It was argued that the aim of guidance should not be to make decisions for people, but to facilitate the process of career fulfilment and promote decision-making competencies.

John Holland's Six Personality Types and Environments (1966, 1973) is an elaboration of Super's self-concept theory, but can also be seen to revert to earlier talent-matching approaches based on individual differences. Where it differs from the earlier approach is in its emphasis on the 'chooser': on the choice or series of choices actively made by people seeking environments congruent with their personalities or self-concepts.

The main instrument (still used today) developed on the back of this theory is the Self-Directed Search (SDS). It exemplifies Holland's contention that people on the one hand and occupational environments on the other fall into six categories, in varying degrees and combinations: Realistic, Investigative, Artistic, Social, Enterprising and Conventional. People tend to search for jobs that match their personal orientations, and which will let them exercise their skills and aptitudes, express their values and interests, and take on agreeable roles and problems. Holland states that a person's primary direction of choice is determined by the type he or she most resembles. The theory and its associated SDS are particularly useful in clarifying vocational preferences and related occupations, as they describe both people and environments in similar language. Ask students to visit the following URL to read the basics of the theory, identify the combination of their first two (or three) types of interest, and what this implies in terms of their current aspirations: http://hrnt.jhu.edu/cmp/HollandTypes.cfm .

You will find a critique of this and other career theories in John Arnold's book *Managing Careers into the 21st Century* (1997). Such theories may be explicitly included in curricula, but the emphasis should be on their practical application to individuals' real worlds, through activities such as reflective audits, psychometric questionnaires, group exercises, feedback and discussion, etc. The role of the tutor is mainly to facilitate open and honest self-appraisal, informing this with relevant information.

Student brief for The Lifeline exercise

The Lifeline is another way of taking stock of past experiences that may have contributed to your present situation. All sorts of factors influence life-career decisions: educational, personal, professional, financial, health and family circumstances. This exercise helps you focus on and gain insights into defining factors and events in your life: how have they affected you; what was your response to them? Thinking about this now can also help when you are faced with tough application form and interview questions such as:

> 'Describe the most difficult decision you have had to make. Tell us how you reached this decision.' (GKN)
> 'Which people, events and experiences in your life have you found difficult to handle? How have you coped and how have you developed as a result?' (Marks & Spencer)
> 'What have been the most important events in your life so far? Indicate briefly why they are of significance to you.' (Lloyds Bank)

1) Get a blank piece of paper, turn it horizontally and draw a line from left to right across the middle to represent your life from birth to the present. You can mark it from 0 years to your current age, and section it off into five or ten-year periods.

2) Chart on this line the significant events of your life at the age they occurred. Try marking positive, happy events and factors in black ink above the line, and sad or difficult events below the line in red, using the distance from your lifeline to indicate the degree of impact the event had on you. Give yourself time to think about this. Note that the same event may be perceived by different people as happy or sad, depending on your experience of it – and you may be ambivalent about some events. Examples of events and influences you might include are:
    • changes, e.g. starting school, university, first job/pay packet, leaving home, etc.;
    • significant holidays or trips;
    • turning points and decision points;
    • achievements and setbacks;
    • meeting significant people.

3) Consider which experiences led to personal growth, character development and discovery of abilities and potential. What were the major learning or turning points and the factors that affected you (whether internal or external)? Mark these with a T. Who and what helped or hindered your progress? Which experiences were most challenging? Which involved you in real choice? Try marking stresses with S, risks with R. Discuss your lifeline with a friend or mentor if you wish.

4) Looking back over your life so far, you may be surprised by the variety of experience and development you have been involved in. This is because we rarely have time to think about this variety all at once. Do you notice any patterns in your response to events and in your decision-making style? What led to your aspiration to come to university and study the course you are on? How do you feel about the result now, in retrospect?

5) What do you think employers are looking for when they ask the type of questions given above? (They can tell a great deal about you from the way you answer. Basically they want to see that you can persevere despite obstacles and setbacks; learn from feedback and failure as well as achievement and success; make good decisions and solve problems; respond appropriately to change.) Use this exercise and your knowledge of career theories to write a sample answer to one of the questions.

6) Prepare a four-minute verbal presentation on the topic: 'Where do my self-perceptions come from? What events, relationships and groups have most influenced me, in both positive and negative ways?'

Transferring self-assessment principles to other subjects

Metacognition is integral and meaningful in the SOAR process, but it could easily be part of any course, by building in reflection during classroom activities, pausing to ask questions that require students to assess their own engagement and think about the process of their learning. For example, I adapted and tried an idea that came from the One Minute Paper (Angelo and Cross, 1993), using this as a 'connecting thread' linking sessions and topics on my module, by concluding each session with a short exercise. Students were asked to write down individually (and share later):

Three things I have learnt from this session:
Some things I will do differently as a result:
Questions I still have about this topic:

I would then pick up the questions at the start of the next session and deal with them, which often usefully linked to the next planned topic anyway.

Building self-assessment into tutor-assessed written work: Assessment enforces student engagement, and I have given an example in Chapter 3 of self-assessment combined with peer- and tutor-assessment, so that it is one element within a mix of strategies. You can also enhance student learning by building elements of self-assessment into the summative grading that is conventional in HE. For instance, in any subject students could be given marker sheets alongside assessment briefs, setting out the criteria you will be using to grade that piece of work (see my example on p. 88). Ask them to use this as a checklist during their draft work, and again before they submit the assignment, to assess themselves by ticking the boxes that best reflect their performance against each criterion. Use the same marker sheet when you assess that piece of work, giving feedback on the extent to which your grades correlate with the student's self-assessment. Award a few marks for honest self-appraisal efforts.

See David Boud for further explanations, reasons and suggestions for incorporating self-assessment in different ways into HE curricula. For instance:

> Some self-assessment practices take students beyond the present context. By reflecting on their learning they gain a greater appreciation of the influences on it and on the nature of their particular experience. In these cases self-assessment is emancipatory. It contributes to the development of the person because, through it, students' self knowledge and self understanding increase.
> (Boud, 1995: 20)

Chapter 4: Summary of main points

- Focus on 'Self' (the S of SOAR) is central within my interpretation of the process of learner development, and in facilitating skills and attributes associated with self-awareness, self-assessment, self-efficacy, self-promotion and self-management. In turn this skill-set leads to other-awareness, interpersonal skills and team effectiveness. Developing this 'skills success cycle' (Figure 4.1, p. 78) actually encompasses beliefs, feelings, experiences and behaviours, and may be difficult to address as part of HE curricula but has benefits for students in all areas of life.

- A personal profile has three main facets: **M**otivation, **A**bility and **P**ersonality (Figure 4.2). Students should proactively discover and develop their MAP, and use it as a map to both navigate and create their life-career journey. They can focus on their MAP strengths to find work and learning opportunities that fit with their interests, values, skills, and personality.

- 'Self' is like an iceberg (Figure 4.4), with only a small part of the human psyche conscious and visible in different environments (above the waterline). Capabilities and interests are reportable but only become observable when they are demonstrated in actions and performance. Going deeper into the subconscious mind, capabilities and attitudes are driven by 'mental maps' consisting of values and beliefs, of which one is often unaware. 'Double-loop learning' (Argyris and Schon, 1978) requires learners to reflect on their deeper values and beliefs in order to break the ice of unproductive mental maps.

- You are in a powerful position to create classroom conditions that can enhance self-esteem and self-efficacy beliefs. I give some examples of theories, exercises, teaching and assessment methods that you can adopt or adapt to develop the 'self-awareness skills-set', and suggest how these may be transferred to good learning in any subject. The theme of 'self-mapping' – blending theory and prac-tice – is continued through the following three chapters, dealing in turn with Motivation, Ability and Personality.

Chapter 5

Motivation in the Self-MAP
What do I want and need?

'Motivation' in self-development

As you are here, reading this chapter, could I ask (being intrusive!):

1 Are you interested in this topic for its own sake?
2 Are you keen to discover what really motivates you? or
3 . . . what drives the performance of your students? or
4 . . . how you can create/maintain/enhance students' desires to learn and improve, and get their best results? or
5 . . . how you can enable them to understand and use their career drivers (value systems, interests, attitudes and beliefs) for the linked purposes of academic, personal and professional growth – both for present and future purposes?

If any or all of these considerations are important to you, read on. They certainly will be important for students, although they may not know this until you point out why – and how – and give them that boost they need to succeed. I suggest you adapt the questions above so that they are suitably addressed to your students – to get them thinking about the type and level of motivation that underpins their performance. Going through an intentional SOAR process can enable students to progressively refine their understanding of their interests and values, and the relative importance of these in their relationships with learning and work situations.

As a starter question, to clarify the terms commonly used when discussing this topic, ask students to underline all the words in the five questions above that represent some type of motivation – e.g. interests, values, drives, attitudes, beliefs, desires, learning and improving. You will probably notice that most of these words represent intrinsic motivation. There are other similar words students may add to this list (e.g. rewards, incentives, 'carrot and stick' – but note that these are extrinsic motivators). The significant difference between intrinsic and extrinsic motivation will emerge later in this chapter.

Clearly the study of human motivation is a complex subject, and one that is a whole field of enquiry in psychology and social science. One could upscale or downplay the level of intellectual challenge in dealing with it. For a purely pragmatic purpose, CDL programmes and vocational guidance models require individuals to identify and consider their interests and values as important factors in career decision making. For example, one session in the module represented in Table 3.2 (p. 52) is devoted to this topic. Students are referred to online case examples and questionnaires to identify their career interests and values. They prepare a short presentation on this topic, stating why they feel motivated on some occasions and not on others – what makes a difference?

Motivation is introduced to students as a vital part of the career profile – the MAP they are expected to build and evidence (Figure 4.2). In constructing this section of their personal map – in their journey of self-discovery – learners are re-focusing the usual job or course-choice question from '*Can* I do this course/job?' to '*Will I want* to do this course/job?' i.e. Will I look forward to studying or working here? Does this opportunity allow me to use and develop my strengths, express my interests and interact with like-minded people? Will I have the lifestyle, terms and conditions that are really important to me?

Taking their type and level of motivation into account can help students to:

- decide which jobs and courses will hold their interest and which to avoid;
- determine an acceptable balance between their study and work roles against other life roles;
- find an occupational sector and employer organization which would fit their interests and values;
- see where compromises in option-choices need to be made and decide whether these are acceptable;
- enhance their personal efficacy beliefs and confidence.

I propose in this chapter to broaden CDL considerations so that students flexibly and simultaneously gain other personal, academic and employability benefits too. The focus here is on enhancing students' motivation in order to:

- improve their attitudes towards learning, performance and academic development so that they achieve better results at university (a key factor in improving retention rates and preventing drop-out from university);
- identify and enhance behaviours associated with their 'drive for results' and enable them to demonstrate this drive to employers and other selectors for future opportunities (an essential generic employability attribute);
- ensure that they identify and consider their motivations, interests and values in choosing suitable work and learning opportunities (an essential aspect of self-awareness and career management);
- enable students to identify what stops them from achieving;
- address their needs for self-confidence and positive self-efficacy beliefs.

Why bother with 'motivation'?

Traditionally and historically the focus on ability and performance in education ignores the fact that interventions to maintain and build students' motivation are key to success in addressing concerns about recruitment, retention and progression, especially in the context of mass HE today. Although performance – in study and at work – is *enabled* by intellectual ability, skills and knowledge, it is *driven* by the values, interests and aspirations of the individual. What I mean here by values are those qualities that represent deep driving forces for what any of us might consider important in life, learning and work. Two of your students with similar capabilities may have had very different reasons for choosing to study their particular subject(s). For the future they may wish to employ their abilities in very different ways. Helping them to identify their underlying motivations can lead to more effective engagement with their studies and future plans.

In careers guidance interviews I notice that few people can say with precision or conviction what they want, why and how they are motivated to achieve this, and how they will derive long-term satisfaction from it. Students may have an *intuitive* grasp of what is important to them in work and life, but many don't act on this knowledge and cannot articulate this when questioned – perhaps because they have focused on ability and never explicitly considered their interests and values to be important determinants along their life-career pathway.

If I may illustrate this point with a personal experience – I recall my own interview from hell when I was not far off graduation and woefully lacking in personal job-search skills (this was in the days before I trained as a careers professional). Having applied for a postgraduate teacher-training qualification, I set off to the interview armed with a first-class degree, a fair amount of self-confidence, but little preparation for the sort of questions I would be asked. I failed miserably to defend my choice of teaching as a career because my understanding of myself was internalized and intuitive, and my ears had never heard my voice saying 'I really want to teach because . . .' in any convincing way. So I came away with no offer, lots of self-doubt – and the need to console myself with vast quantities of chocolate. Maybe you can tell similar stories from your experience.

There is a further consideration implicit in my example: organizations and professions, like people, have their value systems – which are again not necessarily visible if you are not looking for them. So students must identify not only what they want but explore what requirements they *need* to match up to, and find sufficient compatibility between their priorities and those of the organizations in which they might work or study. Failing to do so carries a severe career health warning: in the long term if not sooner, it can severely damage both satisfaction and performance in the chosen job or the course of study. The mismatch is likely to have spin-off effects in other areas of life too.

An understanding of career drivers is also essential because values change – on both individual and collective levels. As we mature and our circumstances change, our values change over the lifespan – so we seek different satisfactions at different ages and stages. This is often even truer for women than for men. In my case, my job as an international airline stewardess became incompatible with marriage and domestic responsibilities, and once I had children everything had to revolve around them. In any case, at the collective level the airline's values at that time were blatantly obvious, as stated in my contract: 'You must resign if you reach age 30 or if you get married, whichever comes first.' A statement like this would be both legally and politically incorrect – and seems incredible – today!

Just one further point to infer from my example: academic success does not automatically transfer into career decidedness and career success. Although the two are linked (because some of the same motivational and competency attributes drive both) they are not equated – not without congruent aspirations and occupation-specific skills.

Moreover, there are cognitive, affective, physical, cultural and social aspects of human motivation and self-efficacy beliefs that interact variably with each other and with different environments, as discussed in the previous chapter and symbolized by my iceberg analogy (see Figure 4.4). Multiple, often subconscious, influences add up to a complexity that is difficult to deal with in any depth as part of HE curricula, and indeed in this one chapter. Many academic staff feel they cannot and/or should not 'plumb the depths of their students' minds'. I am not qualified to do that either, but I approach it differently. I believe we can enable students to discover 'self' – for practical reasons – and it is not necessary for us to be qualified psychologists to enhance motivation in tandem with self-efficacy beliefs.

Some students have an integrated personality, where all the layers of the mind are in harmony with each other: what they are interested in is also what they are good at, and they find an HE environment congenial to what they want and need to achieve. Witness this statement, from a student's written reflections:

> I've been working steadily, whatever task is set for me, because I want to achieve my best results. I know I can get a first if I try. I also need to get work experience in a school so that I can end up teaching Biology and Chemistry – subjects which I've loved since my own Science teachers inspired me at school.

Well, that says a lot! Unfortunately not a lot say that. We are more accustomed to hearing 'reasons' such as 'I couldn't do . . . x . . . because I got decapitated yesterday' – okay, maybe not that ridiculous, but some excuses are very nearly so! And how about this for a giggle: 'Students always give 100%: Monday 15%, Tuesday 25%, Wednesday 30%, Thursday 20%, Friday 10%' (seen on a student T-shirt, originally in German).

An integrated personality calls for adjustment and alignment between interests, capabilities, realistic aspirations and decisions, and above all self-belief that translates into goal setting, sustainable ambition and action (which encapsulates the SOAR process). Students do not need to reveal all their motives to you or to employers (especially if their main reason for job choice is to be a salary slave or fit everything around childcare!) but they need to take account of what really turns them on so they can leverage their chances of gaining satisfaction through study or work.

Anyway the question 'What do I want?' is relatively recent in the history of human endeavour. Before the industrial revolution, one's work was determined by the tasks one had to perform, for example as a peasant, miner, artisan or domestic servant. Even as recently as the 1950s and 1960s, when a new information age was dawning, a company's personnel department had responsibility for planning the careers of the workforce. That is no longer the case, and graduates will need to 'proactively design and manage their life/career progression.' (Miles Morgan Australia, 2003: 5). Individuals need a new set of driving forces for this type of self-managed career (as they do also for thriving in a less-supported, mass HE environment).

Today we could go further than a 'matching individual wants to employers' needs' type of model. Students should think about reconciling their wants and needs in a new way in the contemporary world of work: not so much as a need determined by having to match the requirements of an employer, but a need to understand what their contribution *should* be – to any job, organization and society. They are the potential employers and managers of the future, and there is considerable scope for evolving jobs and projects at the graduate level. Their values will play a key part in the decisions they make. The best of our graduates will not only be adaptable but adaptive in creating opportunities for congruent personal and organizational growth:

> Programmes should continue to produce critical, reflective and potentially transforming students who can help organizations deal with change. However they should not neglect to prepare students to fit into organizational culture and add value through working effectively with others. Graduates need help to be adaptive as well as transformative.
>
> (Harvey *et al.*, 1997: 4)

Employers' perspectives

In matching up to employers' selection criteria, students need to know that employers view the importance of motivation in three main ways:

1   the interests, values and attitudes of applicants that are specific to the job or occupational area (job-fit);
2   the fit between the personal priorities of the individual and those of the company – its culture, ethos, mission and vision (company-fit);
3   the level of motivation that has been and can be demonstrated by applicants, as a general employability attribute (an achievement orientation or drive for results).

The Association of Graduate Recruiters (AGR) conducts regular surveys to find out what skills and attributes are being sought and prioritized by employers. *The AGR Graduate Recruitment Survey Summer Review 2006* (AGR, 2006) was completed by 235 employers with 21,157 graduate jobs on offer – so it was quite a sizeable survey. 'Commitment and drive' headed the table of 'Important graduate skills' followed by 'Motivation and enthusiasm'. In a fast-changing world these attributes are essential because subject knowledge and skills become rapidly dated without the commitment and enthusiasm to learn and change.

Carl Gilleard (CE of the AGR), commented for me on these findings:

> Of course, neither of these qualities are actually skills but it is interesting that employers still regard them as essential attributes for candidates to demonstrate. I say still because they have been around for years.
>
> I think the message for graduates seeking a career is a clear one – you have to show that you are interested, keen and motivated otherwise employers are going to look elsewhere. Why should an employer invest time, effort and money in developing someone who doesn't demonstrate real commitment during the selection process? While employers recognize that graduates will be applying to lots of businesses, they want to be convinced that theirs is the business of choice.
>
> There are lots of ways of demonstrating commitment, from finding out as much as you can about the job and the business in advance, to the way the application is put together. Any candidate who can point to something they have done already to improve their knowledge and prospects (like relevant work experience) will find themselves in the inside lane.
>
> (Gilleard, 2006)

Examples of questions (and answers!) at selection stages

Employers expect to see interest in the job and their company demonstrated throughout the recruitment process. The sections headed 'Personal Interests' and 'Career Choice' on application forms are places where candidates can show interest and enthusiasm. For instance, the 'hobbies and leisure activities' section in CVs is often underestimated for its potential to show how an applicant chooses to spend unstructured time – a good indicator to employers of relevant interests s/he chooses to pursue, and also evidence of a 'rounded individual'.

These qualities surface as high priority in selection interviews, when applicants have been sifted on grounds of ability and only those considered capable of job performance are on the shortlist. Career drivers are at this stage assessed through questions such as:

- What interests you about this job?
- What do you do in your spare time?
- What do you want out of life?

- What motivates you?
- Where do you see yourself in 5/10 years time?

Students need to understand why these questions are asked – i.e. what attributes selectors are looking for, and why these are important to them both in relation to the job in question and as more general employability indicators. There are potential pitfalls in the way they answer. You could ask students to discuss why selectors will not be impressed by such answers (taken from actual graduate applications):

> 'If called to interview I would like to discuss the salary, pensions and sickness benefits.'
> 'I do not have any major achievements that I would consider to be of interest to this application.'
> 'I believe that my choice of dentistry as a career was a natural progression from a youthful affinity with power tools. My current interests are more vacational than vocational but I am looking forward to working with you in order to expand my collection of hi-fi equipment, malt whisky and compact discs.'
> 'My lifelong love of chocolate biscuits is the main reason for my interest in this company' (applicant for a role at United Biscuits)
> 'I have a long term interest in pubic relations' (applicant for a PR job)
> 'I am someone who knows my own destiny, but I have no definate [*sic*] long term plans.'

> Discuss with students: What answers would reveal self-motivation and *intrinsic* interests? Get them to write their responses as if for real, or to record their motivations in a reflective account. (Note that a spell checker does not detect all errors – but employers often do!)

An application form exercise on self-motivation

A common question on application forms asks for evidence of the ability to persevere in challenging tasks, and achieve results despite setbacks. Employer X^1 requests:

> Give an example of a time when you have been self-motivated. Our industry managers are expected to be self-motivated and to learn fast. In meeting these challenges they need to:
> - use their initiative to learn new skills and acquire knowledge;
> - take the trouble to do more than the minimum;

- learn from both positive and negative experiences;
- complete tasks, even in difficult circumstances.

Next, a sample response from a candidate is given, reproduced in the box below. Ask students how they would rate this response, bearing in mind the skill-descriptors and instructions given above.

> 'When I left school, I thought my education was over and I took a job as an export clerk. I had very little idea that I would go on to study for an HND, let alone a degree. After leaving university I started work as a production engineer but after a short time realized that my talents lay elsewhere, and that other careers would give me more room to develop.'

Compare your students' comments with Employer X's feedback on this response:

This candidate probably needed great motivation and initiative to go back into higher education after a spell at work. The trouble with this answer is that his or her motivation is implied rather than clearly stated.

The second part of the answer raises questions in the assessor's mind about the candidate's tenacity and his or her ability to see things through. How exactly has self-motivation been demonstrated? Has the applicant actually used his or her initiative to identify more suitable careers? The tragedy is that unless you can tell us clearly, we cannot give you the benefit of the doubt.

Now it's your turn. Your example will tell us about your competence and potential. Draw on your experiences in education, work or life in general. Remember the key thing is to relate what you write about to the competence we are seeking. Include brief details of important elements of the situation, your approach and actions, and what was achieved.

Motivation as a generic employability attribute

So . . . students need to build evidence not only of *what* motivates them, but also to show that they are *in general highly motivated to achieve positive results*. Although interest specifically in the chosen job is important, 'learning and improving' and the 'drive for results' are also highly valued as generic attributes. Employers such as the Civil Service make no secret of the fact that these attributes are specifically sought in six government departments. They (and many other graduate recruiters across all industry sectors) define them as key 'behavioural competencies' and train assessors to look for these behaviours at interviews and assessment centres.

I see strong similarities in this respect between academics' and employers' concerns – all have a desire to improve general attitudes towards learning and development. Looking at motivational aspects from a skills shortage perspective, the *National Employers Skills Survey 2005: Key Findings* reports that '*staff lacking in motivation is the second most common cause of skill gaps . . .*' (Learning Skills Council, 2006: 11). Apathy is seen as a key reason why staff fail to participate in continuing professional development (CPD) offered by employers.

The same could be said for HE students: their lack of motivation, limiting self-beliefs and negative attitudes probably have more to do with failure, drop-out and under-performance than lack of ability. So most of us working in HEIs want and need to do something about this – not least because these factors are measured by performance indicators and then presented statistically in league tables which may reflect badly on us for all the world to see. And because we love students who bring enthusiasm and commitment to their studies.

Motivation to learn and achieve results

Enabling students to understand what 'results-driven' and 'effective learning' behaviours we expect of them is a starting point in trying to effect changes in behaviour. At this point I am thinking of 'enabling learning' with the primary aim of improving behaviours for better achievement. This is useful for all students but essential for non-traditional entrants to HE, whose experiences and preferences in learning, and expectations of what is required, may be quite different.

The two audits I offer here serve to alert students to ideal behaviours that will benefit them in both learning and work domains, both for the present and the future. 'Learning and improving' and 'The drive for results' contain items expressed in terms of positive goal behaviours. Of course, negative behaviours can be inferred as the opposite end of the spectrum, but in keeping with AI it's best to focus on 'what works'. Briefing and debriefing self-audit activity is impor-tant – please use my briefing on 'Learning from self-audits' (Chapter 2, p. 35). Remind students they should not expect to rate themselves highly at present but simply to identify the extent to which they display these behaviours, and the level of confidence with which they do so in current settings.

In addition, use the following definitions, instructions and cautions for students before they undertake this self-assessment:

Learning and improving may be defined as 'the motivation to seek new knowledge, skills and experience as opportunities for development'. This involves several skills and personal attributes that are key requirements for success in both HE and in employment. They are therefore of high value in your current student role as well as in positioning yourself for any future work role. They can be enhanced once you understand what is expected of you. The skills are reflected in an ability to:

- learn from others and reflect on experiences;
- adapt quickly and effectively to new situations, task demands and people;
- seek continuous improvement in the performance of study and work roles;
- function effectively in a range of roles and contexts, even when these are not clearly defined.

1   Approach this exercise with an honest desire and positive attitude to see what this competency looks like in ideal behaviours.
2   Use it to think about your current behaviours (and remember the aim is not to say you are excellent in everything, but to identify weak areas to work on).
3   Please assess the extent to which you **learn and develop** by allocating ratings to each statement along a four point scale, where:

1 = never, 2 = rarely, 3 = frequently, 4 = very frequently.	
	Ratings 1–4
1 I am keen to develop a range of skills	
2 I participate actively in learning tasks	
3 I understand how I learn best and what motivates me	
4 I select growth opportunities that suit my personal styles and preferences	
5 I take responsibility for improving my performance	
6 I make use of the services available to increase my chances of success	
7 I can identify the level of abilities I need to gain success in my studies and assignments	
8 I can identify the type of knowledge I need to gain success in my studies and assignments	
9 I can identify the appropriate attitudes I need to gain success in my studies and assignments	
10 I seek out opportunities in learning that will help me grow as a whole person	
11 I seek out opportunities in work that will help me grow as a whole person	
12 I seek out opportunities in leisure that will help me grow as a whole person	
13 I particularly target those experiences that will help me develop the skills I need for future work choices	
14 I think about my experiences to identify what I have learned and what I might do differently to improve	
15 I seek out and use feedback from my tutors and others to identify my strengths and improve where needed	
16 I record my achievements and plans for further learning and development	
17 I can help others to develop themselves	

The **drive for results** may be defined as 'the drive, energy, stamina, tenacity and stress tolerance to achieve personal and imposed standards of excellence'. This translates into an ability to:

- plan activities and persevere with them despite competing priorities and obstacles;
- review tasks and prioritize as necessary to meet objectives and deadlines;
- use initiative and stay motivated when problems arise or progress is slow;
- lead a project and motivate others appropriately;
- maintain own performance and good relationships even under pressure.

Students can rate their **drive for results** by allocating ratings to each statement along a four point scale, where:

1 = never, 2 = rarely, 3 = frequently, 4 = very frequently.	
	Ratings 1–4
1 I am prepared to go that extra mile to get the best results of which I am capable	
2 I achieve my objectives and goals	
3 My friends would describe me as enthusiastic	
4 I can experiment with new and different approaches to improve my personal productivity	
5 I set targets that will deliver benefits and desired outcomes for myself	
6 I set targets that will deliver benefits and desired outcomes for others	
7 I can realign my goals to alternative outcomes in the light of changing circumstances	
8 I use support to overcome obstacles to my achievement	
9 I am determined and do not give up easily despite setbacks	
10 I compare and review my performance against high standards in order to improve	
11 I can streamline approaches to save time, energy and other resources	
12 I believe in my ability to find better ways of doing things	

Debriefing on the implications of scores – think, pair, share

Individually, pay attention to high ratings: these indicate your strengths. Look at the items with low ratings: target these for improvement. At this stage your ratings are no more than the claims you are making about yourself. Your next step is to substantiate these claims by thinking about examples from your experience to show, clearly and convincingly, just how, where and with what level of confidence you demonstrate the effective behaviours.

In pairs or small groups, you may want to discuss particularly those items where your scores indicate you have never considered or demonstrated these behaviours. What do these behaviours look like in real-life actions? What stops you from doing these things and/or believing in them, or in yourself? Start with one thing you will change. Decide just how you will do this, and by when.

Discussion usually helps students to identify their agency in learning behaviours – for instance their remarks reveal:

- values regarding study in relation to other values (e.g. socializing, work, family commitments);
- belief in their own ability to achieve good marks or perform well;
- their experience and confidence in:

  1 finding out what is required from tutors;
  2 analysing the requirements from handouts and assignment briefs;
  3 organizing their time;
  4 acting to maximize success;
  5 familiarity with selecting modules on a strategic basis (for intrinsic interest, career purposes, or to suit their learning styles or assessment preferences).

Most HEIs have learning support departments that will provide materials, sessions and/or individual help for students to become better learners. It is increasingly felt that nearly all students need to be inducted into studying their disciplines at higher level.

Ask students to share in plenary: What can be done (by all of us) to create an environment where you would find it easier to develop these behavioural competencies? Remember these will help you perform well in your studies, and you will also need to gather evidence of such attributes to present to future employers and other selectors.

Extension: Role-play an interview

Candidates at graduate job interviews are usually asked to give examples of situations that demonstrate learning and results-driven behaviours. Some typical questions are given below, for students to practise with.

Allocate students to groups of three and ask them to role-play a selection interview, taking turns as the interviewer, the interviewee and observer/ feedback provider. Give them time to prepare answers to the questions, considering (a) what the employer is seeking (b) what might be the potential pitfalls in the response (c) their own personal example from real life.

- For an observer checklist, see Chapter 11.
- For feedback guidelines, see Chapter 3.

1   Give me an example of a time when something didn't work out for you as well as you had hoped.

   a   Did you reflect on the outcome?
   b   What could you have done to make it work better?
   c   What is the most valuable thing you have learned from this experience?

2   What do you usually do when you receive critical feedback? (do you perceive feedback as constructive, difficult to accept, unfair, unhelpful?)

   a   Did this discourage you from seeking feedback again? Why?

3   Give me an example of an occasion when you set out to learn something new. Or when you realized you lacked the skills or knowledge to complete a task.

   a   What did you want to learn?
   b   What options did you consider? (formal training course, personal study, etc.?)
   c   Did you have a personal development plan? What form did it take? How often did you review it? How detailed was it?

4   Give me an example of something that has taken you out of your comfort zone.

   a   Did you know it would be challenging?
   b   Tell me about a situation when you:
      – felt under extreme pressure
      – faced major difficulties and setbacks

 – helped someone else achieve a goal
 – experienced slow progress and you had to meet a deadline.

Students need to record their learning in paper-based formats or e-portfolio personal records, from which they will be ready to construct real-life applications when the need arises and the time comes. At the transition stage, demonstrating these skills in person at interviews and assessment centres is daunting for most job seekers. In future chapters I suggest activities that simulate employers' 'assessment centres', and give students the opportunity to gain hands-on experience and feedback on their performance before they face the real thing.

A fresher's activity: Why am I here?

First impressions and early experience are key to students' views about their HEI, and it's not too early to start motivating students from day one, valuing and developing them as whole individuals for the linked purposes of personal, educational and career development. In student induction you could run a 'knowing me, knowing you' activity in which you get students (perhaps as an ice breaker) to interview each other and ask about each other's reasons for HE choice:

1   Why did you choose this subject/degree/institution?
2   How does your choice fit with how you learn best?
3   How does it fit with the rest of your life?
4   What results do you expect to achieve?

Ask them to introduce each other (if the group is small enough) and follow this up by leading a discussion on general reasons for degree choice.

Amplify discussions with survey findings – suggestions and actions

It is useful to compare students' reasons for degree choice with some research findings: for instance, a large-scale survey (Purcell and Pitcher, 1996) of some 5,000 undergraduates found that HE choice was based on three predominant reasons:

1   interest in and enjoyment of the subject; enjoying student life for its own sake;
2   expectation of career advancement/practical career-related reasons;
3   accepting the advice of others/fulfilling others' expectations.

Ask your students which of these they identify with. The last one rings the most alarm bells with me, as it indicates an abdication of personal responsibility for the decision and a lack of commitment to the choice.

In a recent survey (Allan, 2006) that asked students to rank their reasons for going to university, 57 per cent of humanities students said that their *main* motivation was to improve their chances of getting a job (UNITE, 2005: 4). Career-related reasons for subject choice are even higher for business, vocational and technical degree students, who are likely to see the degree as a means to an end.

However, careers advisers up and down the country report a gap between this aspiration and the subsequent actual preparation for future careers. Student participation in CDL interventions, if offered optionally, is often inadequate and poorly understood even by vocationally motivated students. The 1996 survey also found that students' personal reasons for choice at entry to HE tend to persist and influence the decisions they make at the point of transition beyond graduation.

This is a natural place to tell students about the range of opportunities that can add value to their HE experience, and to emphasize the labour-market realities that make it imperative for them to start and continue developing skills and experience from an early stage. If you can get employers, alumni or professional bodies to reinforce these key messages, so much the better. There are also career publishers who produce material for new entrants to HE – *Fresher Futures* (an annual, Doctor Job publication) and *If Only I'd Known: making the most of higher education*[2] (Hawkins and Gilleard, 2002) are publications that should be available from your Careers Service. These are excellent to show how students can make the most of their studies *and* add employability value to their HE experience.

Give out ideas and details of specific locally available opportunities, ideally those that are relevant to their degree subject, level of study and interests. However, any opportunity can be exploited to develop skills, have fun, make friends and workplace contacts at the same time (see Chapter 8). As skills take time to develop, we are doing students a disservice if we fail to make them aware early on of the opportunities for developing skills – both within and outside the formal curriculum.

Get them to choose some personal goals and write down exactly what they intend to do in the short term, with an indication of medium- and longer term aims, and timed plans of action. Brian Tracy, an inspirational speaker and writer, believes that writing down goals and plans lends power and commitment to their accomplishment. He states that people generally act on their *written* goals, dreams, plans and vision. I think much is made of learning to write, but 'writing to learn' is also a key method of clarifying what you think and what you will commit to: until you communicate and articulate your thoughts and intentions they often remain vague and unformed.

'Career anchors'

Research undertaken by Edgar Schein on the 'career anchors' that underpin people's choices also seems to suggest that basic 'anchors' or motives remain fairly consistent over time. Based on interviews he conducted with 44 graduates in the US over a period of 12 years, via interviews and questionnaires, he reported:

The actual events of the career histories proved to be highly varied, but the reasons that respondents gave for their choices and the pattern of their feelings about events proved to be surprisingly consistent. For each individual, underlying themes – of which he or she often had been unaware – reflected a growing sense of self, based on the learning of the early years. When these people tried jobs that did not feel right to them, they referred to the image of being pulled back to something that fitted better, hence the metaphor of an anchor.

(Schein, 1993: 25–6)

Based on further research with several hundred people in various career stages, Schein and his colleagues developed a Career Orientations Inventory (Schein, 1993: 26) so that an individual can assess his or her career anchors – which consist of a mixture of values, attitudes, needs and interests, and are similar to the 'Career Drivers Card Sort' I give below.

Identifying Values: a Career Drivers Card Sort

Use the box overleaf to create a card sort activity. Print the items onto card, and cut along the lines. You can use this with groups, but have one set of cards available for each student. Alternatively you could put this exercise online, with the facility to drag and drop, and built-in immediate feedback.

Brief for students: There are no 'right' or 'wrong' responses – the aim of this exercise is simply to understand and explore your values, rank them in order of importance for you, and prioritize three things that you feel will bring you the greatest satisfaction in work (relative to the rest of life).

1   First match the 'career driver' descriptors to the examples and meanings that fit them. Make sure you understand the word descriptors (consult with each other in pairs if you like).
2   It may be important for you to add other values if you don't find them on this list – e.g. you may prioritize productivity, honesty, justice and so on.
3   Then place the cards in order of their relative importance to you – it is important you do this on your own. Think about real-life examples that clearly show how your top three values might act as priorities when you come to choose an occupation to enter at graduation. Write these down.

Debriefing, Reflection and Extension

Prompt students: 'Consider your top three values, not in isolation but **in combination**, to see if they support and sit comfortably with each other, producing synergy – or do they conflict with each other and create tension and ambivalence? How do your values relate to your choice of degree subject?'

Career drivers	Examples/meanings
Achievement/abilities	I am excited about work as an opportunity to use and develop my talents, skills and knowledge.
Prestige/status/ recognition	For my friend who works in management consultancy, being in a position of importance, in an occupation perceived as high status, having his achievements recognized and rewarded, is an important consideration.
Authority/responsibility	Leadership and executive positions require this type of motivation: a liking for being in a position of influence, having responsibility or power over others, being an expert in one's field of work.
Advancement/personal growth	Seeking promotion, career development and progression – may be an end in itself or a means to an end.
Autonomy/ independence	For example, barristers have considerable independence of action in handling their own legal cases. People who are self-employed also have autonomy in making their own decisions.
Social interaction/ affiliation	Working with like-minded people, making pleasant, friendly contacts and even socializing within a work community is very important for many people.
Risk taking	Business entrepreneurs need to enjoy (or at least tolerate) an element of risk in making speculative decisions for new deals and business ventures. Working in emergency services also involves enjoying change and chance.
Economic reward	The high salary and earning potential in my son's job in a City law firm seems to be a powerful incentive for him as he likes expensive possessions.
Variety	I worked as an airline stewardess for two years and enjoyed the constant change in environments and crew. In my present job I like the diversity in tasks and try to avoid the same daily routines.
Intellect	A need for mental stimulation and intellectual challenge – again, this was evident in my son's choice to train as a barrister.
Service	I know that many of my colleagues in the Careers Service are motivated to help others, making a direct contribution to society. Caring for others is important in many service occupations, including health, social care and education.
Ethics/altruism	Concerns about the environment, conservation and other moral issues are of prime concern for some people, who may choose to work in non-profit or charitable organizations, in human rights or other 'ethical careers'.
Aesthetics	Making things look good, enjoying beauty is an important part of my life – it takes the form of many different leisure activities that involve playing around with colours and shapes: gardening, interior decoration, embroidery, fashion design, pottery . . .
Creativity	Being original, developing new concepts, designs or things is obviously important in a range of media, art and design jobs – but may be a part of other occupations in a less obvious way.
Work environment	Some people are deeply affected by the physical aspects and conditions in the places where they work.
Security	Stability and safety in job terms and conditions may determine the type of occupation and organization you want to work in.
Work/life balance	This became a high priority for me when my children were young and domestic responsibilities dominated my life. Others may seek simply to have time to enjoy leisure activities.

Take feedback and discuss how values may conflict: e.g. a need for job security and high salary could conflict with the need to do a creative media job, which so often requires stress tolerance for freelancing. The need for high salary is also likely to conflict with work/life balance. Have students considered what they will actually need to do in order to earn a high salary? How do their values translate into real-life experience? How will these priorities affect future choices? Discussing and reflecting on the dynamic meanings of these values through real examples can help to decipher what they stand for, where they will lead, and how they manifest in activities, relationships and behaviours.

Among your students you will have salary slaves, experience junkies, qualification collectors, those who work hard and those who hardly work . . . so should you voice your own value judgements or adopt a laissez-faire attitude? Are some values and combinations of values better than others? Here's your chance to influence values in a positive, developmental direction by sharing your story, thoughts and readings.

It is useful to discuss links between different values – for example the links between earning, learning and achievement. You may want to bring in some facts and figures about graduate starting salaries[3] and greater lifetime earning potential, linked to the contemporary need for lifelong learning. Point out that different types of motivation and ability are needed for different types of career success. For example, not everyone wants to be a high-flying business entrepreneur like Bill Gates or Richard Branson. Interest groupings are best illustrated by Holland's 'congruence theory' of six types of interest related to six corresponding types of environment (Chapter 4). Students on arts courses collectively have different interests from those on business or social science degrees, but individuals should identify their particular combinations of interests and values, which are important indicators of personal job and life satisfactions.

Values in working, learning, playing and giving

Prompt students: 'How do your (envisioned) work values fit with other things that are important to you in life?'

Write down some of the things you most enjoy doing. Think about those activities without which your life would feel incomplete. Peter Hawkins talks about life being shaped by the choices we make each day in four overlapping areas: working, learning, giving and playing. Attached to each of these are values that are represented as key words in Table 5.1. Rate each according to the importance you assign to it, and the level of satisfaction you currently derive from it, using a scale from 1 to 10, with 1 = low and 10 = high.

Debriefing: Compare your ratings of importance and satisfaction to see what this means: you may need to rectify the imbalance particularly in those areas where something you rate highly in importance is low in satisfaction. What might you do and who can help? Write one important goal for each of these.

Table 5.1 Key values in life and work roles

Four facets of life	Key words related to each facet	Level of importance	Level of satisfaction	What does this mean for you?
Working (interpret broadly to include home-working, flexi-working, etc.)	1 Realizing potential			
	2 Fulfilling and fun			
	3 Recognition and reward			
Learning (not just from formal education or qualifications, but learning from any type of experience)	4 Personal growth			
	5 Sense of purpose			
	6 Employability			
Playing (any activity you enjoy – not just related to leisure time)	7 Well-being (physical/ emotional)			
	8 Expressing interests			
	9 Social life			
Giving (not just about donating to good causes but also providing love and support to others)	10 Family			
	11 Other relationships			
	12 Community involvement			

Try projecting yourself five years into the future, and write at least three statements as if you are already achieving these goals in your life. Write as precisely and concisely as you can or draw images to articulate the vision you want for your life and your future.

Mission and vision statements

Bearing in mind your priorities, think about your personal mission in life. Your main values and goals will deserve the greatest attention in your personal mission and vision statements – which you should now write as briefly as possible. Your personal mission and vision statements should act as an explicit guide when you consider to what extent any given opportunity fits with your aims and desires.

You might wish to try these suggestions for yourself, in relation to your current job. What is the extent of congruence between your personal values and those required by your job? If there is imbalance, where exactly does it occur? Is there anything you can do to narrow or close the gap?

Enabling students to find 'company-fit'

At the application stage a little research to find compatibility with potential employers can go a long way. Many large organizations publicize their mission statements on websites, as a precise and concise description encapsulating the purpose for which they exist. They might also have a vision statement, which declares their future focus. SMEs may not so readily publicize themselves but their annual reports and other documents indicate their situation and direction.

For example, currently I work in a university where the strap-line *Education for Life* exemplifies our emphasis on preparing students for real life and entry to work – a mission, vision and resulting strategy that entirely resonates with my interests, strengths and values. My satisfaction comes from working with many like-minded colleagues in collaborative partnerships. This is not to pretend that we are always in agreement over *how* to achieve this, though! At the same time, understanding my own drives and desires helps me to recognize, respect and work with their priorities.

Learning from theories and research: intrinsic or extrinsic motivators?

Further discussion in plenary, if this is possible, can lead to an extension of ideas in many different directions. It is fruitful to look at motivations as either intrinsic – i.e. ends in themselves (considered important for their own sake), or as extrinsic – as means to an end (in order to gain some reward, please someone or avoid negative consequences). For instance, a high salary for some will be a means to attain a lavish lifestyle, status or power. Achievement and the development of competence can be a highly satisfying, intrinsic motivation and reward in itself, or it may be a means to impress a significant other. On the whole, the more intrinsic one's life-satisfactions are, the more chance one has of finding stable self-fulfilment and what Maslow (1954 and 1970, 1968) calls 'self-actualization'.

Maslow's 'hierarchy of needs' model (1954) initially stated that only when basic physiological and security needs are satisfied do we humans move onto higher level social and interpersonal needs for belonging and esteem, and then to 'meta-needs' for personal fulfilment. He later revised his definition of self-actualization (1968). You could get students to visit the *Businessballs* website (www.businessballs.com) to study this hierarchy, illustrated as a pyramid, and to critique the 'theory of pre-potency'. I enjoy Maslow's philosophy – not because it is completely valid in all situations – but because it inspires me with its positive views about the potential for human self-fulfilment.

Self-actualization is arguably the main purpose of personal and career development: enabling students to be(come) fully human and realize their potential. This implies intrinsic desire for freedom to self-develop towards end goals or ideals, rather than an imposed requirement from figures in authority. If we can trust and respect students' natural capacities for growth towards full 'psychological health' (as Maslow calls it), it then remains for us to naturally release these intrinsic drives for growth in a positive direction.

Herzberg *et al.* (1959) were some of the first to make a distinction between different drivers at work: they theorized that achievement, recognition, work itself, responsibility, advancement and personal growth lead to true satisfaction, whereas other conditions such as salary and security do not motivate in themselves, but cause dissatisfaction if they are lacking. Similar conclusions have been drawn from research on the motivations of lecturers to participate in educational development programmes in the US (McKeachie, 1979; validated by Murray, 1999), indicating that extrinsic rewards such as financial incentives, released time and teaching awards do not make long-lasting impact on teaching practices. It is more effective for education developers to tap into intrinsic factors: professional pride, intellectual challenge and curiosity, and the satisfaction that comes from enabling students to learn more effectively (Angelo, 1994: 5).

Angelo goes on to say that programmes likely to result in effective change are those that help teachers become more reflective practitioners, recognize their individual needs and encourage them to adapt new ideas to their existing style of teaching, and encourage ongoing self-assessment and self-development even after the programme has ended. I see this as a direct parallel with what we are trying to accomplish through PDP principles with our students. The SOAR model I am advocating has all these features and, positively interpreted and delivered, will result in sustainable personal and career development.

Another theorist and researcher, McClelland, is known mainly for his research on achievement motivation and personality. His work has led to the development of employee competency-based assessments, in preference to IQ tests. He views motives as three types of goals: achievement, authority or power, and affiliation, which individuals differentially value and seek. He claims that these three in varying combinations characterize both the way in which individuals are personally motivated, the vigour with which they pursue these goals, and the style of managers when they manage and motivate others. His study of 'achievement' is fascinating – especially as we are perhaps most concerned with this type of achievement orientation in our students. Much of what he says about 'results-driven people' implies that for them achievement is an end and a reward in itself. One can make connections between his findings and those of many other recent studies (see pp. 129–30).

Creating the conditions for students to motivate themselves

Increasingly, students in HEIs are from diverse backgrounds, bringing with them very different experiences and expectations. Staff often ask the question 'How can I motivate all these students with their diverse needs?' – and it seems like an impossible task. Instead I suggest we ask the question 'How can I create the conditions in which students are most likely to motivate themselves and each other?' This is still a daunting task, but the diversity issue becomes more manageable, especially if we focus on universal human needs and motivators. For example, what lessons might we learn from a consideration of Maslow's 'hierarchy of needs' model (first formulated in his 1943 paper 'A Theory of Human Motivation', which he subsequently extended in his books of 1954 (updated in 1970) and 1968) to create the right conditions for learning in our classrooms? Whose responsibility is it to create these conditions?

Meanwhile, **a thought experiment for you**:

1   What attributes would you most like to see in an ideally motivated student? Express these in terms of the behaviours and actions you want to see in that student.
2   Jot down your ideas for creating the conditions to enable learner development. Express these as your specific actions and plans. Decide what you will do as a first step and commit to a time plan for achieving your outcomes (do this with a partner if you wish).

In thinking through this I hope you exploited the potential of SOAR as a universal but personalizable model that can simultaneously accommodate diversity and give rise to both process and content that can motivate individuals through AI principles, real-life relevance and constructive alignment, etc. (see Chapter 3).

We must recognize that personal growth, developing skills and improving performance requires our students to have an optimistic sense of personal efficacy as a pre-condition of success: 'The hallmark of successful individuals is that they love learning, they seek challenges, they value effort, and they persist in the face of obstacles . . .' (Dweck, 2000). We must also recognize that the teaching and assessment methods we adopt can do much to motivate (or impede!) that sense of efficacy. My experience is that SOAR, linked with AI principles and their associated enabling methods, can go a long way towards enhancing confidence and motivation – and student feedback from these modules consistently indicates these benefits for the majority.

You may have doubts about setting challenging ideals for students. Some feel that bringing the competitive nature of graduate recruitment to their attention is actually demotivating because the requisite attributes seem unattainable. I believe that it is unfair to keep students ignorant about the challenges they will face at the entry point for graduate employment. Far better to make it transparent and enable them to make progress towards these ideals, by hooking them into the right type of support, guidance, facilitation and resources.

In my experience, students are generally not demotivated by challenging end-goals, provided you point out these are ideals, nobody is or can be perfect – and employers are actually sceptical if you claim to be a wonderful human being in all respects. Many students will then see them as challenges to be mastered, and value the learning activities that help them travel towards these goals. But some students will of course self-select themselves out of activities and situations that they perceive exceed their coping capabilities.

Students who have low self-efficacy beliefs will feel threatened by difficult tasks because they view them as personal threats rather than opportunities to improve. They will typically underestimate their capabilities, let others make decisions for them, aim low and give up quickly when they encounter obstacles. We must therefore help them not to dwell on deficiencies and adverse outcomes, but on what it takes to perform successfully.

Maslow (1954) reminds us of the need to pay attention to the social and affective aspects of teaching and learning. You can reinforce important points about *everyone's* needs for belonging and self-esteem, and assign this as a primary right, not a right that has to be earned depending on one's ability, achievement, appearance or other socially valued criteria. The second half of this question is important – by asking who is responsible for creating the optimal conditions, you are in effect seeking to establish that each individual and the group as a whole should accept accountability for meeting each other's needs for self-esteem and self-actualization. This is essential in diverse classrooms when self-disclosure exercises require trust and cooperation.

In an ideal world you should be able to assume that such lessons are learned in the 'university of life' but in the reality of our classrooms it helps to explicitly create a culture that goes beyond mere acceptance to a culture of valuing diversity, making constructive use of differences, using peer support and affiliation. SOAR principles are consistent with Maslow in offering a rationale for everyone to use and develop interpersonal skills, to ensure the group collectively learns and grows. We also have to accept that some demotivators are beyond our control – but it's useful just to acknowledge that these are universal human needs, even though they are subjectively experienced.

Despite all your efforts there will be reasons for disengagement. You may wish to discuss with your colleagues why particular students are lacking in drives to achieve. Compare with theories: how can theories of motivations and needs aid our understanding of students' behaviours? What are the limitations of theories in explaining these situations?

What do highly motivated people have in common?

You can upscale the level of intellectual challenge in understanding human motivation, personality and competence. There are many studies, books and audiotapes about this topic, and you may wish to substitute the books I am suggesting with other resources you know of – but here's an example of a more demanding assignment, which will require a fair amount of reading, analysis and critical thinking.

The brief

Identify the common characteristics of high flyers and successful business entrepreneurs by reading the following books (or relevant sections thereof):

- Read the chapter on self-actualizing people in Maslow's *Motivation and Personality*. Summarize their main characteristics. Here are some to start with:

    - the ability to see 'the big picture' and locate one's life-mission within a broad frame of reference rather than acting for personal gain;
    - self-determining free agency to act and decide with autonomy;
    - try new things instead of staying within a narrow comfort zone;
    - avoid pretence and 'game-playing';
    - experience life with a child-like 'fully absorbed' quality;
    - stay true to one's own perceptions of reality, feelings and evaluation of experiences and yet resolve tensions or reconcile with the voice of tradition or authority or the majority;
    - take responsibility and work hard;
    - goal-oriented, but the process of achieving goals is enjoyed for its own sake;
    - count one's blessings and feel gratitude for undeserved good luck;
    - try to identify one's defences and have the courage to give them up.

    (and there are many others . . .)

- What does Stephen Covey say are *The Seven Habits of Highly Effective People*? Brian Tracy, author of *Psychology of Achievement*, says of Covey's book that it is 'a remarkable synthesis of important ideas that can lead to dramatic improvements in personal performance and satisfaction. This is a rich, nourishing book with a vital message for business people who are serious about real success and all that it entails.'

    Ask students to see if they agree – you could give them the list below as a starting point or simply get them to find out.

    1   be proactive;
    2   begin with the end in mind;

3   put first things first;
4   think win-win;
5   seek first to understand, then to be understood;
6   synergize;
7   sharpen the saw (this one doesn't state the obvious!).

In *The Prime Movers*, Dr Edwin Locke (2000) reveals the core shared personality traits of 70 of history's great business creators and leaders. Salsman, President of InterMarket Forecasting Inc. says of this book:

> We learn what's never yet been taught about the productive giants of yesterday and today. Better still, we're given a reality-based, time-tested and objective yardstick for identifying the giants of tomorrow. This book deserves the rapt attention of entrepreneurs, business leaders . . . and business students.
>
> It is, in fact, simply a book that can make someone a better person. The traits it mentions include (for starters): independent vision, love of ability in self and others, competence and confidence, an active mind, the drive to action, virtue – and interestingly, such things as spirituality and love: 'I believe the real key to the wealth creator's motivation is, surprisingly, love – not selfless love for others, but a profoundly personal, selfish love of the work' (Locke, 2000: 108). This resonates with Maslow: 'Not only does love perceive possibilities but it also actualizes them' (1968: 98).

Ask students to summarize in a reflective account: What characteristics do highly motivated people have in common? Do you know anyone who has these attributes? Could they act as a role model or mentor for you? How might this help you? Do you have (or aspire to) any of these characteristics? You probably have them in some situations at least. Try writing up to ten statements that begin with: 'At my best I am . . .' and 'At my best I would like to be . . .'. A SOAR process enables you to set development goals for yourself.

Chapter 5: Summary of main points

- Motivation is a major facet of the 'Self-MAP' that contributes to an individual's profile by identifying the part played by his or her interests, values and needs in navigating the journey through life.
- Enhancing motivation is important in terms of students' needs, from our perspective as teachers and from the perspective of employers' requirements. Self-audits such as 'Learning and improving' and 'The drive for results' will alert students to these expectations, and the extension activities can position them for better results in study and at work.
- Identifying early on the reasons for students' choice of HE (see 'Why am I Here?', p. 119) can be reinforced by research findings (e.g. Schein's *Career Anchors*) and

followed up by a card sort activity to discover their most important values and priorities.

- Debriefing and discussion can clarify the differences between means values and ends values, intrinsic and extrinsic motivators – and the real-life implications of their top three values considered in combination with each other.
- A comparison of work values against those in learning, playing and giving, can help students to write a personal mission statement, and decide which occupations and organizations will best meet their interests, needs and priorities.
- Much can be learned about universal motivational and developmental needs, self-esteem and self-efficacy, from theories and research – e.g. from Maslow, Herzberg, Angelo and McClelland. A more intellectually challenging exercise would be to set readings for students and get them to identify what highly motivated people share in common, and write or debate on this topic.

Chapter 6

Ability in the Self-MAP
What am I capable of achieving?

Ability, the second facet in the Self-MAP (Figure 4.2, p. 82) for the purposes of this book is the condition of being capable or qualified; having sufficient skill, competence, knowledge, power, etc. . . . suitable or sufficient for the purpose. . . . Here I use 'Ability' as an umbrella term for the cognitive or mental qualities that students need to recognize and practice, in order to learn, accomplish or achieve results, whether this is for personal, educational or occupational purposes.

In keeping with Appreciative Inquiry principles, let us assume that everyone who enters HE possesses actual and potential cognitive ability – although it will be of different types, at different levels, and gained through different preferences and experiences. I am not ignoring disability – just broadly taking the view that everyone has talents *and* limitations, and SOAR principles should enable individuals to discover and value their unique mix of these. Detail about disability is outside the scope of this book, but you can selectively refer students to available resources and services, e.g. disability officers and the Careers Service at your HEI.

Frequently, the mere mention of aptitude tests and exam results turns some students into jellyfish or some other flaccid form of sea-life. Both 'competence' and 'competition' have the same stem, so actually I place myself in this anxiety-ridden category because I don't really like competing with others, just with myself. However, competing is a fact of life, and judgements about our abilities give or deny access to desired opportunities. The perceptions of other people are therefore critical to success.

Students' perceptions about their competence are usually determined by past experiences and evidence provided by sources such as school certificates, test results, feedback from teachers, parents, peers and work-experience providers. You are yourself likely to be in the powerful position of making judgements about your students' performance and grades. It can be equally powerful to give constructive and formative feedback and referrals – and you may need to counter negative self-perceptions. This is fundamental within SOAR, but not easy to do in a system of mass HE!

I focus on a 'can do attitude', as students will need to do the following.

- understand and achieve the type and level of ability required for success in HE;
- bring unrecognized abilities and 'intelligences' to conscious awareness so that they can articulate and promote their strengths;
- identify the ways in which they learn best, and become more effective and independent learners;
- appreciate different interpretations of terms such as ability, intelligence, competence and skills – and the extent to which these may transfer from their HE experience to (graduate) jobs and life in general.

Given that rapid and relentless technological change in our times now necessitates lifelong learning in order to maintain a competitive edge, it is surprising that so little attention is given in the curriculum to helping students understand how to learn effectively. This chapter contains ideas and interactive exercises that will help them do that, but do advise students first, along these lines:

- You enter HE to learn, not to be taught. This is an important distinction: it is possible to experience HE passively, absorbing subject knowledge at a surface level. However, to achieve good results and make the most of your studies, take control of your learning rather than receiving it simply as facts that are imposed on you. You can undertake inquiries broadly around your subjects and engage actively with your learning to progress through more intellectually demanding levels and become an independent, more versatile, mature learner.
- Lecturers are usually not as available to students as teachers may have been at school. There are, of course, a range of support services and resources, but you will have to seek them out and use them wisely. There is no stigma in asking for help according to your needs.
- Just as you are largely expected to manage your own learning in university, so as an employee in today's workplace you will be expected to manage your career progression, to identify and negotiate your training needs. The learning opportunities offered by university (lectures, seminars, homework and group work projects, field trips, computer and library resources) will be replaced by on- and off-the-job training, perhaps formal professional courses. Your willingness and ability to engage in lifelong learning is fundamental to success in the rapidly changing, technology-driven, global knowledge economy of today.
- It is also your responsibility to spot and exploit extracurricular learning opportunities, and to use these effectively to develop skills and experience, and build your CV.
- Because learning is so complex, no single instrument on its own is sufficient to capture a true and complete picture of all your abilities, but the ones presented here give you opportunities to gain useful insights, and develop your study skills.

- Take into account that your perception of your abilities largely depends on self-concept and self-esteem, which may be influenced especially by past results. You can improve your results!
- Your competence (and your perception of it) is not fixed, but should be fluid and dynamic. HE can play a crucial role in developing your ability (broadly defined). You will benefit enormously if you take full advantage of the opportunities available, recognize and record your achievements, and collect evidence as you go.
- Once you have derived your own Ability Profile, you can put it together with your Motivation and Personality profiles to build a composite MAP. You will in effect have a number of profiles that together reflect a comprehensive, in-depth and analytical picture of yourself from many angles. The best type of career intelligence comes from being able to pull together different bits of information to make meaningful connections, and then use these connections to make and implement sound choices in learning and work.

'Conscious competence'

In our busy lives we do not often have the time or inclination to reflect and assess ourselves realistically, so our self-knowledge may be superficial, subjective and largely subconscious. Critically and consciously becoming aware of personal competencies helps everyone to make sensible choices and explain them clearly to others – to compete effectively in university and at work. Besides, HE will probably develop students' abilities beyond recognition.

> I did not realize the skills I was developing during my Sports Science degree. It was only when I started applying for jobs after graduation that I had to think about skills, and then I was only vaguely aware of them. I had to learn to identify and demonstrate my skills through trial and error, and discover the type of work that would suit me. Now, three years later, I am entering what I see as my first real job, a graduate level position in Human Resource consultancy.
>
> Tamsin Dowding, Trainee Recruitment Consultant, Hays
> Accounting Personnel (comment by one of our graduates)

Many skills are implicit in a wide range of student activity, and are often taken for granted – they can therefore go unrecognized and remain in the lower left quadrant of the diagram opposite – but PDP and (e-)portfolios are a way of capturing them. They are fundamental to effective learning and performance in twenty-first-century life, in education and employment of all types. Increasingly, graduates are expected to demonstrate the capacity to apply skills, the essence of which is that they are transferable: they may be developed in one context but can transfer to others. However, that skills are indeed transferable needs to be analysed and demonstrated – it cannot just be assumed.

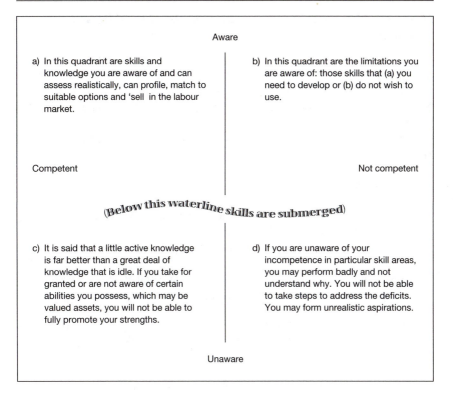

Aware

a) In this quadrant are skills and knowledge you are aware of and can assess realistically, can profile, match to suitable options and 'sell in the labour market.

b) In this quadrant are the limitations you are aware of: those skills that (a) you need to develop or (b) do not wish to use.

Competent   Not competent

(Below this waterline skills are submerged)

c) It is said that a little active knowledge is far better than a great deal of knowledge that is idle. If you take for granted or are not aware of certain abilities you possess, which may be valued assets, you will not be able to fully promote your strengths.

d) If you are unaware of your incompetence in particular skill areas, you may perform badly and not understand why. You will not be able to take steps to address the deficits. You may form unrealistic aspirations.

Unaware

Ability (skills/competence) can be analysed in terms of:

- The *type* or element of skill, e.g. oral communication skills or problem-solving ability.
- The *range of situations* in which that skill can be applied, e.g. the transferability of oral communication to different contexts: the way students discuss group projects is different from the way barristers articulate their cases in court, and again different from the way in which a nurse might explain a course of treatment to a patient. The application of skills is accompanied by different values, an appropriate manner and body of knowledge. Barristers need to be confident and apply their legal knowledge to the case, nurses need to build trust and rapport with the patient, and use their knowledge of medical treatments. Yet to an extent skills are transferable.
- The *level* at which the competence is required or used – for example the Prime Minister fielding questions in the House of Commons is expected to be far more articulate than a student leading a seminar. Performance criteria for both educational and professional assessments are usually defined at different levels to test whether achievement is sufficient for a particular purpose.

Measures of competence (note that this brief is addressed to students)

In a developed society, competence is interpreted and measured in a number of complex ways. Since we are actually talking about several different types of abilities, no single instrument on its own is sufficient as a measure of competence. You will already have formal evidence of your abilities from some or all of the following:

Qualifications: Look back at past certificates, examination awards and current HE choice:

- What do they say about you – e.g. are your results a true reflection of your ability?
- Or do they reflect (in retrospect) the wrong choice of subjects/extenuating circumstances/lack of motivation, etc.?
- To what extent are your perceptions about your abilities influenced by such results?
- Which subjects (or parts of subjects) were you good at and interested in?
- Are you making full use of these strengths and interests now?

Records of achievement or profiles you may have been involved in producing at school or college; or examples and portfolios of your work such as good writing or drawing.

- What are your significant achievements, and what benefits did you gain from them?

Psychometric or aptitude tests and questionnaires are often used by employers when they recruit graduates, but can be used for careers guidance and self-development. Employers test for specific aptitudes (e.g. computer programming, verbal, numerical or abstract reasoning), or for 'business/management skills'. Some are available online – e.g. at www.shldirect.com/ (click on icon 'practice and feedback'). Attempt these practice tests online, and/or find out if practice sessions are run by the Careers Service at your HEI. Not only will they tell you something about your general and specific aptitudes, but you will also develop some familiarity and confidence in taking such tests – useful before you have to do them 'for real' during employers' recruitment procedures. Look at your results to discover your strengths within your overall profile. You can discuss and interpret them with your Careers Adviser, and relate them to jobs.

References from employers and career reviews or performance appraisals at work; also tutorials and feedback from academic staff: what can you learn from these?

These unfortunate quotes are taken from actual performance evaluations (no names named!)

> 'She should go far – and the sooner the better.'
> 'This young lady has delusions of adequacy.'

'This employee is depriving a village somewhere of an idiot.'
'He sets low personal standards and then consistently fails to achieve them.'
'He would be out of his depth in a parking lot puddle!'

These employees were certainly not damned by faint praise! You may on the contrary already have some references from part-time, vacation or voluntary work that you are proud of, which positively indicate your abilities. It is worth asking for an open testimonial if you have impressed an employer, even if this was only at a placement or voluntary work experience. Don't forget you can learn as much (if not more) from mistakes and constructive criticism as from successes.

Add to your Learning Log some notes for this section on any consistent patterns you can detect that emerge from both formal and informal feedback you have received – patterns which indicate your strengths as well as development needs. (End of student brief.)

Discover your teaching goals

Since self-assessment is a fundamental tenet of the SOAR model, one way for you to perceive the relationships between different abilities and purposes is to assess your own teaching aims by undertaking the Teaching Goals Inventory (TGI) (Angelo and Ross, 1993: available at www.uiowa.edu/~centeach/tgi/index.html). Ask yourself: 'What am I seeking to accomplish in individual courses? Are the results I expect from students aligned with my course design, teaching and assessment methods?'

Dr Angelo (an education developer) found through the TGI that most HE teachers across all faculties and disciplines agreed that developing higher order thinking skills (e.g. analysis, application and problem solving) was an essential teaching goal, secondary to teaching discipline-specific knowledge. The latter is seen as a means to achieve the former, which are more lasting abilities.

In this respect a quote from Dr Angelo seems pertinent: 'Many programmes try to "develop" teachers, rather than helping them to become truly self-developing.' He believes that the focus in teacher development should shift from 'improving teaching effectiveness' to 'enabling student learning'; teachers should be judged on their ability to coach students to devise their own effective learning strategies and study habits. This shift is endorsed by the SOAR principles, process and coverage.

Enabling students to access HE curricula

What is thought to be unique to HE is the speed and intensity of the learning experience – the blend of knowledge and skills acquired in a short period of time – in a structured and formal environment. Ability in HE is typically differentiated from tertiary education in terms of 'higher order thinking skills'. Bloom (1956) categorized a sequence or hierarchy of stages through which different types of learning pass. His framework provides a useful set of standards against which

HE lecturers typically design their course and define its learning outcomes. They set assignments and coursework questions within particular levels to assess (a) how well the course is achieving its aims and objectives, and (b) how well students are performing against the set criteria.

Most teachers, however, expect students to abide by the rules without ever saying what they are. Although we are usually good at providing information about the content and methodology of our subjects, students may be left in the dark about the nature of skills they need, how best to learn their subject discipline(s), and how eventually their acquired abilities might transfer into the world of work. Learners need to know what is expected of them, along these lines:

- For most courses in HE there is little room for you to negotiate your learning. Learning outcomes of courses, details of assessments and other expectations are usually set out clearly and made available to you in course handbooks. In addition you may be given specific briefs for particular assignments. Study these carefully – the better you understand what is expected of you, the better your performance is likely to be. Use them also as a means of evaluating your performance.
- You can also approach your learning more creatively and critically: consider those aspects you can perform well in, and those that are more difficult, and try to identify the reasons for this. If the reasons are to do with course provision, teaching methods, lack of support – we welcome your suggestions for improvements.
- Meanwhile, take a look at Table 6.1, and relate it to your assignments to determine what is expected of you. When your work has been marked, use the tutor's feedback comments to improve your next assignment.

Learning in Bloom's hierarchy can occur adequately at any level, but is much more likely to be transferred from surface to deep and integrated learning if it moves right through the hierarchy, from knowledge to evaluation. (As an experiment, you could scrutinize the learning presented in this book under the Bloom microscope, taking SOAR itself or any of its applications as an example.)

It is a good idea to let students see good and poor examples of written work such as essays and reports (without labelling them as such) – get students to discern the difference between writing that is purely descriptive and writing that is reflective, or analytical. You could spell out that you require a well-researched and correctly referenced, balanced argument with evidence that they have understood the question or topic. They may need to know that they should cite evidence from recommended sources to support their case, and to acknowledge the weaknesses or other options inherent in the topic – all this without running the risk of plagiarism.

On the other hand, if you want students to think imaginatively, ask them to give free reign to their creativity. While keeping the bigger picture in mind, they

Table 6.1 Levels of learning and assessment (devised from Bloom's taxonomy)

Level of competence	Abilities required	Question cues
Knowledge	the ability to observe and recall information, facts, jargon, techniques; knowledge of major concepts and key points; expertise in subject matter.	Describe, identify, list, tell, show, collect, name, label, quote, who, when, where, etc.
Comprehension	the ability to understand and interpret information, grasp meaning, transfer and relate knowledge to new contexts, compare and contrast, order and classify, predict consequences.	Interpret, describe, compare, contrast, summarize, predict, estimate, distinguish, discuss both sides of a question, give a balanced view.
Analysis	the ability to see connections and hidden meanings, implications and patterns, structures and organization of parts; to identify components.	Organize, arrange, classify, put into categories, analyse, generalize, separate, differentiate, explain, connect, compare, select.
Application	the ability to use and apply information, methods, concepts and practical solutions in new situations; to solve problems using appropriate skills and knowledge	apply, illustrate, construct, solve, modify, relate, connect, demonstrate, change, classify, experiment, discover, calculate.
Synthesis	the ability to make connections between different areas and types of knowledge and techniques; to combine old ideas to create new ones; extend from given facts and information to predict and conclude.	Create, integrate, design, combine, modify, rearrange, plan, formulate, prepare, rewrite, hypothesize (ask 'what if' questions), invent.
Evaluation	the ability to compare and discriminate between different ideas; assess the relative value of ideas and practical solutions; make choices and decisions based on balanced viewpoints and sound reasoning; weigh up relative merits and disadvantages of a course of action; recognize subjectivity and verify value of evidence.	Assess, appraise, compare, contrast, decide, conclude, grade, rank, test, measure, convince, select, judge, recommend, explain, support, discriminate, summarize.

will need to see relevant links between issues, demonstrate intellectual curiosity and generate innovative ideas or develop practical solutions from them. All students will need to plan, structure, draft and edit their written work – nobody gets it perfect first time round! – but many students fail to allocate sufficient time and effort for refining their drafts.

Study skills and learning styles

Offering study skills in the first year is often seen as particularly important for 'non-traditional students' in HE. There is good material freely accessible on the Internet – e.g. http://dir.yahoo.com/education/higher_education/study_skills/ provides access to sites that offer free guidance, checklists and downloadable handouts on various aspects of study in HE (e.g. listening in lectures, note-taking, time management, stress management and exam revision, etc.). You might also recommend or use material from *The Study Skills Handbook* (Cottrell, 1999) or *Skills for Success: the Personal Development Planning Handbook* (Cottrell, 2003). The online study skills resource is at www.skills4study.com.

There are a number of learning style inventories, many available online with immediate feedback. However, it must be remembered that these are not intended to be used for any predictive validity about learning outcomes – they are best promoted simply as mechanisms to aid reflective self-assessment, and should be viewed as indicators to be linked with evidence from the individual's real-life experience.

A widely accepted conceptual cycle of learning is offered by Kolb (1984) and you will also find a free test and description of seven learning preferences (based on Honey and Mumford, 1992) at www.learning-styles-online.com. General briefing and debriefing in class can encourage students to make effective use of their 'results' – to understand the process of their learning, make best use of their natural styles and also develop non-preferred styles. Identifying one's learning style can help to improve performance only if the insights gained prompt action.

Students will have different ways of receiving, thinking about and using knowledge. One example is that:

- **Visual** people learn best by observing landmarks, maps, pictures and graphics, and creating their own mental pictures.
- **Auditory** people learn primarily through listening and discussing information and ideas.
- **Reading and Writing** styles are predominantly required in Westernized education and developed societies.
- **Kinaesthetic** people make sense of information best when they can feel, touch, do and experience things, actively engage in tasks and experiment to apply the information.

Understanding these styles can help students choose methods of study and assessment that suit them best, and develop other flexible approaches and coping strategies. Direct them to VARK at www.vark-learn.com/english/index.asp (Fleming and Bonwell, 2006) where you will find advice for teachers and a questionnaire for students (which generates feedback).

Specifying a preference for one predominant style does not mean we cannot function in the other styles. Whatever our natural style(s), we can all benefit from learning experiences that present information in different forms, so that we have the opportunity to see, hear, read, write and actively engage in our learning. Being able to benefit from the full range of methods students encounter at university (and at work) will serve to reinforce knowledge and give it deeper meaning.

VARK exercise for students

Take a look at the following quotes describing some techniques students actually use to tackle their studies. Guess which preference they represent (Visual, Auditory, Reading and Writing, Kinaesthetic) – but more to the point, use this exercise as a source of ideas for what you might do to improve your learning.

1 'I attend lectures and enjoy contributing to class discussions and seminars.'
2 'I reduce my lecture notes to pictures, diagrams and flowcharts in order to remember key points.'
3 'I write lots of notes and lists, and re-write my lists again and again when I plan and write an essay or report.'
4 'I highlight important points in my lecture notes and textbooks using bright colours.'
5 'I need to take frequent study breaks to stretch my legs or do something different.'
6 'I enjoy hunting out books and journals in the library related to my topics.'
7 'When I explain new ideas to other people I clarify them for myself and understand them better. I am then likely to remember them for the exams.'
8 'I look for quiet study areas because I find other people's conversations and even background music distracting.'
9 'I can actually study better with some music on.'
10 'I look to supplement my skimpy lecture notes with real-life examples, pictures and case studies. I need to see actual examples to demonstrate principles – such as previous exam papers and solutions to problems.'
11 'I read round my topics for each essay, making notes as I go, enjoying the use of words.'
12 'When I am confronted with tables, charts and other graphic information, I interpret and remember it better if I convert it into words.'
13 'I use videos, TV programmes and multimedia online learning materials whenever possible, related to the recommended reading list.'
14 'I prefer to tape-record lectures rather than rely totally on my written notes.'
15 'I would rather listen to a news bulletin on the radio than read a newspaper.'
16 'I like things I can see, hear, touch, taste and smell – things I can collect on field trips for example, and things I can experiment with in the lab.'

Did you guess that:

- items 2, 4, 8 and 13 were quotes from Visual learners;
- items 1, 7, 14 and 15 were from Auditory learners;
- items 5, 9, 10 and 16 were from Kinaesthetic learners; and
- items 3, 6, 11 and 12 were from those who preferred Reading and Writing.

Are you using your preferences to advantage, but also practising other styles to become a more flexible learner? For example:

- Visual people can turn pictures back into words and practise writing out answers to exams in full.
- Auditory people can leave space in their skimpy lecture notes to fill in later, when they have read round the topic and discussed it with others.
- Kinaesthetic people can reconstruct and recall the 'real' things that have happened during their learning experience, and use all their senses to learn (chew gum while studying, construct a model to learn a concept) – but they could also benefit from role playing situations and practising exam answers.
- Reading and Writing people may end up with copious notes that they could rearrange by summarizing and classifying into key points.

Which of these tips could you feasibly adopt? Record what you have learned briefly now, and use it in your action plan for improving your learning capability at the end of this chapter.

'Competence' and 'graduateness': how have expectations changed?

The personal views and concerns students often have about succeeding at university are mirrored by national concerns about creating and maintaining competitive advantage in a global economy. Increasingly, nations are busy making reforms that will encourage wide participation in HE, and lead to national economic prosperity. We can share with students our understanding that some educational values in HE are now derived from the needs of employers and the national economy.

Large graduate recruiters often specify they want good (and consistent) academic results as a general indicator of applicants' intellectual ability. SMEs have become important players in providing jobs for graduates, and they may be more flexible in interpreting qualifications and results. It is commonly agreed among careers professionals that 'a degree is no longer a meal ticket, it is merely a licence to hunt'. Today it is widely accepted that everyone's education and training should include a combination of general capabilities and specialist knowledge or technical expertise.

It may be easier for students to demonstrate the latter, certified by their formal education. However, general skills and personal attributes often outweigh the HE qualification in relative importance to employers, and they will have to find ways of demonstrating that they possess the right type and combination required for their chosen job. However, continuing debates about concepts of 'graduateness' and employability highlight the complexity of analysing what 'skills' mean to different stakeholders. 'Competencies' are often used broadly to encompass the qualities that graduates should possess in terms of the knowledge and understanding, dispositions, attitudes, values and skills specific to their field of study, and other generic attributes they will be expected to develop as a result of their HE status and experience – all adding up to their unique personal ability profile.

Although we often think of ability in HE as knowledge or intelligence, employers typically demand a mix of skills or a 'competency profile' that is very different from that required two decades ago – but is remarkably similar across occupations, organizations and industry sectors, and even across different countries in which it occurs:

> The intellectual skills of analysis and synthesis should be typical of the competent graduate, as should the ability and desire to continue learning. But graduates will require a wider repertoire of skills to enter and function effectively in modern business. There is much consistency across all sectors in what firms look for from graduates, namely the core skills that the Confederation of British Industry has recommended as the outcome of all learning . . .
>
> (Extract from CBI input to the National Committee of Inquiry into Higher Education, Dearing, 1997)

This consistency is still apparent in surveys conducted today, and I have represented it in column 4 of Table 2.4. Give your students a copy of this Table and ask them to discuss how they perceive the similarities and differences between the skill-sets in the four columns. There is considerable overlap but to be meaningful they really need to be analysed in specific contexts. Resources such as the Employability Profiles[1] show which skills are developed by different degree disciplines, giving learners a useful checklist against which they can rate their developing personal skills. This can aid their understanding of the relationships between different skill-sets, and the transfer of intellectual and other skills learned at university into 'employability'.

Ability and transferability

Recently in conversation with a surgeon from Germany[2] I learned of his participation in the training event he has described for me below. I read this as a classic case of 'transferability' – see what you make of it, and share the example with students if appropriate.

> Although I am a surgeon I had the chance to accompany an aircraft crew on its flight. What does a surgeon have in common with the pilot of a big airbus with more than 300 passengers onboard? What is the profit both may draw

from that? Although aviation is a very different branch from mine I wondered whether there were features in common, because both of us do the same thing: transporting people from A to B, the one from everyday life to holiday, the other from sick to healthy. There should be no accidents either way.

Therefore 'safety' is the uppermost commandment for aviation and for surgery. I accompanied that flight to observe how safety is secured in the very concrete situations during the flight. But not only in medicine or aviation, in many fields safety is important. Safety is a general topic in society. What makes safety come to reality?

At first, many people think that safety mainly leans on technical progress. Actually there has been considerable progress in that field. But even the best technical equipment of a high pressure boiler in a giant power station or of a ventilator in a surgical intensive unit is not fail-proof, because it has been planned and made by humans who are not able to anticipate every critical situation of a power station, or of a patient just having received a heart transplant.

Second, standard operating procedures and precisely formulated rules are considered to secure safety. But medicine, aviation and many other fields can be regarded as systems with a very high degree of complexity. These systems cannot be defined completely no matter how detailed rules are. There are remaining grey areas creating leeway for decision making. Safety in complex systems is a priority that has to be secured continuously. Thus exceptionally, in complex systems it may even become necessary to violate rules for the sake of safety.

Third, the toolbox of safety contains a number of highly developed instruments. Reporting systems for instance are capable of effectively detecting and eliminating latent failures. But it is human beings who need to interpret and act on the messages of such reports, or even decide not to act. Safety reports written to measure quality and safety that have lost their 'history' do not touch people, they are a waste of time.

Daily work in safety-relevant branches is full of remaining uncertainties. They can be regarded as critical situations or crises that require decision making. The Chinese word for crisis stands for 'danger' as well as 'chance'. A crisis can be mastered or not, as the case may be. How these critical situations are handled is crucial for the safety of the whole system. We all are familiar with such situations.

Often there is pressure of time and lack of information needed to completely understand the situation. Beside technology, standard operating procedures, rules and the knowledge of safety reports, these situations require skills to master them. Non-technical skills comprise a number of capabilities: not to be influenced by pressure due to the external circumstances, to realize the main features of an emergency situation, good decision making under pressure, using all available resources, leadership qualities, knowing one's own personal shortcomings, and the capability to accept help by others, etc.

Human skills, such as effective communication and appropriate behaviour, the ability to explore personal views and convictions – and exceptionally the breaking of rules – may become very important for safety. Humans, with their limitations and restrictions (to err is human), but also with their gifts, are the only constant of complex systems. Human capabilities and a profound knowledge of limitations and restrictions are the main pillars of safety. Human capabilities can be trained. On that flight I realized that technical safety standards in aviation are very similar to medicine, but communicating, acting as a team, and leadership are still to be improved in my field – and in many other fields besides surgery.

An application form exercise: analysis and evaluation

Earlier I gave an example of Employer X's application form question on Self-Motivation (pp. 112–13). The same form asks candidates to provide an example of their ability to analyse and evaluate. It describes how managers in their industry use Analysis and Evaluation, to:

- identify the key characteristics of a problem;
- analyse and interpret information, identifying practical implications of research;
- determine if recommendations follow logically from evidence, and evaluate the strengths and weaknesses of alternative proposals and solutions;
- identify the action needed to solve a problem, including any modifications needed to suit specific circumstances.

Ask students to rate this sample candidate response:

I evaluated and analysed a lot of information whilst engaged in rationalizing the stock control system at Weaver Bros last summer vacation. I would look at factors like – when the stock was last ordered, what it was used for, how often it was used. Through my efforts a 15% reduction in stock levels was achieved.

Take feedback from students, then read out Employer X's comments:

This has the potential to be a good answer: however, it needs more detail in it. It is particularly important to state what you achieved by your actions, and clearly here we have a successful outcome to whatever was being done to the stock control system. The applicant does give some evidence of analysis and evaluation skills, but fails to give a clear picture of what exactly was being evaluated and analysed, and how his or her efforts resulted in reduction in stock levels.

Now have students write their individual response: choose an appropriate situation (from work, study, leisure or life experience), describe the task, your individual actions and the results you achieved. Remember the STAR formula: have you covered the four bases represented by the acronym? Have you described a Situation, Task, Action and Result? Write clearly, concisely and correctly.

Multiple Intelligences (MI)

The popular view of intelligence, based on the work of psychologists such as Spearman (1927) and Terman (1975), is that it is a fixed, inherited, general capacity that determines such things as how well we learn and perform, especially in verbal and mathematical tests. The view that intelligence became fully developed by the age of 11 resulted in the 11+ examinations (in the UK) to filter those who should go to more academic 'grammar schools' and those who should go to less intellectually demanding schools. IQ (intelligence quotient) is well known as a measure of this type of general underlying capacity.

Academic intelligence, which manifests in the ability to engage logically with complex, abstract ideas and theoretical problem solving, has historically been greatly valued. Only some types of intelligence are assessed in HE through traditional examination results and the writing of essays, although other skills are increasingly gaining acceptance and being assessed within innovative curricula.

More recently there is a growing realization that intelligence is the result of complex interactions between 'nature and nurture' – between innate genetic aptitudes and the external environment. Harvard educator Howard Gardner (1993) saw that people used many abilities to succeed in everyday life, most of which were not academic. His research, conducted across cultures, identified eight kinds of 'intelligences' that humans generally possess in varying degrees and combinations, and that they apply variably depending on their preferences and situations.

This theory provides a clearer sense of personal abilities within a broader typology. It enables students to value aspects of their abilities they may have dismissed. Once identified, they can match their special profile to work and learning tasks (as with Holland's (1973) interest categories). The resulting self-awareness and self-esteem can add multiple dimensions to the SOAR process.

Handy discusses MI in *The Empty Raincoat* (1994):

> The intelligent society will inevitably be a credential society, one where certificates of competence become necessary passports in a more temporary and mobile workplace. We will move through life accumulating portfolios of competences and intelligences . . .

From personal experience most of us recognize these in ourselves and others. Although they are not necessarily connected, they can interact and be developed. For example, research has discovered that teaching children to play a musical instrument can improve their maths ability. Organizing information visually can in turn help memory and understanding. The following exercise is based on the theory of multiple intelligences. Tick one of the boxes in each row to rate your level of ability in each type.

		Low	High
1	Factual intelligence – the type that excels at University Challenge and Mastermind competitions (depends on good retention and recall of facts)		
2	Logical/analytical intelligence – characterized by a love of intellectual problem solving, crosswords, chess, puzzles, etc.		
3	Linguistic intelligence – possessed by those who communicate well and learn languages easily		
4	Mathematical intelligence – numerical ability		
5	Musical intelligence – that which made Mozart a child prodigy, but which also drives modern pop stars and bands		
6	Spatial or pattern intelligence – the ability to conceptualize shapes and objects in three dimensions, needed by architects and designers		
7	Practical intelligence – which enables one to apply knowledge and skills for useful purposes and to achieve practical results ('common sense' is a misnomer for this!)		
8	Physical/kinaesthetic intelligence – allows an athlete or dancer to be finely coordinated		
9	Psychic or intuitive intelligence – almost a 'sixth sense' possessed by some		
10	Interpersonal or emotional intelligence – the ability to work with and through other people, being attuned to their needs and thoughts.		
11	Naturalistic intelligence – the type that is attuned to plants, animals and natural objects		
12	Intrapersonal intelligence – ability to reflect and analyse one's inner feelings, thinking patterns, strengths and limitations, and relationships.		

In recent times interpersonal or emotional intelligence has received a great deal of attention, probably due to the demand from employers for 'team players' who can work well with others (see Chapter 7). A balanced society with a diverse and sophisticated economy will have room and need for all these abilities. Most jobs (and indeed courses) require particular combinations, at varying levels – for example, entrepreneurial intelligence (business skills and acumen) is mainly a mix of practical and interpersonal intelligence, possessed by those people who see the 'art of the possible' and can work through and with others to get things done.

It would seem that a bulging portfolio (containing anything from word processing, familiarity with the Internet, a driving licence, first aid, leadership skills, swimming, . . .) and not just one lonely HE qualification should be the aim of every student.

?   Ask students:

1   What does your portfolio contain? What evidence do you have in real life that you actually do possess these skills?
2   What should it contain – for the type of learning or work you wish to focus on?
3   Are you currently using your best strengths?
4   Do you wish to avoid using skills that you marked 'low' or will you need to develop them?
5   Do you want to be a flexible generalist or an occupational specialist?
6   What did you identify as your greatest strength? Pick out one thing you are really good at and describe how you became good at it. Either talk to a friend or write about it in your Learning Log. Is there any relationship between your preferred learning style and your best 'intelligence'?

The idea that every individual has MI and personal transferable skills leads to the belief that each individual has the potential to enter several different jobs. It can be an advantage for some people to avoid making major career decisions too early. It helps to keep options open and explore broadly before narrowing one's choices, using a variety of opportunities to develop a range of high-level skills, and evaluating the extent of fit between 'self' and fields of work which are of interest. By generating different ideas and investigating some in depth, students are more likely to form appropriate aspirations.

Combining insights from MI with VARK

Certain types of abilities and learning preferences may go together, but since many other cognitive and environmental factors also contribute to learning it may be too simplistic to assume that this is always the case. However, here are some examples of such combinations:

A strong Auditory preference together with Linguistic intelligence may result in highly developed oral communication and language skills that would fit well with careers in law, journalism, politics, translating, interpreting and teaching.

An Auditory preference together with Musical intelligence may lead to an interest and development of skills in appreciating and producing music and sound effects. Related careers could be singer, musician, composer, poet, arts critic, disc jockey.

A Kinaesthetic preference combined with Physical intelligence is likely to result in good physical coordination, control of and expression through body language, manual skills and dexterity in handling and making objects. Possible careers include dancer, athlete, PE teacher, actor, artisan and firefighter.

A Reading and Writing preference combined with Logical Intelligence can lead to good academic ability, and traditional educational systems seem to favour these. Examples of related careers include teaching, law, journalism, publishing, and accounting.

A Visual preference combined with Spatial intelligence is manifest in the case example in the following box. Read and discuss this. Why do you think Sabrina's experience led to successful learning, while Alex failed to achieve his desired outcomes? List the factors you identify for success and failure, and compare these factors with your own experiences.

Example 1: Sabrina says:

I identified spatial/visual intelligence as my best skill area. When I walk into a room I notice how the furniture and decorative objects are arranged within the space available. I have strong views about colour schemes and can easily visualize how different colours would look relative to each other and to the space they occupy. I also have no problems imagining how objects would look from above, or if rotated.

I think I developed an interest in shapes and colours very early on because there was plenty of visual stimulation at home and school. I grew up with books, pictures and toys, and my school encouraged art and craft work. I loved to experiment with and compare different paints, crayons and any media that I could find. My GCSE grades were very rewarding in both Art and CDT (Craft Design Technology) – not surprising as I had taken every opportunity to learn not only from my teachers but from books, films and videos borrowed from the library.

My current Degree in Visual Communications uses a variety of teaching methods to develop both theoretical knowledge and hands-on experience. It has further improved my repertoire of design skills and techniques. I can now not only produce high quality designs for a wide variety of uses, but also analyse the impact of these and talk convincingly about them.

Example 2: Alex says:

I enrolled on a correspondence course to learn about computers because I felt I was fast becoming generationally irrelevant – everyone nowadays seems to be clicking a mouse right, left and centre with no problems. As for me, I had left everything in the lap(top) of the Gods far too long. Now I am the proud possessor of my own new laptop, and I felt I needed to learn how to use it.

My first manual arrived in the post and I read it straight away. However, when it came to applying the instructions and concepts, I experienced a major block between the written word and the keyboard. I just could not get enthusiastic about doing the assignments and sending them in. I kept wanting to talk to a real human being who would just 'show me how' in a hands-on sort of way. In the past I have always learned best when I am involved in a group situation and can actively do things.

You may have identified factors for success and failure in learning similar to the examples in the following box:

Sabrina: successful learning	Alex: failure to achieve results
Visual learning style congruent with natural talents and interests; appears to enjoy what she is good at and motivated to learn.	No real intrinsic interest in computers – feels he *should* learn rather than *wants* to learn.
Environment favourable for the early development of visual/spatial interests and skills: easy access to teaching methods, resources and equipment.	Method of learning chosen (correspondence course) does not suit his preference for active, hands-on learning in a group.
Encouragement and validation of her interests from family and teachers, who also share her values.	The teaching method (through a written instruction manual) is probably not the best way to learn practical IT skills.
Positive feedback provided by achieving early success and good grades.	Does not have prior experience of computers. It's more difficult as a complete beginner to absorb new and totally unfamiliar information.
Grasped opportunities to learn to a high level, using a variety of methods and resources appropriate to the task.	Lacked the stimulation and feedback that can come from being with other learners.
Sufficient time to study, think and experiment.	Not motivated to tackle the assignments: were they really fit for his purposes?
Any others you can think of?	Any others you can think of?

Developing into a more flexible learner

By now you should have some idea of the strengths and limitations associated with your predominant learning profile. You can choose those subjects and modules most suited to your styles – and recognize why some situations cause you discomfort. However, discomfort in certain learning experiences should not be construed as a bad thing, to be avoided at all costs. Using the styles in which you are less comfortable will develop them. Another way to improve less-used styles and appreciate their advantages is to work with someone who has a different preference – for instance:

> We run a mentoring scheme here for our employees. New recruits are paired with a mentor who will oversee their induction and provide whatever help is necessary. One of the criteria we use to decide how people should be paired is to look at their learning preferences. People with different preferences are required to work together so that they each develop something of the other's style, and begin to see how a different way of looking at things can be useful.
>
> (Chris Worts, Human Resources Manager, Skipton Building Society)

Time to draw the threads together for this section, record outcomes in your Learning Log and draw up an action plan to implement your good intentions. When reflecting on what you have discovered about yourself by using these exercises and models, link their outcomes with evidence from real-life examples to demonstrate your choice of styles. The following box illustrates a suggested format you may wish to use, with some brief worked examples to give you guidelines:

Strengths of my learning styles	Real life examples to demonstrate my strengths	Skills/styles I need to develop	Ways in which I will develop these	Timescale for development (when will you implement/ review progress?)
I am a strong Reflector – which links with my 'intra-personal Intelligence'. I am good at objective observation.	I felt I was quite self-aware, and have taken to this Learning Log idea like a mummy to an Egyptian museum. I enjoy reflecting, analysing myself, and recording.	I need to develop my weakest style – Activist – and develop more extrovert qualities, getting involved with hands-on, here and now activities.	I will interact more 'publicly' in group work and seminars, try to contribute to discussions.	I will try this immediately and review if I am succeeding at the end of one month.
I prefer visual intake of information, and my next best style is reading.	I create mental pictures and I doodle in lectures. I learn well from creating mind maps and can produce good visual aids for presentations.	I need to develop my Auditory style – to listen more carefully and develop a good telephone manner.	I will practise tape-recording lectures and make notes as I play back and listen. I will also use audio-cassettes on topics related to my studies.	Will start next week, and the week after visit the library to find relevant audio material. Review at the end of two months.

Chapter 6: Summary of main points

- Competence is an umbrella term for many different types and levels of abilities (knowledge, intelligence, qualifications, skills and aptitudes), interpreted and measured in diverse and complex ways.

- Bloom's taxonomy or hierarchy of learning defines different levels through which learning develops. The learning outcomes and grading criteria for courses are often defined against such levels, and understanding them should help students see and achieve what is expected of them in HE assignments.

- The HE curriculum is becoming more skills-orientated, but may still encourage relatively passive, dependent learning. Students also need preparation for different needs, forms and styles of learning and work – where more self-managed, independent learning will help them maintain and enhance both their current academic learning and future employability.

- In today's less supported and competitive environment (at university and in the workplace) it is imperative for everyone to take responsibility for their learning, and work towards achieving the status of independent, mature, lifelong learning.

- The skills and personal attributes being developed through HE can often go unrecognized unless they are explicitly identified. Through PDP in the UK many HEIs have provided opportunities for students to reflect and record their achievements.

- Students' perceptions may be unduly influenced by negative feedback and past experiences, and may be superficial, subjective and largely subconscious. In-depth and realistic self-appraisal is a criterion for successfully managing one's relationship with learning and work in the twenty-first century, where lifelong learning for the workforce is an imperative.

- Learning is a complex process, and there are many theories and ways of understanding it. In the main, differences in the way we learn stem from the different ways in which we perceive information and process it (i.e. the sensory intake of data, and how we integrate data to make it part of what we know, understand and can do).

- Personal preferences in learning may be identified and understood through online material combined with classroom discussion and exercises given here.

- Insights gained can be linked with the theory of Multiple Intelligences, validating a wider variety of 'intelligences' or abilities than those normally valued in HE.

- As a result of expansion in HE and changes in the economy, there are now many more graduate job-seekers and not enough traditional 'graduate jobs' to absorb them. SMEs have risen in importance within the economy generally and as providers of jobs for graduates.

- The attributes expected of a graduate are under critical scrutiny and have led to new notions of 'graduateness'. HE qualifications on their own no longer guarantee entry to a career-job, but open doors to apply for graduate positions.

- UK graduate employers are remarkably flexible in their requirements: approximately 60 per cent of vacancies are open to graduates of any discipline. 'Competencies' are highly valued. Students should enhance them through study, work and leisure, and job seekers need to demonstrate them convincingly.
- Employers' requirements are often expressed as a 'competency profile', which includes skills and attributes not strictly related to 'ability' but more in line with motivation and personality (covered in Chapters 5 and 7). Despite certain specific technical differences, there is much similarity in these requirements across graduate schemes.
- Consistently good academic results are often sought for graduate vacancies – especially by large, popular and competitive employers – to attract what they see as 'talent', but are not considered sufficient. Evidence of 'soft skills' will be assessed during the recruitment process.
- All of which makes it imperative for students to understand and develop requisite skills, and achieve the best result of which they are capable.

Personality in the Self-MAP

How do I interact with others and with my environment?

The third facet of the 'Self-MAP' extends the previous work done on **M**otivation and **A**bility to considerations of '**P**ersonality'. This is about gaining insights on how 'Self' interacts with others and with the environment (Figure 4.2, p. 82). For many years it was thought that intellectual ability (measured by the intelligence quotient or IQ) distinguished star performers from average people. More recently, a series of research studies conducted by Hendrie Weisinger (see for example *Anger Work-Out Book, 1985*) indicate that it's not just intellectual ability but effective interactions with people that also make the difference between success and failure. Daniel Goleman (1996) coined a new phrase to balance the emphasis on IQ, and to capture what is meant by interpersonal skills and qualities: 'emotional intelligence' (EI). The quality of our EI, how we interact with others and respond to situations is largely due to personal styles and preferences.

?

A thought experiment for you: Try writing your response as analytically as possible to the following indicative questions:

1. What is your unique contribution to group projects or any work in which you collaborate with colleagues? How do you feel about individual versus collaborative work? Think of a particular example of recent work you did in a group. How would others describe your contribution?

2 What approach do you bring to designing, developing and delivering your lessons?

3 What impact do your preferred teaching, learning and assessment styles have on your students?

4 Which of your work tasks do you find easy and interesting? Which do you find difficult or stressful? What brings you satisfaction?

5 What are the predominant learning preferences of your students?

6 In what way might it help to understand these aspects of yourself and others?

'Personality Type' and MBTI

This chapter explains some concepts and applications related to Carl Jung's 'type theory' and its associated psychometric instrument, the Myers-Briggs Type Indicator (MBTI®)[1] – hereafter referred to by the shorthand term 'type'. In the journey of self-discovery, type is a powerful mapping tool. I would have found it impossible to describe my approaches and personal qualities in any depth before I qualified as an MBTI® administrator and began to observe others and myself through a 'type lens'. Yet when I first heard about type theory and the resulting 16 types into which it sorts people, I was sceptical that the rich complexity of human personality and behaviour could be reduced and labelled in this way. I believe every individual is unique and should be approached as such, with an open mind. At the same time it is undeniable that humans share certain characteristics.

Type concepts, *interpreted in the right way*, actually do allow us to understand and value both similarities and differences in individuals. The insights I have gained as a result have improved many areas of my life. I guarantee you will be better able to answer the questions above if you explore type through the suggestions and references for further reading given in this chapter. A word of warning though – type is a rich, deep and complex model, and to exploit its potential takes far more reading, experiencing and observing than I am able to even introduce in this one chapter. When you have come to grips with type you may want to return to your responses in the thought experiment above and test my assertion.

In identifying their personal styles, students should begin to understand how and why they process information and make decisions in different ways, the characteristics they habitually use in getting along with others and in getting ahead in study, work and life in general. This helps them to choose opportunities where they can 'be themselves' and form aspirations that use their natural preferences. It also helps them to recognize those aspects of life, relationships, study and work where they feel uncomfortable, and have to adapt or develop behaviours that may not come naturally to them.

In practice with students I use the popular application of type concepts rather than the MBTI® psychometric instrument, for three main reasons:

1   I find the greatest benefits come from explaining the concepts in such a way that students understand them and at the same time identify their own type. The majority usually find this affirming and empowering, even if they do not immediately precisely verify their type.

2   My colleagues who are not qualified MBTI® practitioners can use and apply the concepts with their own students.

3   The MBTI® questionnaire is both expensive and time-consuming to administer and interpret on an individual basis, and is therefore difficult to deliver in mass HE situations.

So let's proceed to:

- introduce 'type theory' and its applications;
- provide exercises you can use to verify your type;
- use type to appreciate how other people 'tick', and to value diversity;
- develop communication and interpersonal skills in group work at university, that can transfer into team effectiveness at work.

Once you have done this for yourself you can pass the benefits on to your students, using the exercises and explanations presented below. In subsequent chapters I expand on the type theme, to provide insight into decision making and problem solving.

Background and brief history of type theory

Type has an interesting history and is rich in theory and research. Carl Jung, the well-known Swiss psychoanalyst, first described his theory of personality in 1921 (in *Psychological Types*). In 1923 two American women, a mother and daughter – Katharine Briggs and Isabel Myers – encountered Jung's ideas and became deeply interested in using them to develop a popular instrument that could be used to foster understanding between people. Through their analysis of family and friends, their observations and readings of biographies, they tested and refined a set of user-friendly, jargon-free questions that would ultimately be published during the Second World War as the MBTI. This was developed as an objective, standardized psychometric measure of a sample of behaviour with known properties of reliability and validity. In 1975, the MBTI® was taken on by CPP Inc. in the US (www.cpp.com) and in 1988 OPP was established in the UK as the European distributor and trainer for the MBTI® (www.opp.eu.com).

Type has been progressively refined and researched, until today it is very widely used in the business community (internationally) for skills development in a variety of applications such as management or leadership training and team building. It is described in the OPP catalogue as 'the world's most popular personality instrument', and my Google search (5 January 2007) elicited 1,500,000 results related to it. It has been translated into 19 languages, there are numerous books, websites, research studies and professional associations with type as a central feature. Those that I have found useful are referenced, and I strongly recommend these to students.

'Type talk'[2] with students

In the words of Isabel Myers, 'Whatever the circumstances of your life, the understanding of type can make your perceptions clearer, your judgements sounder, and your life closer to your heart's desire.' (quoted at the MBTI European Conference, 27–9 Sept. 2006). The operative word in this quote is can – yes, type concepts can be applied at different levels of understanding, and the resulting insights can make a significant difference in people's lives. I have met many in the (growing) 'type community' who claim that it has 'saved my marriage', 'improved my relationships', 'developed my skills', etc. However, there are potential pitfalls: I have also met people who misuse type by stereotyping themselves and others. It is therefore very important to position 'type talk' for optimum advantage in terms of personal and career development.

Type is used by many large employers to add useful dimensions to the development of skills such as communication, teamwork, decision making and problem solving.[3] I will be showing how it may be used with students in developing both intra- and inter-personal skills – but (as with any tool) there are guidelines for using it ethically, and cautions against misusing it. Type offers a particularly rich, deep and complex model for self-awareness, and therefore requires effort for understanding, applying and practising with it in effective and ethical ways.

There are no right or wrong answers to type questions. This immediately allays any 'test anxiety' students may feel. The first point to clarify is that MBTI® and Type questionnaires in general are *not tests* – this is simply a way to sort personality preferences into 16 dynamic energy systems that characterize all normal human beings. It does not measure skill, ability or intelligence, career potential, level of maturity or psychiatric abnormality. It does not direct people into choosing specific occupations. Any type can do any work, but a given type is likely to prefer certain job tasks, approaches and environments. People typically begin to see why they enjoy certain tasks and approaches and feel stressed by others.

The emphasis on type is more positive than talking about traits, because (as we know) certain traits are perceived as socially undesirable or unattractive, whereas all 16 types are equally valuable. All are desirable and necessary to well-balanced teams and organizations. It would be unethical to make value judgements about a type because essentially all have associated talents and strengths, and all equally have shadow sides or blind spots that individuals should validate for themselves. Awareness of these can then lead to better use of one's strengths, and development or compensation where it is needed.

The MBTI philosophy encourages individuals to identify their type honestly. I would go further and say that 'type talk' can promote individual and team understanding and effectiveness even if you never manage to wholly identify your exact type. In discovering type people often report a sense of liberation and ownership of aspects of themselves that they may have been unaware of, or felt uncomfortable about. They also learn to capitalize on the gifts and strengths that are associated with their preferences, and to value those of their opposites (see Myers and Myers, 1995).

With my students, especially in large group situations, I find that the main benefits come from the 'aha moments' that are engendered by type explanation, which serves simultaneously for students to verify their own type. MBTI then becomes a non-judgemental self-report tool for enhanced self-perception, and not a psychometric result imposed on individuals. (Having said this, professional administration of MBTI® also requires interpretation by discussing and agreeing the outcomes with participants – they are still the final agents in deciding how the results apply to them.) The most positive use of type as a self-assessment tool is to discover the strengths that arise from one's personal preferences, and to see where compensation or development is needed. Jung believed that the road to maturity involves both nurturing those preferences to which we are predisposed, and learning to deal effectively with situations that require our non-preferences.

I ask students to extend their understanding through reading and experiential exercises. The module question that is set for homework is 'What strengths and blind spots are associated with my personality type? How does this manifest itself in my actual experience?' (see Table 3.2, p. 52). Students are required to write a brief response and present to each other in class, followed by discussion and feedback. If possible get them to ask someone who knows them well: 'What in your view is my biggest blind spot?' This can be revealing if done with sensitivity, and feeds into that dreaded interview question employers sometimes ask: 'How would you (or your peers) describe your greatest weakness?' It also leads to the realization that everyone's greatest strength can at the same time have a corresponding weakness or shadow side.

Finally, it's important to remember that human personality is amazingly complex, and MBTI cannot explain everything. I have come across people so steeped in MBTI that they obsessively reduce every behaviour to type differences. There are many situational and dispositional variables and MBTI does not give an infallible result. Environment and culture are mediators of type expression and development, and people are capable of adapting their behaviours to suit different situations. Jung's comment on the application of theory is very apt: 'Learn your theories as well as you can, then put them aside when you touch the living miracle of the human soul.'

Introducing type theory

Jung, Myers and Briggs all observed that much human behaviour that appears to be random is not random at all. It can be observed as patterns that arise from individual differences on four basic dimensions of human personality that are inborn and natural. At the core of type theory are two basic mental functions: *Perception* – how we (broadly and generally) perceive, take in and process information; and *Judgement* – how we make decisions or arrive at conclusions based on that information. The way in which we *prefer* to perceive and process information is either through our senses in a step-by-step approach (*Sensing*) or through a whole-brain intuitive approach (*Intuition*), expressed by the letters S–N. The way in which we make decisions is either in a logical and objective way (*Thinking*), or in a subjective, values-based way (*Feeling*), represented by the letters T–F.

Added to this are two basic differences in attitude: whether we focus our attention and derive our energy from the external world (*Extraversion*) or our Internal world (*Introversion*), represented by the letters E–I. Jung formulated these first three dimensions, and Katharine Briggs later added a fourth dimension that she observed was implicit in Jung's theory: whether one's orientation to life and lifestyle is of a *Judging* or *Perceiving* nature, i.e. whether we prefer to live in an orderly, planned way (*Judging*) or in a spontaneous, flexible way (*Perceiving*), represented by the letters J–P.

This fourth dimension (J–P) is about approach to life, and is not to be confused with the mental functions of perception and judgement. A potential source of confusion and misuse stems from some of the terms used to describe the preferences. Students must listen carefully and grasp the explanations because common words like 'thinking and feeling', 'extrovert and introvert' are used in 'type talk' with a somewhat different specific meaning, as described in the exercise below.

Type theory describes *preferences* that are common to all normal people, and are therefore universal.

> The MBTI instrument and type have been tried out in almost every country in the world, and with all age groups. Type can therefore be a way to bridge the cultural gaps between countries and generations. Universally, people recognize their type preferences, give examples from their experience, confirm their type descriptions and find type information insightful and useful.
>
> (Barger and Kirby, 2006)

I find that this way of understanding personality equally resonates with international students in the classroom, but the challenge is to present the theory and exercises so that they are meaningful to different cultures (Kirby *et al.*, 2007). We must bear in mind that expression of type preferences is influenced by what is considered acceptable in different environments and cultures – e.g. preferences for extraversion generally appear very different in Italy (lots of hand gestures and overt interaction) than in Finland (more self-contained and less obvious display of emotions). It is good practice to let each student validate his or her own type, regardless of what observable behaviours suggest. Exploring the interaction of type preferences and cultural differences can lead to useful perspectives on behaviours, both in one's own and other cultures.

A basic tenet of type theory is that the four basic dimensions of preference are expressed as opposite poles. The assumption is that everyone's personality falls on one side or the other of each pole, resulting in the identification of an individual as one of 16 qualitatively distinct types. The task you are initially setting your students is to decide on which side of the mid-point their preference lies, on each of the four dimensions. You can give them a handout as in Figure 7.1, prior to starting the 'handedness' explanation, followed by the exercise 'Thinking about Mental Habits' (pp. 160–2).

In order to explain the important concept of preferences, I find it useful to do 'the handedness exercise'. Ask students to sign their names in the normal way on the top line (Figure 7.1), then sign again below using their non-preferred hand. Ask what it felt like that second time. Students usually comment it required more effort, felt difficult, uncomfortable, awkward, 'like I was a child again'. Record

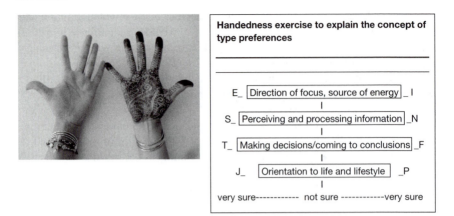

Figure 7.1 'Preferences' and 'handedness'.

these words on a whiteboard or flipchart as you may need to refer back to them to reinforce the concept of preference, and to make the important point about choosing between the poles.

Meanwhile, make the following points: We use both hands but one usually naturally feels easier. Because we use our preferred hand a great deal it tends to be better developed than the other. However, if my non-preferred hand was tied behind my back I would soon miss it – I do use it for balance. And so it is with type preferences: we use both sides of each dimension but not both at once, and not (in most cases) with equal ease and confidence. Choosing one side does not mean the other is irrelevant, it simply means that for you it is more comfortable.

For now you will be trying to discover your innate preferred approaches, where you generally feel at your best. So think how you typically feel and behave rather than what you have to do in particular situations, or to please others. Choose your response as your 'shoes-off self', as if you had free choice, divorced from constraints. If it is difficult for you to decide, think how others might describe you.

Exercise: Thinking about Mental Habits[4]

Which pattern describes you better, E or I?

E	I
• likes action and variety	• likes quiet and time to consider things
• likes to do mental work by talking to people	• likes to do mental work privately before talking
• acts quickly, sometimes without much reflection	• may be slow to try something without understanding it first
• likes to see how other people do a job, and to see results	• likes to understand the idea of a job and to work alone or with just a few people
• wants to know what other people expect of him or her	• wants to set his or her own standards

E's interest turns mostly outward to the world of action, people and things. **I**'s interest turns more often to the inner world of ideas and private things. Everyone turns outward to act and inward to reflect. You must do both, but you are more comfortable doing one or the other, just as right-handers are more comfortable with the right hand, but do use the left one.

Circle the **E** or **I** at the top to show which pattern fits you better. **E** stands for extraversion, which means outward turning. **I** stands for introversion, which means inward turning.

Next, which pattern describes you better, S or N?

S	N
• pays most attention to experience as it is	• pays most attention to the meanings of facts and how they fit together
• likes to use eyes and ears and other senses to find out what's happening	• likes to use imagination to come up with new ways to do things, new possibilities
• dislikes new problems unless prior experience shows how to solve them	• likes solving new problems, and dislikes doing the same thing over and over
• enjoys using skills already learned more than learning new ones	• likes learning new skills more than practising old ones
• is patient with details but impatient when the details get complicated	• is impatient with details but doesn't mind complicated situations

S pays most attention to the facts that come from personal experience. **S** can more easily see the details, while **N** can more easily see the 'big picture'. **N** pays most attention to meanings behind the facts. **S** and **N** are two kinds of perception, that is, two ways of finding out, or giving attention to experiences. **S** stands for sensing and **N** stands for intuition. Everybody uses both sensing and intuition to find out things. You use both, but you use one more than the other.

Circle the **S** or the **N** at the top to show which pattern fits you better.

Next, which pattern describes you better, T or F?

T	F
• likes to decide things using logic	• likes to decide things using personal feelings and human values
• wants to be treated with justice and fair play	• likes praise, and likes to please people, even in small matters
• may neglect and hurt other people's feelings without knowing it	• is usually very aware of other people's feelings
• gives more attention to ideas or things than to human relationships	• can predict how others will feel
• can get along with little harmony	• values harmony; feels unsettled by arguments and conflicts

T makes decisions by examining data, staying impersonal and cool. **T** stands for thinking judgment. **F** makes decisions by paying attention to personal values and feelings. **F** stands for feeling judgement. You make **T** and **F** judgements every day, but you use one kind of judgement more than the other.

Circle the **T** or **F** at the top to show which pattern fits you better.

Next, which pattern describes you better, J or P?

J	P
• likes to make a plan, to have things settled and decided ahead	• likes to stay flexible and avoid fixed plans
• tries to make things come out the way they 'ought to be'	• deals easily with unplanned and unexpected happenings
• likes to finish one project before starting another	• likes to start many projects but may have trouble finishing them all
• usually has mind made up	• usually is looking for new information may decide things too slowly
• may decide things too quickly	
• wants to be right	• wants to miss nothing
• lives by standards and schedules that are not easily changed	• lives by making changes to deal with problems as they come along

Circle the **J** or **P** at the top to show which pattern fits you better. **J** stands for judgement and **P** stands for perception. **J** people run their outer life with settled judgements. **P** people run their outer life in an open, perceiving way.

Type comes from patterns

Now you can put together the four letters of the patterns that describe you best. Write your four letters here: ___ ___ ___ ___ . Place a cross on your handout (Figure 7.1) along the lines between E–I, S–N, T–F and J–P dimensions, to indicate the extent to which you are sure about choosing the letters you circled in doing this exercise.

The four letters together make up a whole pattern called a type. It may be your type. There are 16 different 'people types' as shown by the 16 combinations of the letters in the following type-table. Find yours.

ISTJ	ISFJ	INFJ	INTJ
ISTP	ISFP	INFP	INTP
ESTP	ESFP	ENFP	ENTP
ESTJ	ESFJ	ENFJ	ENTJ

Each type is different from the others in important ways. As you come to understand the type ideas better, you will see how type affects your life with your friends and family, at work or in study.

Debriefing and recommended extensions for developing type understanding

Thinking about Mental Habits was written by Gordon Lawrence in simple language, with young students in mind. Use it only as a discussion starter, as a first step in thinking about type. This exercise is NOT a Type Indicator, nor does it replicate the Myers Briggs Type Indicator® which is a validated instrument developed by research.

In my work with MBTI I have found that some people verify their four-letter type quite easily, whereas others find it impossible to choose a preference on one or more of the dimensions. Tell students that there are no prizes for immediately verifying one's type – it's fine to use MBTI as a working hypothesis, to look through this 'lens' to observe and experience behaviours related to type – both in oneself and in others. When people are 'very sure' about their preferences this does not indicate ability or maturity – it simply indicates clarity of preference. Personally, it took me ages before I could find a comfortable 'home-base' as an ENTP. I learned much in the process of exploring the concepts and validating my type, however.

It is important to remind students about the ethical uses of type and equally how it should *not* be used and interpreted. Occupational psychologists specify that it is not validated for use as a selection tool – and employers should not recruit or reject anyone for jobs or career progression on the basis of their type. Students should similarly be instructed not to misuse the outcomes to label or typecast themselves or others. For example, it is not acceptable to say or think that 'I'm an Introvert so I can't initiate conversations with people I don't know at a party.' Or conversely, 'I'm an Extrovert so I don't do reflection!' For some it seems natural to think that their type is the best, and although it's healthy for them to nurture their type preferences it is not an excuse to feel 'superior', or to denigrate others.

So . . . human personality is different on the four basic dimensions outlined in the activity, but the theory holds that validating one's type preferences as separate dimensions is just the start. The real advantages come from considering how these dimensions interrelate and develop (type dynamics and development). I extend insights about and from type in further sections of this book, but have limited space here (and usually also in the curriculum) to go into detail about type dynamics and development. However, it's important not to settle for shallow interpretations of type. OPP advise that these can be damaging. On the other hand, over-analysing and over-generalizing is a sure source of stereotyping. Use tentative words such as 'when you are expressing a J-preference you would typically be systematic and planned in your approach.'

Students should be encouraged to read web articles and books to extend their understanding through whole-type descriptions and interpretations, in order to further clarify and decide on their 'best-fit type' – and understand the strengths that arise from other types too. Give them access to the following link to *Looking at Type and Careers*, by Charles Martin (1995), to read their type description and construct personal meaning from it: www.capt.org/using-type/workplace.htm.

Alternatively, or additionally, if your HEI has the licence to use the web-based psychometric material from TeamFocus, have your students take the TDI, and the LSI. Both are based on MBTI; both generate very useful feedback delivered directly by email to the student. Whatever the instrument used, it is useful only when students construct personal meaning from the feedback by thinking about how it manifests in their real-life experiences, and acting on the suggestions for development. If you ask students to do the TDI or LSI in their own time, you can follow through with general debriefing and discussion in class to ensure it is appropriately understood and used.

Experiencing S–N differences

A further way of experiencing and verifying type is through exercises. A common, simple exercise for S–N is to divide students into S and N groups, and ask them to describe an object – either something in the room such as a telephone, or something familiar such as an apple. I usually project the picture of an apple and say 'Write about this.' (The actual words you use in instructing them are important.)

Take feedback from the N group first. A typical outcome is that students with a preference for N use the object as a jumping-off point for memories, associations, uses and metaphors. They will usually have some sensory words in their list, but they say things like 'An apple a day keeps the doctor away', 'Reminds me of the apple orchard I used to play in' or '. . . of my mother's apple crumble'. Other associations are Adam and Eve, William Tell, Newton and the force of gravity, etc.

The S group provide rich sensory detail, practical and factual information. Their list is typically down to earth and contains words such as round, red, green, sweet, juicy, Cox's English apples, Golden Delicious, cooking apples, etc. – with fewer mental leaps and comparisons, if any. This serves to illustrate the difference.

You can try a variation: ask all students to write two lists about the object: first describe it in a sensing way and then in a creative or intuitive way. S people will find themselves more comfortable with facts and N people with associations. This also serves to reinforce the important point that most people can do both but usually have a way that feels more natural to them.

Experiencing E–I and J–P differences[5]

Divide your class into EJ, EP, IJ and IP groups. Ask students to:

a think how they would go about tackling an assignment to write an essay or report;

b discuss this in their type-alike groups, observing the extent to which they agree.

Each group then reports back in turn, while others listen and note similarities and differences.

A 'true to type' outcome would indicate that EJs tend to start discussing the assignment with others, plan the essay and begin writing early on. IJs tend to read more narrowly and specifically about the topic and make copious notes. IPs start quite early to notice relevant ideas, references and news items, but tend to put the actual writing aside until the deadline is near. EPs tend to put the whole task aside until the deadline is looming really large – they have lots of competing priorities that they may not have worked out systematically anyway.

You might also observe the noise and energy levels in each group's interactive process as they discuss this (or any other) topic: Es tend to initiate discussion earlier and talk more, while Is typically reflect for longer and are more self-contained. This is because Es 'bake their ideas' externally by bouncing them off others, while Is think things through internally, so that their ideas or plans come out more fully formed when they do speak.

This outcome would illustrate type differences well, but remember there are always variations in behaviour depending on the actual situation and environment. As Carr (1997) says, 'Type clarification is a sifting process, in which the practitioner tries to help the client to isolate their basic, enduring preferences from other influences on their behaviour.' In practice this can sometimes work very effectively, and sometimes not!

Type and preferred methods of communication[6]

Understanding and accommodating the different preferences of types in their ways of communicating can help all of us to develop our skills in this important area of human functioning. I have used the descriptions in Table 7.1 as an exercise with students – again to do double duty: to explain communication differences, but also to have them tick all the items they identify with, regardless of which side of each pole they occur. Counting the number of items on each side serves as yet another way of validating their Type, but they can also see where they 'use the other hand', or act 'out of preference.'

Table 7.1 Type and communication

Extraversion	Introversion
• Communicate energy and enthusiasm	• Keep energy and enthusiasm inside
• Respond quickly without long pauses to think	• Pause and reflect before responding
• Converse about people, things and ideas in the external environment	• Thoroughly consider ideas, thoughts and impressions
• May need to moderate expression	• May need to be drawn out
• Seek opportunities to communicate with groups	• Seek opportunities to communicate one-to-one
• Prefer face-to-face over written communication, voice mail over email	• Prefer written over face-to-face communication, email over voice mail
• In meetings, like talking out loud to build their ideas	• In meetings, verbalize ideas that have been thought through

Sensing	Intuition
• Like evidence (facts, details and examples) presented first	• Like global schemes, with broad issues presented first
• Want practical and realistic applications shown, with any relationships between the facts clearly explained	• Want to consider future possibilities and challenges
• Rely on direct experience to provide information and anecdotes	• Use insights and imagination as information and anecdotes
• Use an orderly step-by-step approach in conversations	• Rely on a roundabout approach in conversations
• Like suggestions to be straightforward and feasible	• Like suggestions to be novel and unusual
• Refer to specific examples	• Refer to general concepts
• In meetings, follow the agenda	• In meetings, use agenda as starting point

Thinking	Feeling
• Prefer to be brief and concise	• Prefer to be personable and in agreement
• Want the pros and cons of each alternative to be listed	• Want to know an alternative's impact on people and values
• Can be intellectually critical and objective	• Can be interpersonally appreciative and accepting
• Convinced by cool, impersonal reasoning	• Convinced by personal authenticity
• Present goals and objectives first	• Present points of agreement first
• Use emotions and feelings as secondary data	• Consider logic and objectivity as secondary data
• In meetings, seek involvement with the task first	• In meetings, seek involvement with people first

Judging	Perceiving
• Want to agree on schedules, timetables and reasonable deadlines	• Willing to discuss timetables but resist tight deadlines and unchangeable schedules
• Dislike surprises and want advance warning	• Enjoy surprises and adapt to last-minute changes
• Expect others to follow through and count on this	• Expect others to respond to situational requirements
• State their positions and decisions as final	• Present their views as tentative and modifiable
• Want to hear about results and achievements	• Want to hear about options and opportunities
• Focus on purpose and direction	• Focus on autonomy and flexibility
• In meetings, concentrate on task completion	• In meetings, concentrate on the process being used

Using type in self-development

Awareness of type will take you only so far – it must be followed by action if you hope to function more effectively. Tell students they will perform best and most comfortably when using their preferences, but they should also consider two alternatives:

a   Learn to be flexible, to use an opposite preference when you choose or the situation demands it.
b   Recognize your limitations and take steps to compensate, or use someone from an opposite type to evaluate or help whenever this is possible and appropriate.

By way of illustrating this I can think of nothing better than the example Rob and I gave students when we were co-delivering the module I have referred to in Chapter 3. Rob was new to MBTI so he verified his own type when I introduced students to MBTI concepts – and we discovered that he was exactly the opposite from me on every dimension: Rob has ISFJ preferences, and my home-base is ENTP. That didn't really come as a surprise to me, as I had noticed these differences from our very first meeting. I turned up to this meeting with my strong preference for NP, expecting us to discuss the module in a fairly open-ended way, wanting to start with the 'big picture' and look at possibilities. When I said 'What would you like to do?' however, Rob responded 'You tell me – you're the expert!' With his preference for SJ, he wanted to structure lesson plans step-by-step within a specified timeframe, and expected closure and clarity on what we would deliver. He was more attuned to practical constraints and here-and-now realities, whereas I am open to experimenting with creative ideas.

I plan lessons too, of course, but consider plans more a life-jacket (to use when needed) than a strait-jacket. I like being flexible, open and receptive to students' ideas. However, I saw that Rob was more receptive to students' wants and feelings in the classroom – he respected their comfort zone perhaps more than I did. I tend to deal more objectively with the class as a whole, and to challenge students with what they need to do. This reflected our respective preferences for F vs T. Our E–I differences showed up in my expectation that there would be lots of energy, activity and discussion from the students, whereas Rob is comfortable with giving them more space and time to reflect and absorb ideas before plunging into action and discussion. I have learned to adjust my style of questioning (N), which is not very effective with S students: instead of showing a video and making mental leaps afterwards, asking 'what do you think we should do . . .' or 'what were your impressions of . . .' I might ask concretely: 'what did you see happening . . .' etc.

In our practices as teachers, I think we learn to flex our methods, often quite naturally through experience in the classroom, students' reactions, peer observation and feedback, and our own reflections. Looking at all this through a type lens has given me valuable additional depth of understanding, and I hope that sharing some of this here will translate into improved practices for you and your students, too.

Developing skills in group work and team effectiveness

Type understanding and exercises that enhance self-awareness can lead naturally to 'other-awareness': an acceptance that others have their preferences that are as natural and valuable to them as yours are to you. This can be particularly useful in developing the group-work skills that students need at university, as well as those that applicants are expected to demonstrate during the selection process for graduate jobs. HEIs sometimes set group projects and assignments, grading the group's achievement as a whole, instead of (or in addition to) individual performance. Students are usually then left to deal with any problems that arise. They often complain that others in their group did not pull their weight so they ended up doing all the work, etc. – resulting in a poor grade for no fault of their own.

If students are to develop group-work attributes for success in such projects at university *and* simultaneously for team effectiveness at work, they need to become aware of this dual purpose and rationale for engaging in group activities. Give them examples to illustrate your own academic expectations, as well as employer perspectives. Ask students: 'Why do you think employers today value team-playing ability so highly?'

   Make the following points:

- Working with others is more important than ever in a complex and competitive global knowledge economy, where project teams are often set up to work on a specific project or 'problem', and then disbanded when the project finishes – only to go on to yet another project team.
- Due to 'globalization', team members, clients and customers may be internationally spread. Workers need to communicate with people of different backgrounds, have cultural awareness and possibly foreign language skills. Communication may be via email, telephone, fax or videoconferencing. Many companies make a business case for valuing diversity and seek employees with an international perspective.
- The skill-sets associated with teamworking have changed and risen in importance due to sophisticated consumer demand for services. For example, working with others is imperative in the service occupations that are predominant in developed societies. Education, health, hospitality, travel, leisure, finance and legal services are all sectors where interpersonal skills are vital for building effective relationships with co-workers, managers, customers and consumers.

Basically, employers want to see if candidates display the behaviours that are itemized in the teamwork audit given below. They explicitly seek evidence of

Figure 7.2 Team essentials.[7]

such behaviours throughout the job application and selection process. Before students undertake this self-assessment on teamwork, give them instructions and cautions suggested in *Learning from Self-Audits* (Chapter 2).

Teamwork Audit. Working with others: how effective am I? (Note that this is addressed to students)

Group work or teamwork (I am using the words 'group' and 'team' interchangeably here) may be identified as the ability and motivation to work cooperatively and flexibly with others, making respectful and constructive use of differences while also striving to achieve common goals. You will also see this ability referred to as 'interpersonal skills' and 'emotional intelligence'.

This is important at university, at work and in all areas of life. You will need it for group work in HE. Employers look for team effectiveness when they recruit. Many questions on application forms and at interviews ask applicants for specific personal examples that demonstrate interpersonal skills. Sixty-seven per cent of graduate recruiters use group discussions as part of assessment centre exercises that are designed to 'test' team skills. They expect to see the behaviours itemized in this audit.

Please assess the extent to which you understand and display effectiveness in working with others, by rating each statement along a four-point scale, where:

1 = never, 2 = rarely, 3 = frequently, 4 = very frequently.	
Ideal group-work behaviours	**Ratings 1–4**
1 I am aware of my core strengths in contributing to a group project	
2 I offer support and share information freely with my group/team	
3 I am aware of the role I tend to adopt when working in a group	
4 I appreciate and use the different roles and strengths of others in my team	
5 I take group projects at university seriously	
6 I know why project teams are important in the workplace	
7 I understand how collective effort can be more productive than isolated individual efforts	
8 I am aware of the factors that make groups dysfunctional	
9 I adapt my ideas and views to suit the collective group aims	
10 I help to create commitment to common goals among group members	
11 I ask for support or information appropriately when I need it	
12 I adjust to changes in team members, goals and values, as and when necessary	
13 I accept personal responsibility for my contributions to the team	
14 I respond to requests from others in a timely and helpful way	
15 I keep my promises to others in the group	
16 I admit my limitations and mistakes and take steps to rectify them	
17 I challenge dysfunctional behaviours in others – e.g. intolerance and divergent personal agendas	
18 I involve team members in decisions and plans that affect them	
19 I encourage others to express their views and listen respectfully	
20 I challenge unsound or illogical ideas tactfully	
21 I give credit where it is due	
22 I facilitate a win-win solution or compromise when conflicts arise	
23 I focus on resolving a problem or addressing an issue rather than blaming others	

Debriefing (addressed to students):

Remember that these are ideals, and nobody is perfect. High ratings indicate you demonstrate frequent good behaviours that make you very effective in working with others. You will need to think next of real-life examples you can use to show this convincingly on application forms and at interviews. Continue to build your skills through participation in different groups and project teams. Try to diversify your role – e.g. try chairing or leading a team if you have not done this, perhaps using different approaches and styles to see what works best.

Low ratings indicate development needs. Seek support and opportunities to practise good team skills. Gather evidence of your progress, using opportunities through study, work and leisure activities.

Some reflections on group work

It is important for students to become more intentional in how they enter a new group and become part of it. Enable them to recognize and deal with both *group processes* (setting up and managing the roles and tasks: who will do what, by when) and *group dynamics* (interactions and relationships) that contribute to effective group functioning. Equally they need to see what makes a group dysfunctional. A challenge and an ideal end-goal would be to have all your students valuing and making constructive use of individual differences in interactions with others.

Why work as a group or team?

Discuss with your students: What can teams do better than individuals?
  For example, ideally, teams can:

- pool ideas and produce more and/or better solutions to a problem;
- share and make more efficient use of resources;
- contribute from the specific roles, strengths or areas of expertise of different team members;
- eliminate impractical ideas more effectively and produce better judgements;
- compensate for individual limitations by using others' strengths;
- increase productivity;
- increase the motivation of members;
- learn interpersonal and communication skills through group dynamics;
- share sense of responsibility for the results to be achieved, and therefore reduce stress on individual team members;
- use 'collective clout' in lobbying or influencing externally.

When you ask people about what it is like being part of a great team, what is most striking is the meaningfulness of the experience. People talk about being part of something larger than themselves, of being connected, of being generative. It becomes quite clear that, for many, their experiences as part of truly great teams stand out as singular periods of life lived to the fullest. Some spend the rest of their lives looking for ways to recapture that spirit.

(Senge, 1990: 13)

Are 'dream teams' non-existent?

The most visible and obvious examples of 'dream teams' come from the world of sport or music: e.g. a football team or a jazz band, where every member has a valued role and responsibility that is appreciated by the others as contributing to their shared end-goals. Every member accordingly appreciates and communicates with the others, putting the group's success above any individual agendas. Unfortunately, however, 'dream teams' rarely exist, and one has to focus practically on the circumstances in which teams have to function. What might go wrong? Why are some teams dysfunctional? Have your students think: 'How could I wreck group sessions and make sure they are an ordeal for my classmates and for the teacher?' Think of a group activity where things haven't gone as well as they might have, and write down your thoughts on this particular experience:

- What was the team task: what were we trying to achieve?
- What worked?
- What went wrong?
- What could be improved? Or done differently in future?
- What part did I play in all this – what did I learn or realize from the experience?
- How did I help the group in its task?
- What did I not do that would have helped?
- What stopped me from being more effective?
- Were my team role and personality preferences reflected in my group contribution?

Have your students refer to Figure 7.2 and consider 'team essentials' as a group process. Individual members can complete these statements to identify their own patterns and habitual behaviours in groups:

1   In a group I tend to . . .
2   In a group I prefer not to . . .
3   I like groups where . . .
4   In this group I'd like to be . . .
5   How I'd like this group to be for me . . .

Arriving at an agreed group contract

Ask students to share collectively their thoughts on the last statement above – this does not have to remain a wish-list on paper, it should form the basis of a written group contract that students discuss and agree to abide by in every class. Formulating ground rules that everyone signs up to and is clear about can be particularly useful in groups where there are disruptive elements. Type it in large font and display it for reference. Clarify expectations regarding your role as facilitator, and also negotiate with students that it is everyone's responsibility to ensure the smooth functioning of the group, not just yours.

A typical group contract for in-class sessions might look something like this:

- Attend, arrive and finish on time.
- Cooperate on the task at hand, be supportive to each other.
- Take on a specific role when required.
- Bring enthusiasm to the shared topic or goal.
- Refrain from irrelevant private conversations, turn off mobile telephones.
- Attempt to communicate clearly.
- Give constructive and objective feedback with sensitivity and consideration, to help others improve.
- Accept constructive feedback without taking it personally, and act upon it to improve.
- Listen actively and respectfully to others, seek others' views.
- Be aware of each other's personal space and create a safe environment to share and discuss personal information.
- Judge each other not on 'ability' measures but by motivation and contribution to team objectives, as defined by generic and specific criteria for the task in hand.
- Notify each other of reasons for absences and failures to deliver agreed work.
- Accept that differences of opinion are normal and sometimes necessary to improve productivity.
- Deal appropriately with conflict or unsound behaviours within the group.
- Take responsibility for the effective functioning of the whole group.

(This contract can be amended and developed in the light of increasing experience and new needs or changing goals.)

Type knowledge and Belbin team-roles

You can extend the teamwork audit in other ways too, for example by enriching type knowledge by administering a Belbin questionnaire (Belbin, 1981, 2004), or get people to use www.teamtechnology.co.uk/belbin.html to identify the team roles that they habitually adopt. Visiting this site can enable students to make connections between their identified personality type and their preferred team role.

Although there is no such thing as a perfect team, you may be able to continuously improve how your team functions by paying attention to its process and to individuals within it. Usually the trouble with teams arises from a failure to define and share common understandings, goals and values related to the tasks and actions needed. Every group member needs to understand others' roles, responsibilities, strengths, limitations, aspirations, feelings, needs and resources. If all members have an understanding of type this obviously gives them a common vocabulary and an added dimension to appreciate each other's preferences and make constructive use of them. For example, is everyone on the team being heard, being valued, able to contribute fully in a way that honours their type preferences? Ensure everyone has a chance to input, but respect the sensitivities of others – especially those with a preference for Introversion, because they are inclined to be quieter, and to keep their best strength somewhat hidden, like a fur coat with the fur on the inside.

At the same time, students should avoid the tendency to judge each other based on type knowledge or Belbin team-roles alone. Failure to listen, keep an open mind and communicate clearly, to participate and contribute as required, to follow agreed directions and procedures – all are cited as reasons why teams fail. Students may enter their names onto a type-table (as on p. 162) if they are comfortable with disclosing their types, or enter a tick if they wish to remain anonymous. You can then total the number of times each preference occurs and see what the dominant team-type is, and if there are any types that are scarce or missing.

A team's greatest weakness usually comes from under-utilizing its scarce type-functions, which often remain blind-spots. For team decision making and problem solving, type can be used to identify strengths and potential weaknesses as a checklist to evaluate each team decision or product. The team can then develop strategies to counter its limitations (more about this in Chapter 10).

Application form questions on teamwork

To motivate your students to engage in group work, and simultaneously develop application skills, give students examples of questions such as the following (taken from recent application forms):

> Tell us about a time when you demonstrated leadership skills while working as part of a team. How did you identify the needs of your group? How did you address these needs to achieve success? – *British Airways*

> Please tell us about an occasion when you have worked as part of a team or group. Describe your personal contribution to the group and explain how the group functioned as a whole. – *NHS Management Training*

> Describe a situation where you worked together with other people to achieve an objective – we are particularly interested in your personal role in these situations, and the specific actions you took. – *Nestlé*

In the following exercise, Employer X asks applicants to provide an example of a time when they worked in a team, but first helpfully tells applicants how managers in their industry use interpersonal skills:

Our managers work with a wide range of people, so they need to be able to:

• interact with all types of people to enable results to be achieved;
• work cooperatively and constructively as a member of a team;
• sensitively challenge decisions and other people to improve performance;
• give and receive feedback to promote relationship building.

The form then provides a sample candidate answer to this question, reproduced here:

'As a member of the Rock Society, which I joined because I play the guitar and wanted to improve, I was involved in setting up and operating the PA for some concerts in the Students' Union. Setting up a PA requires teamwork, due to the large amount of equipment needed, the requirement that it should be set up quickly and adjusted accurately to give optimum sound balance between vocals and instruments.'

Ask students to assess the extent to which this sample answer shows that the candidate has:

1 answered the question clearly and concisely;
2 provided an appropriate example to give evidence of having the required competence;
3 covered the four bases represented by the acronym **STAR** – i.e. described a Situation, Task, Action and Result;
4 used plain language free of errors.

The employer's comment on this response gives us clues as to what they expect:

Teamwork is vital in our industry and through your experience of working in groups we can learn a great deal about your interpersonal skills. Unfortunately in this answer we learn far more about the challenges of setting up a PA system. We would like to have discovered what this candidate contributed to the team, how he or she communicated with other members and how disputes were resolved.

Ask each student to write their own example now, of a time when this competence was used or developed. They can draw on their experiences from education, work or life in general, including brief details of important elements of the situation, the team task, their individual action and approach, and what was achieved or learned. They should use the same checklist of STAR criteria given above.

Mock interview

Extend the exercise above (perhaps in the final year) to prepare for interviews:

a   Interview each other, practising in threes and rotating the roles of interviewer, interviewee and observer (using the Observer Evaluation Form, Chapter 11, p. 267).
b   Share with the whole group what you have learned from this exercise, what you will do differently as a result, and any questions or concerns you have.

Question 1: Tell me about your best team experience. (What was your task/role/aim in this team? Who were you working with? What made it work so well?)

Question 2: Give me an example of when you had to work with someone with whom you found it difficult to establish a relationship. (What made it so difficult? What did you do? What was the outcome?)

Question 3: Tell me about a group project where you ran into serious disagreement or conflict. (What was the nature of the difficulty? How did you respond/did you seek help – how did others respond? What happened?)

Question 4: Tell me about a situation where you had to work with people from a different cultural background, or people who had different experiences and values to yourself. (In what precise ways did they differ? What issues did you have to deal with? What did you learn from the situation?)

Try a group discussion or activity

You can set up a fun group exercise, role play or experiment, although it has a serious purpose behind it. Remind students that observed group discussion is the most frequently used method to assess candidates during recruitment for jobs. Almost any topical subject will do. International students in HE offer rich opportunities for learning about different ways of studying, working and conducting business in their home countries. You can choose topics with an explicit international dimension, which require participants to make the most of such opportunities for multicultural learning from each other. An example of such a project is given in Chapter 9.

Often the topics set by employers in assessment centres are fairly general and not strictly related to any particular job or course. They will be looking for generic behavioural competencies such as communicating with impact, building effective

+	Positive behaviours you should try to emulate	–	Negative behaviours you should try to avoid
	Who talks clearly and assertively		Who doesn't talk at all or very little
	Whose points are well received		Whose views are ignored
	Who encourages others to join in		Who interrupts or squashes others
	Who introduces relevant ideas and suggestions		Who makes little or no positive contribution
	Who listens well and builds on the ideas of others		Who is insensitive to the feelings and views of others
	Who monitors the time available and keeps others on track		Who is unaware of the time constraints
	Who strives to meet the objectives of the exercise		Who loses sight of the exercise brief and wanders off the point
	Who uses appropriate body language and eye contact		Who looks down when speaking, appears to lack confidence

relationships, being a team player and the drive for results. If you are facilitating this type of activity, you should explain what these competencies look like (e.g. show clips from the assessment centres video and use the observation and feedback sheets given in this book). Allocate students to discuss the topic in groups of four, while others use the checklist of competencies to observe group interactions and provide feedback on their performance. They should try to write down exactly what a participant says, so that they can refer to specific examples when they give feedback.

Use the checklist above of positive and negative indicators for group behaviour.

Relationship between personality and temperament

The Temperament Theory espoused by Kiersey and Bates (1984) is among the most popular of alternative – or additional – approaches to personality. This approach introduces some variations on the theme, has only four type classifications, and is considered simpler than MBTI but is also very helpful, preferably used alongside MBTI to enrich type with temperament. Students who have used it on its own still report those 'aha moments' of recognition – a free version of the Kiersey Temperament sorter is available at www.advisorteam.com/temperament_sorter/.

Pulling the Self-MAP together

Having come to the end of Part 2, students should by now have used the resources and gathered all the material needed for completing the assignment *Finding My Profile*, given in Chapter 4. Remind them to return to that brief, especially to the last bit, which requires them to make connections and find patterns between the separate sections of their MAP – i.e. how does their Motivation, Ability and Personality create synergy – or create tension if misaligned. In my experience they find this the hardest part of the assignment, and often turn in weak analyses – but then this picture is never complete, and we are all travelling hopefully, finding direction and creating our futures with our MAPs in continual flux.

The next part of the journey (Part 3 of this book) enables students to take their MAPs into the external world of **O**pportunity (the O in the SOAR process), and assess how the requirements of various occupations, employers, study and training opportunities might fit with their identified strengths, interests and attributes.

Chapter 7: Summary of main points

- Understanding and verifying one's 'personality type' through Jung's theory and MBTI readings and exercises is very useful in developing skills related to self-awareness and 'other-awareness'. 'Type' is widely used in business and increasingly available through books, websites and communities of practice – some of which I have used for practical exercises and referred to in this book.

- The second part of this chapter gives many practical examples of activities for developing group-work skills in HE that can transfer to team effectiveness at work.

- Through work undertaken in Part 2 students should now have the material they need to find their composite profile, drawing together the three main facets of 'self' – Motivation, Ability and Personality. This enables them to complete their assignment for this section. For real-life purposes, they have a MAP they can map against the world of Opportunity in Part 3. In this way, the Self–Opportunity reflective–active dynamic continues as part of the SOAR process.

Opportunity in the SOAR process

Chapter 8

Researching and engaging with 'Opportunity'

Connecting **S**elf with **O**pportunity (the **S** and **O** of **SO**AR) now brings into sharper focus that external world where students can explore and exploit options within the curriculum and outside, and research occupations and organizations that may fit their strengths, interests and priorities. They have more opportunities than ever before, and more freedom and flexibility to choose. The flip side of this situation is complexity of choice: we risk discharging students into a sea of confusion unless we prepare them to choose sensibly. Constructing their Self-MAP in Part 2 gives them a springboard for action: students typically report that having this MAP makes them more confident in charting the 'sea of confusion' and navigating through it.

The vital need for information is conveyed well in the words of Richard Froeschle, Career Resource Network Director with the Texas Workforce Commission: 'labor market and career information is to students and job seekers what market research data is to business – invaluable' (p. 2 of Jarvis's (2002) paradigm shift). Jarvis extends this:

> High quality, current and comprehensive information is more important in today's workplace than ever, but it's not enough. Special career management skills are needed to use available information effectively to make sound choices. People need skills that give them legitimate confidence in their ability to construct fulfilling lives. They need:
> * *focus* on who they are, what they have to offer and what is important to them;
> * *direction*, knowing their options, what appeals to them, and how to qualify for suitable learning and work opportunities;
> * *adaptability*, the skill of making the best of ever-present change; and
> * healthy *self-esteem* and *self-knowledge*, to counter uncertainty and doubt.

Employability is also closely related to Opportunity, as in the following definition put forward at an employability conference: 'Employability is how individuals engage with opportunities, reflect and articulate their skills and experiences.' This emphasizes not so much the context but the quality of learning, wherever it occurs.

The learning that can take place outside formal education and training also usefully builds skills profiles towards an experience-rich CV. Taking my cue from these perspectives, this chapter is about enabling students to:

- understand the usefulness and relevance of a range of options and opportunities, directly and indirectly related to their HE studies;
- spot and engage with wider opportunities to develop needed skills and experience;
- reap the benefits of those opportunities more fully (e.g. work experience or placements);
- use and evaluate a range of information sources – print and Internet-based, multimedia and people;
- develop information literacy skills that transfer to future potential jobs;
- assess the extent to which their MAP or 'profile' (identified in Part 2) may fit with and transfer between different options and occupations;
- narrow their options down to the choice of an occupation/employer/sector or course to enter when they leave HE;
- undertake a personalized, analytical study of a chosen occupation (or alternative choice) and present their findings in report format;
- gain insights through sociological theories of career choice.

Students who already have clear aspirations for the future can clarify and review their aims, and test their readiness for implementation. They can use suitable opportunities to develop the attributes required for successful entry to their chosen destination. Others who are still exploring options can 'test the water' with different types of work-sampling, and develop the skills needed by most graduate employers. All students should gain information skills through researching options broadly and a chosen occupation more specifically.

But first – some theory!

Students can benefit from considering two main theories related to Opportunity-awareness:

a   'Opportunity structure theory' speaks of the type of work that is available to people in their particular social positions – and emphasizes external cultural and socio-economic constraints acting on them (Roberts, 1977).
b   Community interaction theory stresses the importance of influences in the individual's environment, and the fact that social encounters can enrich experience and lead to new opportunities (Law, 1981a). This gives an impetus to practices such as mentoring, networking, work experience and work-related learning.

The main psychological theories of career choice outlined earlier emphasize or imply that individuals have virtual freedom of choice to implement their 'self-concept'. It is notable that career theories have been historically heavily dominated by psychologists in the US, whereas in the UK the contributions of sociologists have been more prominent. This may be partly because the US is perceived as being the land of freedom and opportunity, formally committed to the proposition that 'all men are created equal' – a philosophy that encourages belief in social mobility, with a corresponding focus on individuals and their capacities. British writers have generally been more preoccupied with the constraints of social structures.

Sociological theories have one thing in common: they tend to put a strong emphasis on external 'cultural' or sociological influences and constraints acting upon the individual – sometimes acting in such a way as to restrict choice substantially. You can have your students read about the two main sociological theories, take the same critical approach to them, and answer the questions that follow.

Opportunity structure theory

The best-known exponent of the 'opportunity structure theory' is Ken Roberts. He concluded that the American theories did not fit the British scene at all, as they implied a freedom of choice that is irrelevant to most people. He argues that people do not choose jobs in any meaningful sense, they simply take what is available to them. So work entry is determined not by individual differences or preferences, but by the external constraints of opportunity structures.

'Opportunity' is therefore differentially available to individuals. For example, the occupations open to graduates will be structured by a number of factors, the most important of which is educational attainment. Roberts stressed that limitations are inherent in the structures of the educational institutions that learners are leaving and the occupational institutions they seek to enter. He points out that everyone is subject to a process of socialization – first within our families, then in the schools we attend, in our communities and cultures. Inevitably socio-cultural influences adjust our expectations and aspirations by means of gender roles, ethnic stereotyping and social class images within the family, the education system and the media.

Roberts is of particular interest to careers advisers because he discusses their role at some length. He feels that careers guidance should concentrate on helping people to adjust successfully to whatever is realistically available to them instead of raising naive aspirations. If advisers encourage young people to develop aims that conflict with their backgrounds this could leave them maladjusted to the occupations they are practically obliged to enter.

Roberts has usefully helped to balance the personal choice side of the equation by drawing attention to the importance of the social side, reminding us that social stratification is a significant factor in channelling people in the labour force. Periods of unemployment, labour market restructuring and inequalities all serve to strengthen his arguments. His theory is based more on common sense observations than a sound empirical investigation, and it certainly does not fit all cases.

? Have 'opportunity structures' imposed constraints on your choices in the past? How do you think they will affect you in the future?

Community interaction theory

This theory, formulated by Bill Law (1981a), is attractive because it adopts a composite, mid-range focus between the psychological and sociological positions, drawing upon both types of approach. It is much more optimistic and full of enabling possibilities for individuals. He says that it is not the macro-level structure of society that determines the occupations people enter but a whole range of small-scale influences. It is in the exchanges that occur between ourselves and the different groups of which we are members that crucial determinants occur.

The evidence Law produces from his study gives foreground significance to the plurality of personal exchanges that occur between individuals and the people with whom they are in community contact – notably family, neighbourhood, peer group, ethnic group and teachers at school. To these groups I have added staff at university, employers, work experience providers and other contacts (Table 8.1, p. 186).

Law identifies two main types of external influence:

Community as a transmitter of motivation: We are all subject to a spectrum of influences ranging from those that are psychological in terms of the innate needs we pursue to those that are sociological in terms of the rewards and incentives offered by the labour economy. A great deal of the process of identifying motivations for career development and choice occurs in the mid-range transactions involving the participation of parents, family, neighbourhood, peer groups and ethnic group – the rag-bag of community, territory or patch.

Community as a modifier of social functioning: Community interaction processes do not simply *transmit* the influences, they also *modify* their effects. For example, social class attitudes are transmitted to youngsters through their families, but not in a way that you can rigidly use to predict what their aspirations and achievements will be. The community mediates and modifies structural influences upon individuals. It also transmits its own influence on individuals. It does so in a variety of overlapping ways that can be identified.

Applying theory to practice – and to real life

People involved in advice, guidance and education need to acknowledge that their interventions are interwoven in complex and sometimes subtle, covert ways with a wide range of other sources of help, influence and experience. Different people do, can and should contribute to the SOAR process for our students, and informal sources are often influential in ways we cannot control. We can, however, get students to understand how these influences affect them. Even more important, we can proactively intervene to set up positive experiences to compensate for a limitation, or to meet individual development needs. Finding a mentor, organizing work experience and placements, etc. can act as significant 'modifiers of social functioning', and these can be made available to students regardless of their background. I know of many cases where such opportunities have served to broaden students' horizons and adjust their aspirations while developing their capacity.

Staff at the University of Bedfordshire increasingly acknowledge the value of more interaction with local business and volunteering. In a recent staff workshop they suggested the following activities could enhance students' employability:

- real briefs where students go out to external companies to do their projects and assessed presentations;
- employers contributing to the curriculum, telling students directly about the world of work and their own requirements;
- students writing reflective reports, for example on what they learned from work placements, paid or unpaid work;
- students undertaking trans-disciplinary projects that simulate the world of work and bring them in contact with students from other faculties, employers, alumni, professional associations, etc.;
- refreshing their skills for writing tailored CVs and covering letters, completing applications effectively (including online);
- scheduled sessions for preparing and practising interview skills and assessment centre activities, with facilities for video playback;
- enhanced resources so that students can participate more in organized external activities such as 'CRAC Insight to Industry' or 'Careers in Focus' events, the National Mentoring Consortium scheme, and others that are specific to fields of study.

Student exercises: community interaction

Using the framework represented by Table 8.1, identify the main sources and types of influence in your life: how significant have they been in shaping your life-career so far? (Do this in conjunction with the Lifeline exercise. It will help you to answer some tough questions at selection interviews – see Chapter 4, p. 102).

Is there anything you can proactively do now to make 'community interaction' work in your favour?

The wheel of opportunity

Consider the benefits you might gain from each option shown in Figure 8.1. In the inner wheel are HE learning opportunities, module and course choices. The intermediate white wheel shows short-term, extracurricular opportunities to add value to your HE experience. Which of these appeal to you? Those represented in the outer wheel are longer-term choices for transition beyond HE. Finally, all this takes place in the context of a changing world. In this journey we are travelling outwards, looking beyond the immediate curriculum to co-curricular and extracurricular experience, and then beyond to preparation for the future.

Table 8.1 Sources and influences of community-interaction

Sources:	Influences:				
	Expectations	Feedback	Support	Modelling	Information
Parents					
Extended family					
Neighbourhood					
Peer group					
Ethnic group					
Teachers at school					
Staff at university					
Employers and other work experience providers					
Any other contacts					

Making the most of academic opportunities

All traditional forms of academic coursework and assessment also develop a range of skills (touched on in Chapter 6) but you might work with your students to explicitly identify the skills they are developing through these. For example, **examinations** may cover a range of variations including open/closed questions, time-limited or open, multiple choice, short and long questions, computer-based assessments (CBA), etc. A quick brainstorm with my colleagues identified the following indicative skills students develop in preparing for and taking examinations:

Self-management: Managing self, time and pressure – in preparing, using anxiety positively, then getting to the venue and completing the paper; working alone and taking personal responsibility; concentration for extended periods; being 'task-focused'.

Written communication: Extensive writing by hand, although IT skills are a component in CBA.

Analytical ability and information literacy: Identifying and memorizing salient features of subjects/topics from a range of sources, synthesizing and communicating (without access to those sources); selecting and structuring knowledge.

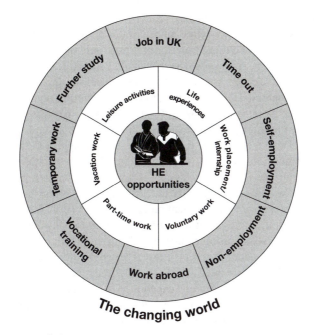

Figure 8.1 The wheel of opportunity.

Creative and critical thinking (depending on the subject and mode of examination).

In a similar vein you could try identifying the transferability of skills gained from writing essays and reports, doing presentations, group work, producing portfolios, field work . . .

Group projects and presentations using the wheel of opportunity

Either allocate groups, or allow students to self-select themselves into 'interest groups' to investigate the different options, and prepare presentations for an assignment. The aim is for each group to evaluate and promote the benefits of the opportunity, using real-life examples wherever possible. The volume of material on each of these options, even just on websites, seems to grow exponentially each year, but students should venture into the 'real world' in this quest. They will also learn from each other through the presentations – which you could give them free reign to create as imaginatively as possible.

Alternatively, have them organize a fair for opportunity providers to visit your HEI. Careers Services sometimes do this, and students could then collaborate in that venture. They can get involved in organizing and marketing the event – it will develop a different set of skills.

Those options in the inner white wheel would be relevant in their first year, when they generally have more time for part-time paid or voluntary work, etc.

In the penultimate year you could have them do a similar exercise for the longer-term transition choices represented in the outer wheel. In the section starting on p. 194 is an example of an assessed Job Study, which ensures students choose and analyse an occupation in depth. I have also itemized some benefits of postgraduate study – the second most popular destination for graduates in the UK.

Early in the final year (when they actually need to apply) they can research employer-organizations and industry sectors in which their chosen occupation occurs. Point out that this inquiry should be approached without preconceptions about 'jobs' as they are evolving all the time, and the same job can be very different depending on the sector and organization in which it occurs. There may also be possibilities for self-employment that some will want to consider.

Additionally, you can reinforce that undertaking this inquiry as a student-group replicates workplace conditions where teams are increasingly set up to work on projects, and may be disbanded when the project is completed. For success in team situations, individual values and capabilities should constructively align with the team aims and tasks, and in turn with the mission and functions of the organization – which has its own structure, and must undertake its business in a broader political, cultural, economic, technical and geographic climate. This is well represented in Figure 8.2.

Make it a requirement that students should collect information from a variety of sources on their chosen option. Suggest visits to the Careers Centre, library and Internet, and an interview with at least one person doing the job in which they are interested, as below:

Print materials: books, journals, newspapers, etc.
Multimedia: DVDs, websites, radio and TV programmes, etc.
People: e.g.

- family members, friends, alumni;
- providers of work experience or part-time jobs, voluntary work, summer placements;
- employers at careers fairs;
- representatives of professional associations.

Indicative examples: making the most of a year out

If students are burned out or stressed out after the intellectual rigours of university life (!) and not yet ready to join the rat race, they might fancy a year out on *The Beach*, with Leonardo DiCaprio as their role model – but they should think again! There's a veritable wealth of opportunity available. Several graduates take a 'gap

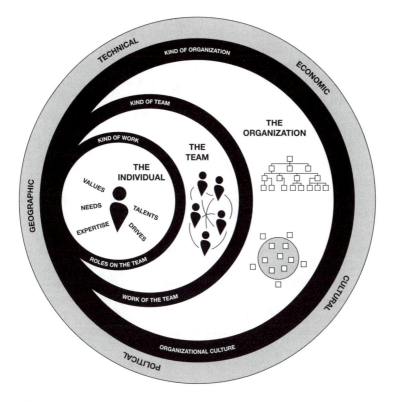

Figure 8.2 Interface between the individual, the team and the organization.[1]

year' to earn, learn and/or travel – often in some combination of these options – both in the UK and abroad. Any of these can count as valuable experience: a chance to apply, test and improve skills, prepare for the future, learn about other people's ways of living and conducting business, and enhance that skimpy CV.

An employer viewpoint

Most employers view time out favourably provided it is constructive, but the onus is on applicants to translate the benefits into 'employability', or relate them to specific job requirements. Have them think about their reasons, and plan with a purpose – for example to strengthen their chances of successful entry to a chosen occupation or simply to try something unusual, challenging or adventurous. Many students who broaden their horizons in this way report benefits of increased confidence, independence, maturity and adaptability – precisely those qualities that employers value highly. Here are some glimpses of constructive 'gap year' experiences:

Kishore's paid work experience:

During my year out I worked on various projects for a medium-sized company. I had already worked in student-type 'McJobs' before, but I felt I was really able to get into the life of this organization and make a valuable contribution. People were very friendly and helpful, and I will be able to use these contacts for future references and networking. I developed many transferable skills and gained in confidence, which will really help with job hunting. In my CV I analysed and 'marketed' this experience, as follows:

> **Assistant to Managing Director**, ABC Electrotech, July 1998 – August 1999
> Successfully contributed to marketing projects and undertook a variety of administrative tasks in this medium-sized electronic engineering company during 'year out' after graduation.

- improved word-processing, desk-top publishing and Internet skills;
- updated and revamped a small library;
- learned to use office equipment, information and communications technology;
- developed insights into business administration and organization;
- learned the principles of marketing and public relations;
- gained confidence in communicating and working with people in a team;
- classified and organized publications, paying attention to detail;
- developed good time management and self-management skills.

Loren's volunteering in Nepal:

I taught children aged 5–15 in a government-run school in Nepal, but I probably changed more from the experience than they did! It was humbling to be so readily accepted as a friend from a foreign land, and my host family welcomed me into their lifestyle and culture. I learned to see from the inside and understand my children's attitudes and situations. I was thankful for the short and simple English teaching course I had taken as a volunteer before I went. I put my teaching skills and aptitudes to the test, and adapted teaching methods to scarce resources. I discovered methods that worked well and those that didn't. I will be able to speak convincingly from experience when I apply for teacher training on my return to the UK.

Researching options

'Information is Power' – however, 'many students make career decisions with much less research or effort to obtain accurate information on occupations and employment opportunities than they would invest in writing an essay' (Ball and Butcher, 1993: 9).

? How can you ensure information is reliable, accurate, up-to-date and relevant to your needs?

Note that this question is broader than 'careers research' – it applies to any type of information.

Evaluating information

When was the material produced?
How often is it updated: can you rely on its currency and accuracy?

Who produced it and for what purpose?
From what sort of viewpoint or perspective is the information presented?
Is it fact or opinion: objective and rational, or subjective and emotional, even perhaps glossy and glamorous?
Is it formal and expert or informal and amateur?
Does it give only the positive aspects of the job and/or employer, or a balanced picture?
Was it written for marketing or recruitment purposes, or to inform and guide?

Who was it produced for?
Does it meet your needs as a graduate?
Does it have age-related information if you are a mature student, or special sections on disability/equal opportunities? Interpret its relevance for your purposes.

What is the scope?
Is it local, national or international in coverage?
What scope are you looking for? If you are an overseas student you may want to find out about occupational opportunities back in your home country; or you may be a home student interested in studying and working abroad.
How much information do you need in order to do or decide something – in what sort of depth or level of detail?

What type of information do you find?
Think about the nature, form and function of any item of information you discover.
Is it news, comment, analysis – a practical report, historical account, financial or statistical knowledge presented in graphs or charts?
What type of knowledge are you seeking?

How accessible is it?
There are two main aspects relating to ease of access:

a   how easy is physical access – for example, the Internet is not readily available to unemployed graduates who do not have computers at home;
b   how accessible is its meaning for your level of comprehension?

Information literacy and employability[2]

Information literacy focuses on cognitive and transferable skills deemed essential to learning and employability. It has been defined by the Chartered Institute of Library and Information Professionals (CILIP), the professional body for librarians, as 'knowing when and why you need information, where to find it, and how to evaluate, use and communicate it in an ethical manner.' (CILIP, 2006).

In a knowledge-age economy, knowledge management can be critical to a company's success. Information is increasingly available in different formats and in abundance, amounting to 'information overload'. It is of no use to individuals or to companies if they cannot cope with this. They need to find ways of storing and recovering relevant information when they need it. New data-management systems are replacing paper records, which seem to get out-of-date almost as soon as they are written – but companies then need to provide substantial training for staff.

In relation to the key principles identified in CILIP's definition, ask students with what level of confidence they can honestly claim that they demonstrate the following capabilities, where:

1 = very confident 2 = confident 3 = somewhat confident 4 = not at all confident	
	Confidence ratings 1–4
I can identify what type of information I need to find or locate in order to solve problems.	
I can identify appropriate information sources to find the information I need.	
I can identify suitable keywords and phrases that describe the topic I am trying to research.	
I can create relevant search strategies to search for information on appropriate resources, both print and electronic.	
I can employ a range of search tactics to ensure my searches retrieve relevant results.	
I can critically evaluate the information retrieved in terms of reliability, accuracy and authority.	
I can handle a diverse range of data to identify key themes and arguments.	
I can cite my references in an appropriate and recognized way.	
I can analyze and interpret the information I have found, to communicate my ideas and arguments in a variety of formats and for different audiences.	
I can organize and store the information I've found so that I can retrieve it easily when I need it again.	

These information tasks are not confined to the HE environment, students will need the same competencies in the workplace. Kubler and Forbes (2005, cited in HEA, 2006) suggest key competencies that employers look for in graduates, and many involve information literacy to some extent. The following are some examples.

Cognitive skills: the ability to identify, question, analyse and solve problems using a wide variety of information and data.

I use the reference material online to check definitions and undertake basic research on a topic.	
I use the full text journal collections to find journal articles.	
I use the bibliographic databases to find journal citations.	
I spend time identifying keywords and phrases that best describe my topic.	
I use search techniques such as Boolean truncation and phrase searching.	
I use the Internet to find my information.	
I use library resources to find information.	
I use the print journal collection.	
I assess whether the information I have found is accurate, and is obtained from a reliable source.	
I use a wide range of resources to undertake a literature search.	

Technical ability: the skills and knowledge to use work-related equipment and services.

I use the library catalogue to find books on my topic.	
I use the reservation option to obtain material out on loan or only available at another campus.	
I renew my books online.	
I use the library catalogue to check if the library takes a particular journal.	
I ask the librarian for help and advice.	

Business and/or organizational awareness

I keep records of the resources I have searched.	
I keep records of the keywords and phrases I have used in my searching.	
I reference the work and ideas of others that I use in my work.	
I organize the information I have found so that I can easily find it again.	

Truthful assessment will help students to identify their weak areas in terms of information literacy, both in education and later in the workplace. Once identified, students can start to address those weak areas by using appropriate guidance and learning development activities provided by the university via study skills and the library.

Understanding jobs and transferable skills – student exercise

If you are facilitating this exercise you will need to collect a range of occupational profiles that are directly and indirectly related to the subject you are teaching. These are printable from www.prospects.ac.uk/ (click on 'Explore types of jobs'). Give a different profile to each pair or small group of students, together with the following brief.

This exercise should enable you to:

- define different types of skills and how these might be applied in a range of occupations;
- explain how skills relate to various job functions, and the extent to which they may be developed in one context and transferred to others.

Each small group will have a different occupational profile.

- Read and understand your job within your group, focusing especially on two sections: Typical Work Activities and Entry Requirements, making links between the job functions and the skills required – e.g. 'In this job you have to gather and analyse all available data. . . . You must therefore have excellent "information skills" and analytical problem-solving ability.'
- Make notes to enable you to present a concise description of your job to the rest of the group, preferably in the form of a visual aid you can project and speak to.
- Note: Do not mention the job title – the others must guess which job you are describing!

You will have 20 minutes to prepare, 5 minutes for each group to present. You will need to be quick with turnaround time and guessing the job!

A module assignment: analysing a chosen occupation (as in Tables 3.1 and 3.2)

Assignment: personalized job study and report briefing

Weighting: 50%   **Hand in date:** ....

A   Purpose and learning outcomes   This job project should enable you to:

- choose, investigate and understand an occupation/job and industry sector of your choice that links in with your interests, abilities and personality;
- assess your suitability (strengths and development needs) for the job you study;
- use and appreciate a range of careers information sources in terms of accessibility, reliability and usefulness;
- gain insights into different industry sectors in which your job occurs;
- practise informational interviewing skills; start making contacts you can build on later;
- develop the language for describing, analysing and comparing jobs – useful when you come to apply for employment;
- write a well-structured 2,000-word report that uses appropriate language and layout.

B   Preparation for the assignment   Steps to take before you write your report:

- Choose a particular occupation or alternative opportunity you want to explore, preferably related to your personal career goal and one you can enter as a new graduate, e.g. one of the occupations described in the occupational profiles at www.prospects.ac.uk (choose the link: 'Explore types of jobs'). You may study this job in your country of origin if you are an international student or if you intend to work abroad, and compare it with the UK if you wish.
- Identify appropriate employer organizations that provide this type of occupation.
- Research the occupation systematically using a range of reliable information sources, as suggested above.
- Plan, negotiate and undertake at least one visit to interview one or more employees as examples of people working in this occupation. Find someone suitable to interview using any contacts you may have, possibly through work experience, placements or family connections. You may wish to use the questions suggested later in this chapter, as guidelines from which to select, adapt or add your own questions.
- Put all your findings together – from the interview and your research – compare, analyse, and verify the accuracy and reliability of the information you have gathered. Recognize when key information is missing. Select the most reliable and useful data to include in your report.

?

- Refer back and reflect on your 'Self-Mapping' insights, and match your personal profile to the job requirements. Ask: 'What does this mean for me? How do I relate to it?'
- Bring together your 'self-assessment' and 'job knowledge', making pertinent, personal connections.
- Present your findings in a word-processed report format (2,000 words), using the guidelines on writing a report – see below.

C   Please familiarize yourself thoroughly with the criteria for assessment and the report-writing brief below.

Criteria for assessment and marking scheme: We expect the report to contain the following elements:

An **Introduction**: briefly explain your reasons for choosing this job to study and indicate what methods you used to conduct your investigation.   **5%**

The **main body of the report** should present findings, evidence and conclusions drawn from your research, *linked with your Personal Profile*. This should be divided into appropriate sections with sub-headings. As the length is restricted to 2,000 words, please present only relevant content concisely here. Do not include transcripts of interviews or lengthy quotes from employer brochures for example – all supporting material can be attached as appendices, but again, please be selective in what you decide to include.

We will expect to see a job study which is **not just descriptive but analytical**, in terms of:

- **the job**: *Interpret your findings* (do not just report them), make comparisons, connections, and independent judgements about the different aspects of the job: its tasks and responsibilities, entry requirements, training opportunities and prospects, terms and conditions, environment and lifestyle, growth potential and availability within different employment sectors and types of organization.
- **your sources of information**: We will expect you to use and compare a variety of sources intelligently, e.g. original research in the real world of work (your interview), knowledge of current affairs, resources available in our Careers Resource Centre and on the Internet.   **50%**
- **yourself in relation to the job**: Make pertinent links between your assessment of your motivation, ability and personality, and the requirements of your chosen job or occupation. How do your interests, skills, values, personal attributes and experience match up to this job, and to the demands of the contemporary world of work generally? **Give evidence of this match.**   **30%**

Your **concluding paragraph** should draw together and summarize key observations, and indicate what you might do or develop in relation to what you have learned from your investigation.   **5%**

Overall presentation: style and layout, correct spelling and grammar, **system of referencing** (criteria which generally apply to university written work). **10%**

D Guidelines for writing this report A report is different from an academic essay in its **structure, language and presentation**. We do not want a rigid business style for the purposes of this job study – this is a personal report about you in relation to a job of your choice, so use the first person, e.g. 'I have chosen to investigate the job of a Market Research executive because I found marketing the most interesting part of my degree in Business . . .', etc.

We will be looking for a clearly structured format, using sections and sub-headings so that the information is easy to locate and follow. The style of writing in a report is less discursive than in an essay, with a more direct and economic use of language. We expect you to write with a clear purpose, presenting and analysing specific information and evidence applied to a particular investigation. So, allow yourself time to:

- read and understand the report brief given here, adhere to its specifications – and draft and redraft until you can present the final version;
- gather, evaluate, analyse and present accurate and **relevant** information from a variety of sources;
- acknowledge and reference sources throughout and in your Bibliography at the end. Avoid plagiarism (see guidelines and examples in your Module Handbook);
- structure material in a logical and coherent order;
- present your report in a manner consistent with the job study brief;
- make the connections between self-knowledge and job knowledge that are required;
- draw appropriate conclusions that are supported by evidence from your findings;
- make effective use of appendices; include supporting material here, for example any printouts from questionnaires on the Web, interview notes, etc. (Appendices will not be included in the word limit.)

Aim for the 2,000-word limit and don't forget to include your Word Count and Bibliography at the end of the report.

E Demonstration of analytical skills as opposed to describing facts To achieve grades in the A range, you must demonstrate ability to describe the job in some depth and balance, locating it within the contemporary labour market, and critically analyse your ability to enter and thrive within it. This would involve:

- using a range of information sources to build up as complete and reliable a picture as you can manage (of yourself as well as of the job you have chosen);

- interpreting the information you gather, making independent judgements based on sound data;
- making connections and comparisons between different facts and aspects;
- analysing the extent of the fit between your 'career profile' and the various requirements of the job;
- drawing some conclusions as to what you might do or develop in order to enter this job – or what other jobs you might investigate if you conclude this one does not suit you.

Note: Grades in the F range will demonstrate no more than ability to describe the job.

F   Researching jobs: what questions will you ask?   Researching a job of your choice will only help if you research actively and analytically. What are you really trying to find out? Here are some questions to ensure good coverage of the basics:

1   Questions about **job tasks and responsibilities**: (Job descriptions, often supplied as part of recruitment literature, are a good source of information about job tasks.)

- What actual tasks does the work involve?
- How much routine and variety is there?
- What is a typical day like?
- What opportunities are there to specialize, take responsibility, develop procedures, use equipment, etc.?
- What are the most and least enjoyable aspects of the job?

(Consider your profile: Do these activities and ways of working use your strongest abilities and interests?)

2   Questions about **entry requirements**: (A 'Person specification' may be supplied together with a job description when you apply for jobs.)

- What typically are the qualifications, skills, qualities and experience required for entry to this work?
- How competitive is it for new entrants to this type of work?
- How flexible are the rules, written and unwritten, about prior qualifications, experience, age on entry, etc.?
- What is the normal method of application: answer a vacancy advertisement, write speculatively, network and seek work experience first, use an agency . . .?

(Consider your 'abilities': Could you meet the entry requirements when you graduate, or would some type of postgraduate course be necessary or desirable?

Marker sheet for personalized job study

(can be used for both self-assessment and tutor-awarded grades and feedback comments)

Name of student: ....

**A: Outstanding   B: Very Good   C: Good   D: Satisfactory
E: Further work needed   F: Unsatisfactory/weak**

	A	B	C	D	E	F	
Effective introduction							Poor or no introduction 5%
Thorough and systematic investigation of job							Superficial investigation of job
Evidence of labour market intelligence							Poor or no investigation of employment sectors/firms
Range of appropriate sources of information used							Basic or too few sources of information used
Only relevant and accurate facts included							Inappropriate/superfluous/inaccurate facts included
Analytical approach to material							Material regurgitated without comment 50%
Pertinent self-assessment in relation to the job							Poor matching of self to the job's requirements
Claims are supported with convincing evidence							Unsupported claims
No waffle or irrelevant material							Rambling; irrelevant material included 30%
Pertinent conclusion							Inadequate or no conclusion 5%
Report style and layout, succinct and precise							Inappropriate style, prone to waffle
No errors of spelling, typing, grammar and syntax, etc.							Many errors 10%

COMMENTS

MARKS

What further skills may you have to develop? What type of experience would help?)

3   Questions about **terms and conditions of work**:

-   Is the work typically offered on a permanent or fixed-term contract? Is flexible working possible or expected? Can one be self-employed, work freelance?
-   What are the arrangements about pay and pension, hours and holidays, job-sharing, career breaks . . .?
-   Are there any perks such as bonuses, company car, childcare?
-   How typical for this work are these terms and conditions?

(What conditions of work are you expecting or willing to settle for?)

4   Questions about **training/induction/further development**: (Again, recruitment brochures and employer websites may tell you about this.)

-   What type of training is offered (if any!) – is it on- or off-the-job, informal or formal? Do opportunities exist for sponsorship to external courses and training events?
-   Is training necessary or desirable for promotion?
-   Does it lead to professional qualifications/membership of a professional association?
-   Will training and experience in this work help you to develop your career with other employers or to transfer your skills to other areas of work?
-   Is there a clear promotion path?
-   What are the implications in terms of job security and advancement?

(Looking back at the work values you prioritized, and your learning styles, how congruent are they with the opportunities offered?)

5   Questions about **relationships and social interaction** at work:

-   Will you be working mainly with other graduates or with people from a wide variety of ages and backgrounds?
-   What sort of relationships are there in this work – with customers and clients, superiors, subordinates, etc.?
-   Does this work involve leadership and/or teamwork? In what way?
-   Who will you report to? How flat or hierarchical are the layers of management?
-   Is the relationship between colleagues formal or informal?

(Consider your personal style and preference in interacting with people.)

6   Questions about **work environment and surroundings**: (A visit to, or work experience with, a company will give you a good idea of the work environment.)

- Where is the work based – city centre, science park, industrial estate, clients' premises . . .?
- In what type of environment is this work typically carried out? Office, laboratory, school . . .? Open-plan, shop floor, out-of-doors . . .?
- Do people doing this work normally work in one place, or are they travelling about as part of the work? If they travel, how often and where? Do they get a company car?

(Consider what sort of work environment would suit you.)

7   Questions about **labour market trends** and **different types of employer organization** in which this work occurs:

- In what types of organizations is this work available: multi-national, small- or medium-sized business, public/private/voluntary sector?
- Is self-employment or freelancing possible?
- How many people in my part of the country are employed in this type of job?
- What is the local availability of jobs of this kind?
- Are jobs in this field increasing or decreasing?
- What are the current issues/future trends facing the company (or this industry generally)?
- What is the status or reputation of the employer (and the work)?
- To what extent is this reputation based on fact?

(In terms of your preferences and values, what type of organization would you fit into best?)

8   Questions about the **underlying values of the work/identity of the employer**:

- Are moral values challenged at work? e.g. experiments on animals, environmental concerns, arms trade, exploitation of developing countries, etc.?
- What is the employer's attitude? e.g. public service, aggressive profit making?
- Do they have an equal opportunities policy with evidence that they act upon it? What is the age and gender profile of the organization? What opportunities are there for ethnic and other minority groups, people with disabilities, older entrants?

(Do the employer's values conflict or conform with the values you identified as being most important to you? Is your identity congruent with that of the employer? Will you have to overcome any barriers to employment in this field – such as age, disability, gender or race?)

Finding out about specific employers and vacancies

When students have decided on an occupational area they will need to investigate relevant potential employers in some depth, to discover if they are interested in working for them and to prepare for application and interview. Again the Internet abounds with employer and professional body websites and other relevant sources of such information – but they should again think about the questions that they want answered. They could structure their inquiry around those suggested below, and select some to ask in an informational interview with someone working in an organization of interest to them:

- products and services (is it predominantly a manufacturing or services organization, or a mixture of both?);
- location(s): where are its headquarters and branches?
- is it in the private, public or charitable sector?
- philosophy and purpose, e.g. profit/non-profit corporate culture, funding source, clientele, functions and activities;
- number of employees (break this down by location if appropriate);
- management structure/management style;
- ownership, e.g. if you join a family-owned business, consider the impact on your potential for career development;
- working relationships/atmosphere/workload;
- induction, training and development programmes offered;
- typical career path;
- recruitment and promotion policy/evidence of 'equal opportunities';
- involvement of subordinates in the decision-making process;
- use of technology, amount and type of equipment and facilities;
- annual sales for the past year(s) compared to industry trends and to major competitors;
- recent trends and potential future growth for the employer and the industry.

A quiz about employment sectors

Remind students that the same job can be very different in different organizations and sectors. Although you do not have to be an expert in all of this, activate them to find out in which sectors their chosen occupation or job can be done, and how it might be different.

Employer organizations can be grouped by:

- location/geographical reach and scope: local, national, international;
- description of how financed, or by goals: public, private, voluntary or charitable sector;
- size: large, or small- or medium-sized employer;
- industry sector: e.g. manufacturing, services such as health, education, leisure, media, etc.

The following statements can stimulate discussion; do you think these are true or false – or 'it all depends'?

1 It is more exciting to work for a large, multinational organization.
2 You get to travel if you work for an organization that has branches overseas.
3 Small firms offer better training prospects.
4 There is greater job security in the private sector.
5 You need to have altruistic motives to work for a charity.
6 Jobs in the voluntary sector are never advertised.
7 Self-employment is not an option for young graduates.
8 Working in the public sector is poorly paid and offers few benefits.
9 Civil Service jobs are based in London.
10 Most graduates want to work in multinational companies that pay high salaries.

What about postgraduate qualifications – do they enhance employability?

Students may choose further study or training for 'the love of a subject' – or on the assumption that it will give access to a 'better' job, higher salary or more status. Many academic higher degrees do not guarantee improved job prospects, except in occupations such as lecturing in HE and research. Statistics consistently provide general evidence that people with higher and better qualifications have a lower rate of unemployment, but postgraduate vacancies in the UK – for most fields of work – are not officially different from those for graduates. There is a significant grey area where work experience may be more useful. Much depends on your chosen field of study, your particular background, your personal skills and qualities and your future career intentions. Other factors will have a strong influence, such as availability of opportunities and competition from others. So low unemployment rates among higher degree holders do not equate with high employer demand.

Many postgraduates go into jobs for which their qualifications are neither prerequisites nor even desirable. The exceptions are in careers such as lecturing in HE, or scientific research and development. And, of course, vocational post-graduate training is essential in order to convert an academic first degree to professional qualifications – e.g. teaching or law.

The great advantage of many postgraduate courses is that they offer further opportunities to develop employability, but again these are often implicit and go unrecognized. For example, you can develop the ability to:

• think laterally and creatively; develop alternative approaches;
• locate your work in a wider field of knowledge; study the field extensively, sift through large quantities of information, take on board other points of view, challenge assumptions, question procedures and interpret meaning;

- gain access to specialist resources, find your way around libraries, etc.;
- present work through seminars, progress reports and the main thesis (seminars should develop confident presentation and group discussion skills; dealing with criticism and presenting cases ought to become second nature.; report and thesis writing should develop the skills needed for composing not only reports but also manuals and press releases, and for summarizing bulky documents);
- cope with isolation: develop qualities of self-direction, self-discipline, self-motivation, resilience and tenacity;
- plan and manage own time effectively; prioritize and juggle a number of tasks;
- use IT appropriately – for word processing, information retrieval, database management and desk-top publishing. In addition, statistical analysis and text concordance software adds convenience when studying and analysing the masses of data generated;
- network with others; make and use contacts;
- work on group projects (should be able to claim advanced teamworking skills).

Persistence and perseverance – seeing a prolonged task through to completion – and adaptability are highly valued qualities in the contemporary workplace. Employers need people who are able to anticipate and lead change in a fast-moving world, yet resist inappropriate change, and higher study can develop these valuable qualities.

Chapter 8: Summary of main points

- The focus shifts here to the external world of opportunity, broadly viewed as a place to explore options for immediate and future choices, research a chosen occupation, organization, industry sector or alternative choice, and develop 'information literacy' in the process of completing an assignment on producing a personalized job report. Assignment briefs and marking criteria are given, together with suggested questions to ask when analysing self in relation to the requirements of jobs and organizations.
- Exercises, inquiries and examples are formulated around a 'wheel of opportunity', starting with immediate learning opportunities in HE, then moving to extracurricular opportunities to develop skills and experience – then further beyond and longer term, to prepare for transition beyond HE.
- Questions and exercises formulated around two main theories can help students view their aspirations and choices in different frames. Sociological Opportunity theories limit individual choice to those opportunities that are perceived to be available within the culture or society. Opportunities are structurally defined, so choice is determined by various socio-economic constraints.

- Community Interaction theory is a holistic, mid-range approach that stresses the importance of the exchange which occurs between the individual and other members of the groups to which he or she belongs. This opens up possibilities for positive interventions that can influence students' choices and aspirations while developing their capacity.

Chapter 9

Understanding the changing world

This chapter contains key messages about the need for introducing SOAR processes into HE curricula in the first place: it is precisely the nature and future of our changing world, the complexity of our lives, the choices we are faced with, and the competitive nature of the graduate labour market, that make *intentional* CDL and PDP (as previously defined) so essential – for ourselves and our students.

In this leg of the journey the individual 'Self' encounters 'Opportunity' in a global perspective, and here I take a big-picture, broad-brush approach, looking at macro-economic concepts in the changing world of our times. I include here an example of 'a project approach' that values and includes the interests of international students, and particularly invites them to contribute viewpoints and knowledge from their countries of origin.

There are whole degree programmes or modules devoted to understanding the spirit of our times, but my summary here necessarily skims the surface of a wide area. You may wish to cover the topic with students in more detail or from a different angle, depending on their interests and the disciplines they are studying. You can approach it, for example, from the more specific perspective of business, economics, social science, history, media or technology subjects.

The shape and feel of learning and work is subject to continuing change that, according to many expert commentators, amounts to a shift that will be recognized in retrospect as radical as the 1950s Industrial Revolution in Britain. Business models and economic theories can be used to enhance students' understanding of the changing world of work, and how to maximize their opportunities within it – e.g. Reich's concepts of globalization in *The Work of Nations* (1991), William Bridges' books on the new knowledge economy, and Charles Handy's writings from 1991 to now. 'Change is not what it used to be', says Charles Handy (1995: 5) – a sentiment echoed by many economists and writers on business affairs. Arguably, previous centuries were not exactly dull and static either – in fact the Greek philosopher Heraclitus (*c*.500 BC) is widely quoted as having said, '*Nothing is permanent but change*'.

So in this chapter we will explore:

* What is different about change in our times?
* What impact is it having on the nature and future of life and work?

- How might we reflect 'globalization' in the 'internationalization of HE'?
- Are the intentions and aspirations of students realistic in this changing context? What abilities and attitudes will be needed at a personal level to remain employable?
- How might individuals need to change in order to be(come) effective in coping with – and ultimately creating – the kind of world we want to live in?

These are large questions, and some students do not see personal relevance in them, but it is important for all students to understand the conditions in which they will be implementing and managing their life-career choices – even if they choose not to work. The exercises suggested here are likely to motivate them to develop the skills they need in order to face the demands of a rapidly changing, high-tech world.

For immediate, practical reasons also, understanding the impact of change on the UK labour market is relevant to applicants for work placements or graduate positions. Recruiters often seek what they call 'commercial acumen' or 'business awareness' and organizational awareness: an ability to understand general business principles as well as specific issues relevant to their business and organizational functions, to keep the knowledge up-to-date and use it in their decision making and action planning.

Although this differs depending on the occupational and organizational context, employers usually expect (and are impressed by) applicants who understand the climate in which their business has to operate and the trends affecting them. Applicants are well advised to show that they have researched their business of choice in this broader frame, to understand broad social and business issues as well as more immediate factors. At interview they may be asked questions such as:

- What are the most pressing challenges facing our industry?
- Tell us about a job or a placement where you gained insight into the factors affecting a business.
- Give an example of how this business could be further developed (ways in which workers could be more effective or profitable, or ideas on developing activities/improving outcomes).
- How do you keep up-to-date with the business news? (by reading the quality press? watching or listening to the media?)

Businesses today have to respond more rapidly to change, which is more global in its process and impact, and driven by increasingly complex technologies. In fields such as advertising, media and marketing a critical appreciation of changing consumer needs and behaviours is a distinct advantage. In journalism and politics, general knowledge about current affairs is essential. Graduate labour markets are highly diverse, and it is easier to make sense of this diversity if students explore how they reflect general global economic and business trends. So at both a general and personal level, developing an understanding of the changing world is important and relevant.

The nature and future of the changing world

Signs of change are all about us – in newspaper headlines, TV news 'stories' and in the everyday conversations of people in staffrooms, barrooms and boardrooms. It is effective then to set up an investigation of this topic in the spirit of Appreciative Inquiry-based Learning: give students a glimpse of the outcomes you expect them to achieve, by way of the knowledge and performance benefits they should gain (as outlined above). Since this is a complex subject the ideal is to discuss it in classroom sessions and/or online material to introduce the main points, and to build it into some form of assessment. These measures should ensure engagement and serve as prompts for students' enquiries.

Divide the class into groups of three or four, and get each small group to investigate a different aspect of the changing world (see suggestions below). Each aspect can be further approached in terms of the challenges or opportunities it offers, with a focus on finding positives – i.e. what should we aim to replicate and 'appreciate'. Ask each group to prepare a short report or poster and an oral presentation, and be ready to present their findings in class. Remind them that 'information is power' and each group will be empowered to the extent that they collaborate to gather information on their assigned aspect of the larger topic. To the extent that they use the first-hand knowledge brought in by international students, they will be further empowered. The idea is to focus on separate parts of the global picture, and then to pool the information through classroom presentations to form a more complete picture so that the 'power' is more evenly shared in plenary.

It's a good idea to revisit with students the ground rules for working in groups, finding information from a variety of sources, interviewing a manager or human resource professional, etc. – as suggested in previous chapters. This exercise will extend their critical appreciation of the global labour market and also develop a range of personal and interpersonal skills such as group working, information retrieval, making workplace contacts, research and discussion skills, planning and communicating in a variety of contexts, cultural awareness, making a formal presentation – all of which they may have to demonstrate through the recruitment process when they apply for work.

Suggested questions for student exercises

Give students some questions, quotes and/or pictures related to the different aspects of change you wish them to explore, just to start them thinking about the pace and nature of change, and the skills and experiences they will need to develop as a result. For example, in Figures 9.1 to 9.3 I have combined quotes from Hawkins with some graphics, which you could use to start a discussion. The four

Figure 9.1
The career ladder.

Figure 9.2
The disappearing
career ladder.

Figure 9.3
'Career flexibility'.

main ways in which change is different today relate to the pace of change, the technologies driving that pace and type of change, globalization, and the vast increase in service sector jobs in developed countries. These main factors can again be subdivided in various ways as they have several implications, or you could just look at the challenges and opportunities presented by each. The following is a simple summary that gives students a basis for their project. It includes some words that have crept into 'business-speak' relatively recently: have your students find out what they mean.

1   'Change is not what it used to be' (Charles Handy, 1995: 5):
    • career paths are becoming increasingly unpredictable/fragmented/varied;
    • requiring ever greater flexibility/awareness of trends/decision-making skills.
2   What is a 'normal' working lifetime/working week/working day?
3   Changes in the type of work available:
    • shift to a knowledge economy;
    • shift to services;
    • shift in skills and attitudes needed
    • is it so simple, however? (what about outsourcing and offshoring?);
4   The international dimension:
    • the 'global web';
    • 'knowledge workers';
    • what about those who cannot compete?
5   Change in organizations:
    • flatter structures, fewer managers;
    • devolved responsibility and authority;
    • smaller units;
    • temporary project teams;
    • temporary contracts;
    • contracting work out;
    • tele-commuting.
6   Gender issues:
    • increase in women working;
    • increase in 'women's jobs';
    • increase in part-time, flexible work.
7   Class issues:
    • high premium on access to education and training;
    • no security, even in professional areas;
    • self-identity via 'career'.
8   Age and demographic issues:
    • ageing workforce, fewer young people;
    • new legislation against age discrimination;
    • increase in part-time service work;
    • lack of investment in training for older people.

9 'Ultimately to manage change we must anticipate it' (Alvin Toffler, 1970):
- To what extent do you understand the nature of change?
- What skills and attitudes do you need for coping?
- How well developed are your skills for coping?
- What would be the consequences of failing to develop the attributes required?

For example, student groups could look at these aspects and prepare presentations based on them, or use the following related questions:

1 'My father had a working life of 100,000 hours. I could now produce the equivalent output in 20,000 hours. And my son will be able to generate the same amount in 1,000 hours' (Helen Vandevelde, 1997).

Advancing technologies are bringing about an ever-increasing pace of change and productivity. Can you think of examples where this is happening? How do you personally respond to such change?

2 As the world shrinks through efficiencies in telecommunications and transportation, groups in one nation are able to combine their skills with those of people located in other nations in order to provide the greatest value to customers located almost anywhere. The threads of the global web are computers, facsimile machines, satellites, high resolution monitors, and modems – all of them linking designers, engineers, contractors, licensees, and dealers worldwide . . .

Consider some examples: Precision ice hockey equipment is designed in Sweden, financed in Canada, and assembled in Cleveland and Denmark for distribution in North America and Europe respectively, out of alloys whose molecular structure was researched and patented in Delaware and fabricated in Japan. An advertising campaign is conceived in Britain; film footage for it is shot in Canada, dubbed in Britain, and edited in New York . . .

In such global webs, products are international composites. What is traded between nations is less often finished products than specialised problem-solving (research, product design, fabrication), problem-identifying (marketing, advertising, customer consulting) and brokerage (financing, searching, contracting) services, all of which are combined to create value.

(Robert Reich, 1991)

What do Reich's observations tell us about the impact of the 'global web'?

- Bearing in mind that he wrote this in 1991, in what way has the international trade dimension changed since then?
- What might be different about the skills and attitudes you will need if you work in a multinational company?

3 Thomas Friedman, author of *The World is Flat*, says that the advice he gives his daughters 'is very brief and very blunt: Girls, when I was growing up, my

parents used to say to me, 'Tom, finish your dinner – people in China and India are starving.' My advice to you is: Girls, finish your homework – people in China and India are starving for your jobs' (Friedman, 2005: 217).

? New words, 'outsourcing' and 'offshoring', have crept into business-speak. We hear them more and more frequently in connection with jobs being outsourced (mainly from the US and UK/Europe) to India and China.

- Why has the trickle of companies outsourcing work become a flood in recent times?
- What types of work are being outsourced?
- What factors are contributing to its success?
- What are the challenges and benefits of this trend?

4 'Your most precious possession is not your financial assets. Your most precious possession is the people you have working there, and what they carry around in their heads, and their ability to work together.' (Robert Reich, American writer, economist and politician, quoted in *The Times*-KPMG supplement, 'Managing in Uncertain Times', 19 February 2002: 3).

The human resources or 'intellectual capital' of a company – in other words the employees – are increasingly acknowledged to be the company's greatest assets.

? What audience do you think Reich is addressing in the quote above – senior managers? Human resource managers?

- In what way have views about company assets changed over time?
- What do employers do (or what should they do) to show they value their 'intellectual capital'?
- What implications might this have for you as a worker?

5 As predicted by Charles Handy, an influential management thinker, the twenty-first century is seeing an explosion of part-time, flexible, temporary and self-employment opportunities. According to the Electronic Recruiting Exchange (an online US news/analysis source), one in three new workers is seeking alternatives to full-time employment, feeding into a phenomenon dubbed 'portfolio careers', whereby workers seek to combine multiple part-time occupations.

Increasingly, portfolio careers are being seen by some not only as a means by which more senior workers can revitalise their work life, but also as an option for those new to employment, unwilling to commit to any one path, but nevertheless strongly motivated by considerations of financial and social status.

(Claire Adler on the rise of portfolio careers, 'Mix and match',
The Guardian, 4 November 2006)

The authors of the new website You Unlimited (http://youunlimited.net/) argue that a portfolio life offers people more satisfying options to pursue interests that would otherwise be squeezed out by a more conventional career. Being 'unlimited' is about having roles that suit your latent talents best, rather than being constrained by somebody else's job specification.

?

What technologies and attitudes contribute to the rise of flexible and alternative ways of working?

- What evidence can you find that 'portfolio careers' are becoming more widespread? Does this really spell the end of a 'job for life'?
- What implications might this have for you as a new graduate job-seeker?

Discussion points: (your students should come up with these in their enquiries and presentations).

The pace of change and technology

Cheaper and more sophisticated Information and Communication Technologies (ICTs) are changing the *way* we work, *where* we can work, the type of work available and the skills required to do it. For example, I can send an email with attached documents to commission a web design, or piece of research, or an inventory of accounts, from anywhere to anywhere in the world, and receive a reply within minutes. Even ten years ago I would use 'snail-mail' (send letters via the postal service) – and wait at least a week before I could even hope to receive a reply.

Moreover, I can work anywhere, anytime – I could use a laptop computer and send email even while I am on a flight 30,000 feet in the air. And the background research for writing this book can be done largely from my home or office PC through information available on the Internet, whereas I would once spend days unearthing nuggets of wisdom in library books and print material. My friend was able to start a business from her home in Goa, India, purely because she is connected to worldwide opportunities through her Internet site: she can attract business, design logos and web pages, and transmit them to her customers with never a piece of paper passing hands. But even laptops and computers are now being superseded by 'Blackberries' that provide easy access to email for business professionals wherever they go.

Advancing technologies are a double-edged sword, however, cutting both ways, presenting opportunities *and* challenges for individuals. For employers, they reduce the number of hours needed to carry out the same volume of work. For workers, there is an expectation that more will be done in a shorter time, and skills will be continually updated to keep abreast of changing technologies. We live in a 24/7 world where '24-hour businesses' (e.g. airports and call centres) are growing in size and number.

Even outside these types of business, analysts now talk of '24-hour occupations' – no longer just the traditional shift work of nurses for example, but the pressure for many managers and professionals, in companies that are part of an international network, to extend their working day so as to deal with clients and customers spread around the world in different time zones.

The engineering firm Honeywell is a good example of how technology is passed round companies worldwide to make the most of a non-stop working day. Engineers from the US and Asia, UK and Europe, complete their project tasks by the end of their day shifts, and pass on the work to be continued by colleagues at different design centres in other time zones. 'To remain competitive as a company, you have to find and use the best, most efficient people in the world – no matter where they are', says Todd Thompson, chairman and managing director of Citigroup Global Wealth Management, and 'If the best design people are in Italy you put your design centre in Italy. If manufacturing is better in China, you put your factory in China' (quoted in Brennan, 2006: 111). This reinforces the previous quote from Reich about the twin forces of global competition and collaboration.

'People now work all hours, right across the world', says Bill McCarthy, a director of Penna, one of the UK's leading HR consultancies. He believes that people are required to be more accountable: 'At work we are scrutinised and assessed in a way that was unimaginable five years ago. Jobs are graded and pay and promotion tied closely to performance reviews. But most staff are happier because good work is rewarded' (quoted by Brennan, 2006: 113). The long hours work culture in Britain means that managers often still expect to see 'the jacket on the back of the chair', despite the fact that technology should liberate many people to work flexibly from home, to travel less, to achieve better work-life balance.

On the other hand there is evidence from an IES (Institute of Employment Studies) analysis (Huws et al., 1999) that 1 in 17 British workers in spring 1999 were using a computer and telephone link to their employer or client to work from home at least one day a week – a growing phenomenon called teleworking (linked with flexitime and homeworking). Towards the end of 1999 I myself joined the ranks of teleworkers when I went to the University of Reading on a four-month-long secondment. I was able to write web-based tutorial materials to support the Careers Advisory Service in launching a major CMS initiative, working from home four days a week and only having to commute down the busy motorways once every week. I was a happy bunny – but not everyone is lucky enough to have the right working conditions at home, as you would quickly realize if you had to fit your work round a two-year-old! Teleworking (like everything in life) offers advantages and challenges.

Employers have to respond rapidly to the relentless pace of change, so they seek people who can adapt flexibly to a variety of tasks – people who are multi-skilled, willing and able to engage in lifelong learning.

Employers indicate that what they want now, and in the foreseeable future, are intelligent, flexible, adaptable employees who are quick to learn and who can deal with change. . . . In a future world of uncertainty employers do not want people who are unable to work on a range of tasks simultaneously, people who are resistant to new approaches or who are slow to respond to cues.

In the de-layered, down-sized, information technology-driven, innovative organisation there is likely to be less and less time for new recruits to get up to speed. Employers want people who can rapidly fit into the workplace culture, work in teams, exhibit good interpersonal skills, communicate well, take on responsibility for an area of work, and perform efficiently and effectively to add value to the organisation – they want adaptive recruits.

(Harvey *et al.*, 1997)

Other types of mechanization have also reduced the time it takes to carry out work – e.g. 'electronic point of sale' (mechanized checkout tills) in shops and supermarkets allows more customers to be processed through, more quickly and accurately. In almost all sectors the lowest level jobs have been automated almost out of existence, but we see this especially in the manufacturing sector where robots do routine jobs and sophisticated computer-aided-design/engineering processes have made a marked difference. A decade ago it was becoming popular to proclaim that cutting-edge technologies were fast replacing the workforce in virtually every sector and industry – in agriculture, manufacturing, government, retail and financial services. Jeremy Rifkin (1995) argued that we were entering a new phase in history – one where jobs would steadily decline as a result of ICTs and robotics.

At the start of the IT revolution people predicted computers would make the workforce stupid if not redundant. Machines would do the thinking and the work, while people would watch and wonder. In reality the reverse has happened. IT has not only increased the demand for engineers and scientists to manufacture and develop hardware and software, but for managers to put these to work intelligently, and for competent workers in all walks of life to adapt and acquire new skills, in order to get the most out of these sophisticated machines. Just as one example, the job of a motor technician now requires higher-level skills in order to understand and put to use the complexity of electronic systems in cars.

Globalization

Division of labour on a global scale has become possible as never before because of cheap telecommunications, email, the Internet, fax machines and video-conferencing – the 'threads of the global web'. Throughout history trade between countries has been an important feature, but globalization is a new term coined in the 1980s to describe economic (and sometimes even political and socio-cultural) trends that have gathered momentum in modern times. The World Bank (2001) defines the term simply as 'the growing integration of economies and societies around the world.'

Friedman (2002) says it means:

> the inexorable integration of markets, transportation systems and communication systems to a degree never witnessed before – in a way that is enabling corporations, countries and individuals to reach around the world farther, faster, deeper and cheaper than ever before.

Jobs are indeed migrating at an alarming rate: many manufacturing jobs have been 'outsourced' from Western developed countries (US, UK) to developing countries – especially to China, now commonly referred to as 'the factory floor of the world', and to India, 'the office of the world'.

I asked my students to find definitions of globalization and feel compelled to share with you one email that was sent to me:[1]

> Princess Diana's death is a true example: An English princess with an Egyptian boyfriend crashes in a French tunnel, driving a German car with a Dutch engine, driven by a Belgian who was drunk on Scotch whisky, followed closely by Italian Paparazzi on Japanese motorcycles. She was treated by an American doctor using medicines clinically trialled in Brazil. This is sent to you by an Indian using Bill Gates' technology, and you're probably reading this on your computer that uses Taiwanese chips and a Korean monitor, assembled by Bangladeshi workers in a Singapore plant . . . .

And so it carries on, probably getting a little fanciful and silly, but forcefully making a point!

Just as people feared advancing technologies, there are now fears of jobs migrating from developed to developing countries. But economic forecasters believe the reverse will happen: as the world sees a more even distribution of wealth through trading not only of goods but services and jobs, more affluent consumers and a new middle class will create increased demand for these products and services.

The impact on graduate job opportunities in the UK

Students are generally aware that the number of graduate job opportunities overall has declined, yet the AGR tells us that their members report a relatively healthy buoyancy in the UK graduate labour market.[2] The situation is more complicated than it first appears. There are approximately three times more graduates now than 15 years ago, so more of them are entering the labour market than there are traditional graduate positions to absorb them. Yet the unemployment rate hasn't changed much, so what exactly is happening? Students need to be aware of five interrelated factors.

1 SMEs have become key players in job creation and graduate recruitment. For example, between 1989 and 1991 (when the job market was buoyant) SMEs employing less than 250 staff created over a million extra jobs – twice as many as large firms. The views of students may be skewed however by the fact that graduate jobs and training schemes are most vigorously promoted by large companies that are often well-known names.

In reality many graduates find satisfactory employment in SMEs rather than with the larger organizations, but the disadvantage here is that small firms have fewer resources to invest in their people and to adopt modern management methods.

> An increasing number of graduates are now finding employment with SMEs, who have traditionally little experience in providing the kind of human resource development which has been routine among the larger graduate employers. Not only may graduates joining an SME be expected to 'hit the ground running', they may also be expected to take responsibility from day one for their own development.
>
> (Coopers and Lybrand, 1998)

2 New firms are springing up, and jobs are evolving all the time. This means that our students need to approach job investigation and job choice with open minds, to look beyond job titles and divest themselves of outmoded perceptions about 'opportunities'. Graduates are now to be found in a vast array of jobs that have evolved to require higher-level skills but do not need a degree, e.g. skilled trades such as plumbing and construction.

3 Self-employment is on the increase. In a recent survey by the Future Foundation (www.futurefoundation.net/), two-thirds of A-level school leavers in Britain reported aspirations to run their own business at some stage in their lives. Entrepreneurship courses are offered in many universities, and enterprise skills are recognized as useful attributes not only in business but also in modern life generally.

4 Under-employment is a somewhat depressing feature when we examine the first destinations of graduates: many are in jobs that do not require their higher skills or even prefer a degree – jobs which were previously filled by entrants with sub-degree-level qualifications. The degree is not an automatic passport to a high-status, highly paid job, but it opens many doors especially if students grasp opportunities to add value to their HE experience and develop the required skills and attributes (www.hesa.ac.gov/).

5 However, there is also evidence from longitudinal surveys that many graduates who start in lowly jobs move on to higher-level work within two or three years (Elias and Purcell, 2004). Salary surveys consistently indicate that it is still financially lucrative to invest in a degree: graduates typically earn an average of £100,000 more over their lifetime.

Whatever happened to Rifkin's predicted work revolution then? If it had all come true I am sure Monday mornings would have a qualitatively different feel about them. You and I and our students would be free to watch a cricket match being contested by Microsoft vs IBM in the virtual world – or to play out our stories in the real world under real sunshine. If the optimism of management gurus were justified, drudgery would be a thing of the past and work in the post-industrial era would be a gloriously rewarding experience.

A debate: Gross Domestic Product (GDP) or General Well-Being (GWB)?

An interesting way of looking at losses and gains in our changing world is to consider the speech made by David Cameron, Leader of the Conservative Party (the largest opposition party in the UK Parliament at the time of writing):

> Too often in politics today we behave as if the only thing that matters is the insider stuff that we politicians love to argue about – economic growth, budget deficits and GDP. . . . Wealth is about so much more than pounds, or euros, or dollars can ever measure. It's time we admitted that there's more to life than money, and it's time we focused not just on GDP but on GWB – general well being.
>
> (22 May 2006)

In his speech Cameron touches on a vital truth: that the spirit of our times requires social values as well as economic value, and that wealth creation does not necessarily spread happiness and fulfil people's deepest needs and aspirations. We have become accustomed to bracketing being rich with being happy and successful, but you might challenge this assumption with your students: discuss the cost of environmental degradation, loss of community, relationship breakdowns, drug dependency, stress at work – many factors that militate against happiness – and which we cannot quantify in monetary terms. Alternative ways of thinking about life satisfactions are to be found in *For the Common Good* (Daly and Cobb, 1994). The UK government is also rethinking strategy – see *Life Satisfaction* (Donovan and Halpern, 2002).

Discussion based on Maslow's 'hierarchy of needs'

One could return to a basic model such as Maslow's 'hierarchy of needs', and get students to start by brainstorming jobs or occupations they know of in connection with Maslow's different levels of need. Are these jobs growing or declining in our economy? Moreover are they contributing to the general well-being and happiness of people in different countries (international students are bearers of cultural knowledge here), or are there significant issues to contend with and a price to pay for the way we live in affluent countries today?

At the basic biological level of Maslow's hierarchy, even though the agricultural sector has steadily declined because we import so much food into the UK, the variety and sophistication of food and drink available in our supermarkets continues to create service sector jobs, driven by consumer demand. Importing, distributing, preserving, packaging and retailing food and drink commands a major market share.

We might note that in this respect there are vast inequalities on a global front – with scarcity and malnutrition in some countries and surplus in others. Despite some inequalities even in developed societies, on the whole here it is not deficit but surfeit that is causing new health and social problems such as obesity, alcohol abuse, diet fads and (perversely) conditions such as anorexia nervosa and drug dependency. Even as I write there is yet another newspaper headline, 'The obesity time bomb' (Woolf, 2006), and news presenters are making the point that in the UK 14 million of us will be seriously overweight by 2010 – in all age groups. Coping with the problems of surfeit also, of course, creates jobs.

What about Maslow's next-level needs for security, shelter, warmth, housing? Many jobs exist in construction trades, surveying, property valuation, estate agency and interior decoration. Here again though, the rise in crime leads us to spend more on security needs: burglar alarms, security and surveillance systems, bouncers and security guards, insurance, lawyers, police, prison, probation and armed services. We seem to be more threatened globally too, from the depletion of energy and natural resources, pollution, climate change or terrorism.

At the next levels of social and interpersonal needs, there are a whole host of jobs in hospitality, leisure, team sports, clubs and pubs. Conversely, difficulties and breakdowns in relationships frustrate the needs for belongingness, love and esteem and create jobs for matchmaking services, divorce lawyers, psychotherapists, counsellors and manufacture of medicines such as antidepressants. Concerns with image and keeping up appearances (esteem needs) create jobs in cosmetics, home improvements, fashion design and lifestyle products – but again, there is evidence in society today that such concerns can become obsessive.

Maslow's initial research sample was with only that extremely small proportion of the population that he considered to be self-actualizers, but he later revised his views and redefined self-actualization to be more inclusive. Enabling students to find self-fulfilment in their own way through the SOAR process I present here is definitely my purpose in life – and maybe part of yours. I like to think that everyone in HE is at least potentially motivated towards self-actualization – even though this may begin as a lower-level need in Maslow's hierarchy, and not an end in itself.

Reflecting globalization in the internationalization of HE curricula

An increasing number of HEIs are promoting 'global citizenship' or the development of global values and intercultural perspectives among their students. In the UK, most universities are already internationalized by virtue of the increasing numbers of international students within classrooms and across campuses, and also by virtue of opportunities for external exchanges – for both staff and students, live and virtual. We are uniquely placed to encourage in students an appreciation of our common humanity while also learning about and respecting differences. This may be demonstrated simply in the attitudes of teachers, and the many interactions – overt and covert – that take place in class, but may also be reflected in specific curriculum interventions. At the same time ICTs and e-learning may be used innovatively to reach beyond traditional classroom boundaries.

Beyond the classroom: international collaboration[3]

This paper describes an e-communication project involving staff in seven HEIs across the UK and the US, and 375 students all studying criminology and criminal justice. I refer to this here as an example that may be transferred to practices within your discipline – and may take in different countries. The authors contend that the project:

> represents a significant innovation in learning and teaching within criminology yet it is also transferable to other associated disciplines that hold the pedagogic desire to stimulate critical awareness, analytical thought and reflective practice.

The project's aims are fourfold:

- to change modes of student communication (individual and group);
- to extend communication across cultural and national borders;
- to develop students' potential to think across such borders;
- to develop students' ICT mediated interaction skills.

The pilot project in 2004–5 gave a small number of students a chance to exchange emails to discuss issues – but expanded by 2006 onto a WebCT platform with space for discussions and supporting materials. Student groups were required to discuss specific structured topics of relevance and interest, set with clear guidelines, linked to assessment, supported by lectures and seminars, and monitored by staff. All these factors were considered important in enhancing participation, as also the initial introduction, a 'getting to know you' week, and practice opportunities to familiarize students and build their confidence in using e-learning and e-discussion.

On the topics of this chapter I could go on and on – as I am sure you could – but this is (as ever) about making students proactive and responsible; in this case to analyse different views and their own attitudes to their changing world, and ultimately to create a positive graduate identity within a world which presents both great opportunity and great challenge.

Chapter 9: Summary of main points

- It is widely claimed that change today is more technological, more rapid and more global in its reach, process and impact.

- Understanding these changes is important for students because they will implement the choices they make now in a world of greater competition, opportunity and challenge.

- Applicants will usually be expected to have 'business awareness' or 'knowledge of current affairs' in terms of both generic and specific 'employability'.

- You can facilitate various types of inquiries into topics related to the nature and future of the changing world: set up a project, activities, exercises, debates prompted by questions, quotes, pictures, news broadcasts or articles. These might trigger discussion on the pace of change and technology, globalization and the impact on graduate job opportunities in the UK.

- An interesting consideration is whether affluence is making us happier: should we focus on Gross Domestic Product or General Well-being? This question could be linked to the satisfaction of our basic human needs, as (for example) represented in Maslow's 'hierarchy of needs'.

- HEIs are themselves reflections of globalization: ICTs, e-learning, VLEs and the presence of international students offer opportunities to transform the 'knowledge economy' of HE, and broaden our classroom interactions and curricula. One such collaborative project is outlined, to spark your own ideas.

Part 4

Aspirations in the SOAR process

Chapter 10

Aspirations, decisions, plans

The process of forming and implementing personal and collective aspirations, deciding and planning ahead, essentially determine the quality of experience in every area of life – practical, academic, personal, professional and organizational. The habit of making connections between 'Self' and 'Opportunity' (the **S** and **O** of **SO**AR) often naturally extends to forming, clarifying and testing Aspirations (the **A** of SOAR), so that students can make decisions and plans along their life-career pathways (see Figure 10.1).

The SOAR process is essentially one of forming and implementing aspirations, where students are progressively channelled through self-assessment and opportunity awareness into more narrow, focused targeting of suitable options in further study, training, work or life in general. This stage of the process – as set out in this chapter – can aid clarity of thinking and help us to:

- understand the steps, stages and factors involved in making decisions;
- implement personal aspirations but remain flexible where necessary;
- see the connections between decision making, information gathering, problem solving, goal setting and action planning;
- become aware of related theories and apply them to personal situations;
- evaluate the effects and effectiveness of our own and other people's decision-making styles;
- see why decisions can never be made with 100 per cent confidence as to outcomes;
- explain or defend our decisions if this is called for (as in selection interviews).

Can 'decision-making skills' be improved?

Poor decisions can cost us dearly in time, effort, emotional upset and money. Not all 'poor' decisions can be avoided (indeed, it is valid to ask 'what makes one decision "good" and another "poor"?' – a question we will tackle later), but implicit in this chapter is the belief that decision-making skills can and need to be improved.

We usually make simple, everyday decisions on autopilot, but complex decisions need careful consideration. As an academic ability and cognitive process, decision-making is inter-linked with information gathering and data analysis, problem solving, goal setting and action planning. In this section I deal with these together as it is useful to identify one's personal abilities and approaches to this skill-set. In this broader framework, decision analysis is a relevant key area in business education and management (e.g. Bazerman, 1986; Huber, 1980) and is the subject of study in many different contexts (e.g. Kaplan and Schwartz, 1975; Hammond *et al.*, 1980).

I present the topic in this chapter through theoretical models and research evidence, and as usual I configure practical examples and activities around the voices and viewpoints of employers, too. Although a career perspective is central here, my main aim is to enable you to consider decision making from a variety of angles, in partnership with students – so that they are motivated to improve their skills and understand the variety of factors and influences that are present in complex decisions. Students' needs may be future-focused for dealing with transition beyond HE, but developing this skills-set is relevant for current academic purposes as much as for future life and employment.

CDL approaches

In CDL terms, this is essentially a normative approach that assumes choices ought to be made rationally, and students can learn to weigh up objectively both the psychological and sociological factors impacting their choices (Figure 10.2). Career action planning may be defined as a written statement of intention setting out the route one intends to take towards achieving means-goals and end-goals in fulfilment of certain targets and chosen career aspirations.

However, occupational choices are embedded in total cultural identities and implemented in socio-economic contexts, so empirical factors are part of the equation in matching Self with Opportunity to arrive at personal decisions. An empirical or descriptive approach aims to determine the factors that actually lead to the choices individuals make. Some relatively recent studies have attempted to understand and explain the dynamic nature of the variables and the process by which decisions are reached. My contention here is that students themselves need to understand what and who influences their choices, so that they might modify the values of the variables that adversely affect them.

A career transition point forces a decision, and becomes a practical necessity as students approach their final year and need to prepare for transition beyond HE. UK employers and postgraduate courses invite applications for vacancies a whole year prior to actual entry, and many deadlines for these come up in the first semester of the final year. Those who have firm, clear aspirations, and possess the skills to implement them, are at a distinct advantage. Empirical experience however – and evidence from sources such as the annual UK National Student Survey (www.thestudentsurvey.com/) – indicates that many students are unprepared.

I will confess that I, too, was so busy enjoying my studies that my 'transition' from university was more a case of Father Time taking me hostage and spewing me out into ... nothingness. I was an optimistic opportunist, but 'travelling hopefully' has its limits. The problem is that graduates usually don't get headhunted into their dream jobs. 'The future has a way of arriving unannounced', says George Will (American newspaper columnist), so obviously the first step is simply to recognize there is a decision to be made. Sometimes students react with mounting anxiety – and a sort of paralysis – as they approach the end of their student days. If they are 'cruising' in this ostrich-like state, refusing to take control of life, life may begin to control them in ways they do not like.

Preparing students for transition may not be as easy and logical to achieve as simple normative models suggest. Some students break out in allergic reactions when faced with difficult and complex decisions. Life is not simple, and it would be misleading to pretend otherwise. In fact, recognizing complexity in our environment is one of the fundamental principles in good decision making, so I make no apologies for pointing out that complexity here (Figures 10.1 and 10.2).

It will be obvious that a major decision consists of a series of mini-decisions, varying in degrees of importance and complexity. Psychological theories of career choice (as outlined earlier) emphasize 'Self' and explain choice predominantly on the basis of internal factors and influences. Sociological theories put the emphasis on external constraints or factors. A career decision is therefore not a one-off, rigid or irreversible decision, and in fact – given the instability and

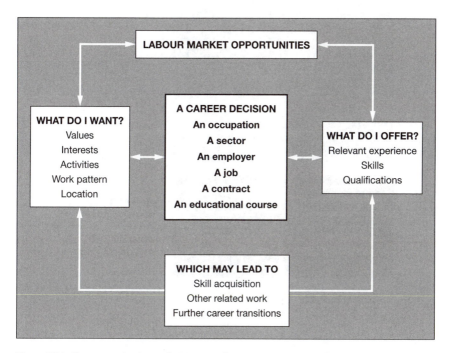

Figure 10.1 Career aspirations, decisions and transitions are complex.

unpredictability of working lives today – remaining flexible, being prepared to review, revise and adjust one's decisions when necessary, is essential when responding to change (Hall and Richter, 1990).

The structure and dynamics of CDL factors

Law (1996) has drawn together the valuable lessons from both internal/ psychological and external/sociological theories, overlaid with a developmental

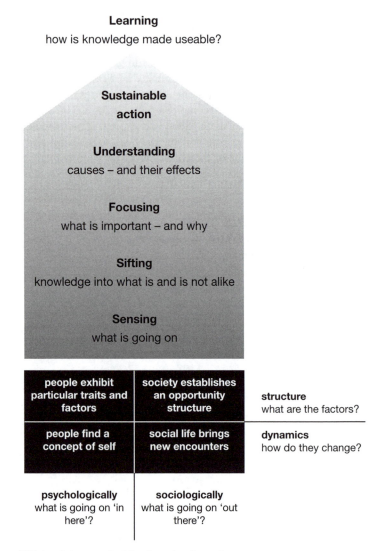

Figure 10.2 Law's 'career decision learning theory'.

or progressive approach. He has put forward a synthesis of all the major theories of the past, and introduced a dynamic concept of learning over a period of time, as a method by which individuals can take control of their career pathways. He says this process can begin at primary school. Individuals go through the elementary stages of sensing information before the sifting and focusing stages that lead ultimately to implementing their decisions in 'sustainable action'. If you feel the urge to stand these ideas on their theoretical head then by all means do so.

Career decisions and self-efficacy

One variable that has been researched is that a person's self-efficacy beliefs are a primary mediator of behaviour and of perseverance in the face of change and adversity (Bandura, 1977). A study by Betz and Hackett (1981) started with the hypothesis that: 'Low levels of career decision self-efficacy (CDSE) will lead to avoidance of career decision-making tasks and behaviours, higher levels will lead to increased engagement in career decision-making tasks.' Taylor and Betz (1983) developed a questionnaire and a five-point scale to measure the extent of confidence with which a person approached the tasks involved in choosing a career.

The tasks were built around five career choice competencies:

- accurate self-appraisal;
- gathering occupational information;
- goal selection;
- making plans for the future;
- problem solving.

Their findings and later studies (Luzzo and Taylor, 1994; Foltz and Luzzo, 1998) confirmed that college students who experienced positive interventions, such as careers guidance interviews or workshops designed to encourage and enable them through these tasks, demonstrated significant increases in CDSE. Note that these are congruent with SOAR principles, which are generically concerned with increasing motivation, recognizing personal accomplishments and preferences, and reducing anxiety. Facilitating and fostering personal growth towards vocational maturity enables individuals to make wise choices whenever they come to a major transition or decision point in life.

Career decidedness and goal setting

A study by Greenhaus et al. (1995) examined the relevance of goal setting to career management, and the conditions under which goal setting is beneficial in relation to career decidedness. They conclude that 'the usefulness of a specific career goal depends on the circumstances' (p. 4) and flag up the need for today's employees to be flexible in their planning, but 'vigilant' in their decision-making style. They see career management (from an organizational perspective) as 'an ongoing decision-making process designed to promote employee well-being through compatibility of work experiences with personal qualities. Information is acquired, awareness is heightened, goals are set, strategies are implemented, feedback is utilized, and adaptation is sought' (p. 5).

Career goals do not have to be overly rigid, but can serve as a route-map towards the future if students balance concrete, intrinsically motivating objectives with flexible planning. Career indecision can be the result of a lack of information and experience, or a more chronic inability to make such commitments, often due to situational constraints or lack of confidence. The Greenhaus research found that the goal selection of 'vigilant employees' is based on 'sufficient personal and environmental information, and is made with a comparatively lower level of stress and anxiety'.

A philosophical view

Can there be 100 per cent certainty about decisions, and is there such a thing as only one 'right' decision? Why do some decisions turn out wrong even though they are apparently sound and rational? The answers to such questions have exercised the minds of many a philosopher, psychologist, business analyst – and careers adviser. For example, the Danish philosopher Kierkegaard (1813–55) saw religion as something essentially mysterious. In defining faith as 'a leap in the dark', he was reacting against the scientific, rational tradition. He believed mere humans cannot aspire to the sort of total knowledge that belongs only to God. We can never attain the judgement that will allow us to know where we belong in the universal order of things, or what line of action we should take. We must make our choices always in the light of partial knowledge and limited experience, never able to foresee all the consequences (for good or evil) that a particular choice might have.

As human beings, however, we have the freedom to choose, so each of us must take responsibility for creating our own future in the face of the unknown. He summed up the human predicament nicely when he said that life had to be lived forwards but could only be understood backwards. He therefore described decision-making aptly as 'going forward in reverse'.

In many ways our past experience will have taught us lessons that serve us well in deciding our future, and that is why it is useful to reflect through exercises such as the Lifeline. But it is also true that, however much 'self-awareness and opportunity-awareness' we accumulate, data only tells us what has happened in the past. To make predictions for the future we need judgement, to assess the predictive value of available data. Given that both self and jobs are subject to change, we cannot expect to make long-term career decisions with cast-iron infallibility. Shifts in views of 'Self' and 'Opportunity' are normal in the light of emerging experience. That is why, as pointed out earlier, it is important to gather fresh information, keep an open mind and know when we must flexibly adjust our plans.

How much information do you need?

We also need to judge how much information is sufficient in order to decide or do something. If we do not gather information extensive enough to form mental concepts, to sift out what is important, and to disentangle order from chaos, we run the risk of making stereotypical assumptions. Having mental maps or concepts also helps us to decide what factors to consider and how much importance to give the different factors. Relative weighting of factors is fundamental to assessing chances of success and failure – and to the further evaluation of outcomes – but we must also know when to stop gathering information and start implementing an aspiration.

Take the example of choosing a holiday destination: you cannot possibly look at all the travel brochures and conduct an unlimited search on the Internet, you would get stuck in endlessly evaluating possibilities and still be here in a month of Sundays! So you reduce your search to something manageable by setting out your requirements: do you want to stay in an expensive hotel or cheap B&B, for instance? Are you interested in active winter sports or relaxing on a sunny beach? Are you looking for adventure, a safari, a wonderful gastronomical experience . . .?

Your answers to these and other questions will enable you to structure your search and focus on the most promising parts of the total search space. It is still unlikely there will be a single optimal or perfect solution, but there may be a few places that would suit you. If you have prioritized your needs, you will know what factors can be compromised – and some degree of compromise is almost inevitable. With any decision you need to find a workable solution in a reasonable time. In the words of Samuel Butler, 'Life is the art of drawing sufficient conclusions from insufficient premises.'

Given such limitations and complexities, Herbert Simon (1976) coined the word 'satisficing' to say that the most common decision strategy was to simply accept a choice that is good enough, rather than seek the best optimal solution. This strategy is often based on what has worked in one's experience: it is therefore a continuous process of searching, implementing and reviewing. If this is not working for us, to break this cycle and find genuinely new decisions and solutions one must 'think outside the box' and define the problem itself differently. Double- and triple-loop learning (Argyris and Schon – see Chapter 4, p. 93) can help us do this.

What judgement do you need when faced with dilemmas?

Discussion: Here are two choice dilemmas: the first involves an element of risk, to be weighed up against benefits. When you are considering the options and alternatives, difficulties can arise when there are conflicts of intentions and interests involved. Consider the following case, and discuss them with a friend or in a small group:

1 Sal is currently in her final year on a psychology degree. She intends to continue her studies, and has been offered a Masters place at psychology departments in two universities. The first has considerable status and an excellent academic reputation. However, a high proportion of its students are failed. The second department does not have such a good reputation or status, but most of its students are successful.

2 Sal and Dave are both in their final year at university and engaged to be married. Sal wants to go on to a Masters degree, but if they want to stay together her decision will have implications for where Dave gets a job. Dave has, in fact, been offered an excellent job in Hereford, but there are no Masters courses available in Sal's field at any nearby universities.

1   Define the problems precisely: what are all their options?
2   What are the possible decision-making strategies they might adopt?
3   If you were advising Sal and Dave, what aspects would you discuss with them as to the most satisfactory way of resolving this situation?

In the first example there are options/alternatives where you have to assess risks by weighing up the probability of obtaining a particular result versus the likely benefits and costs. What is the lowest probability of getting her Masters that you think Sal should accept in order to study at the first university? When studying decision analysis as a subject, the words used for such value judgements are 'Probability' on the one hand, and 'Utility' on the other – i.e. you are asking yourself, 'What are the chances of success or failure? Is it worth the risk and/or the costs? What is riding on my decision in the way of benefits? Who will be affected by my decision?'

The pitfalls and complexities of decision making

The above exercises have been included here as examples of the complexity of making decisions in the real world. Reality is always 'complex, multiple and constructed', as Robin Hogarth points out in his book *Judgement and Choice* (1987). He says that the best we can hope for (in the face of uncertainty) is to look upon decisions as 'time and context-bound working hypotheses'. An example of such a hypothesis or supposition might be 'If I do some conservation voluntary work while I am still an undergraduate, I will have a better chance of getting into an environmental career.'

As we set about realizing our aspirations, we should take action expecting to gather fresh information and experience. If we change our opinions in doing so, we should be prepared to revise our hypothesis as well. On the basis of what you might learn while engaged in conservation work, you may decide that environmental careers are actually very competitive to break into. You might revise your hypothesis to 'If I do a Masters degree specializing in Pollution Control, and choose an industry-based project while I do this, I will stand a good chance of entering a related job.'

Hogarth also says we should be aware that we are not merely at the mercy of 'reality' but that each of us has the power to act upon and construct reality. So as you enter work experience, a job or a course, you could change it in some way by your actions. Your own attitudes and motives are intrinsic and crucial in carrying out and reviewing your decisions.

When all is said and done, however 'rationally' we may weigh up the probability of success or failure against utility, we may end up being right for the wrong reasons or vice versa. We are perhaps limited in our capacity to analyse success and failure. When something goes wrong we are apt to say things like, 'Bad luck' or 'You can't win them all' – but seldom do we explain success by saying, 'You can't lose them all'. There appear to be psychological double standards in our reactions to and analyses of these aspects of our experience.

Hillel Einhorn (1989) gives an example of how our predictions can be based on false value judgements, and how some false assumptions can actually reinforce themselves in inaccurate ways. Take the example of a busy restaurant where a waiter, rushed off his feet, cannot give good service to all his customers. So he makes judgements as to which diners look like good tippers, and concentrates on giving them friendly, efficient service. These customers therefore reward him with generous tips. Other diners, deprived of his attention, feel they have had poor service and accordingly tip poorly. The waiter's predictions are borne out by experience, and his initial opinions reinforced, but for the wrong reasons. His predictions turned out to be self-fulfilling prophecies.

I sometimes think of myself as that waiter, and the busy restaurant as the world out there. Am I unwittingly inviting poor returns and rewards from certain areas of my life and environment, by making a poor investment in these areas? It's certainly true to say that usually what you put into something is what you get out of it.

Decisions and plans – a cyclical process?

An important previous decision common to all students in HE is their choice of course and university. Have them think through how they actually made that decision. Would it have helped them make a better decision if they had rationally followed the stages in the normative process given below?

1   Confront the decision: focus clearly on the elements of choice or the problem(s).
2   Gather information relating to the decision or problem.
3   Consider the facts; weigh up the pros and cons; assess the consequences and risks.
4   Find alternatives (if necessary).
5   Compare alternatives and options.
6   Choose one course of action.

At this point your decision making turns into action planning.

7   Plan how to pursue this course of action.
8   Implement your decision – take action.
9   Evaluate the results; adjust or revise your decision – which takes you back to (1).

You could think of decision making and action planning then as one seamless and iterative process. We are not usually aware of engaging in this process and may not need to proceed through these steps with simple, everyday decisions such as 'what shall I have for breakfast today?' – assuming you have a choice at all! On the other hand, complex business decisions and plans generally have to go through a lengthy, carefully considered process, with different employees being given responsibility for different parts and stages.

Discussion: what makes a decision 'good' or 'bad'?

1   Think of one good and one bad decision you have made. Refer back to your Lifeline (p. 102) and Community Interaction (pp. 184–5) exercises and pick up on decision or turning points you identified there. These do not have to be related to education or work. They can be any significant choices, maybe the choice of a leisure activity or holiday.
2   Now look back at your good decision and write down what factors made it good.
3   Next write down the factors (e.g. family, sociological, educational, psychological, etc.) that led to your bad decision: who or what influenced you?
4   Do you detect any patterns in your own approaches to decision making and planning – consistency of personal style, or development over time?

If you judge decisions by their consequences, you can only see whether your decision was good or bad in retrospect, i.e. at the stage in the cycle where you have taken action and can evaluate the results. Students can benefit from discussing or 'interviewing' each other, and offering peer support on the obstacles and conflicts they have faced in arriving at or implementing effective decisions. I think a good outcome is for them to conclude that all decisions can lead to good learning and new opportunities, depending on one's response to the experience – and that they should 'feel the fear and do it anyway' (Jeffers, 1987). Rubin (1990) is in agreement with Jeffers, judging by what he says: 'It is almost always the decision-maker and not the decision that makes it work. . . . An option becomes a decision through the process of dedicating ourselves to it.'

Personality type, decision-making/problem-solving and planning styles

You will have identified your 'best-fit' four-letter personality type code from the self-report MBTI exercise in Chapter 7, so this is a good place to refer back, refresh and extend your understanding about the dynamics of the mental functions in type theory. You may recall that there are two ways of perceiving and two ways of judging:

a we perceive and process information either through 'sensing' or 'intuition' (S–N);
b we use that information to arrive at decisions or solutions either through objective 'thinking' logic or subjective 'feeling' values (T–F).

These Perception and Judgement processes are basic tenets at the heart of type theory. Many troubles and failures obviously stem from faulty perception and poor judgement, and conversely progress is made through clear perception and sound judgement. Everyone uses the S–N, T–F mental processes – but from our preferences for two of these four (the two middle letters of our personal type code) each of us will rely on these two more than the others. In particular, type theory predicates that one will be favoured and dominant, and the other will be used as an auxiliary to support and balance the dominant.

The dominant function is described in type language as the centre-post of the personality, and can be the core around which students organize their other functions and attitudes in their learning and work roles. It tends to be the most trusted function, and the more we use it the less we exercise its opposite – which therefore becomes the inferior (or least preferred and developed) function. The function which is opposite to the auxiliary is known as the tertiary – so the two letters which do not appear in your type code still play a part in your mental functioning, in a 'hierarchy of preferences' as you will see from Table 10.1.

This is best explained through a metaphor that is commonly used in the type community. Think of the four functions as a family of four people in a car:

1 the dominant function is the driver, who has overall and ultimate control, sets the direction, controls the speed, guides the car . . .
2 the auxiliary function is in the front passenger seat – helpful, may read the map and the driver may appreciate advice to navigate the route, point out obstacles, provide good company . . .
3 the tertiary is the teenager in the back – mostly just there, listening to the iPod, but sometimes helpful and pleasant, sometimes immature and irritable . . .
4 the inferior is like the baby – usually sleeps quietly and goes unnoticed, but when it wants something it causes such a disturbance that the driver is disrupted and may even have to pull over. This baby can scream and fuss – it wants to take complete control of the car but of course has no idea how to do it! Nobody else can get on with anything until its needs are met.

The inferior function is thought to be largely subconscious, and to surface in uncontrolled ways when we are under stress. Understanding the inferior can help us to recognize when we are 'acting out of character' or are 'in the grip'[1] – as observers of our behaviour might say. Although fascinating, type dynamics and development can feel complex and time-consuming to deal with in a normal HE situation, so I usually give students a type table with the order of preferences already worked out. Take a look at the order of your type preferences in Table 10.1 and see if you can relate them to your personal experience.

To give a superficial personal example from my ENTP perspective, in writing this book my dominant N prompts me to start with the big picture, conceptualizing many connections and possibilities between the different concepts of SOAR. I constantly have to remind myself to include practical, step-by-step approaches, and to structure all this into a coherent plan, chapter by chapter. Since this uses my inferior S, and the J non-preference, I find it takes more time and effort. It helps me to understand why I have such problems with time management – and prompts me to ask a friend with a strong J preference to help keep me on track. You will notice that you share your order of preferences with another 'type'. There will still be differences in the expression of the preference, however: those with E in their type code will express the dominant in their favourite External world, and those with I in their code will express it primarily in their Internal world. MBTI gets even more complicated when you factor in the attitudes (E–I and J–P).

As explained in Chapter 7, type can be used at varying levels of understanding and advantage. In terms of their career aspirations, or choice of HE subject(s), or with reference to the Job Study questions given in Chapter 8, you could ask students to discuss what feels most important to them in each of the four functions, moving from S to N, then T to F. They often gain insights into why particular questions seem more natural and relevant to them, and how ignoring other factors has perhaps led them into difficulties.

A typical personal response to decisions is to home in on one's dominant and auxiliary, and only consider the other functions very superficially, if at all. MBTI

Table 10.1 Order of type preferences

ISTJ and ESTP	ISFJ and ESFP	INFJ and ENFP	INTJ and ENTP
Sensing	Sensing	iNtuition	iNtuition
Thinking	Feeling	Feeling	Thinking
Feeling	Thinking	Thinking	Feeling
iNtuition	iNtuition	Sensing	Sensing

ISTP and ESTJ	ISFP and ESFJ	INFP and ENFJ	INTP and ENTJ
Thinking	Feeling	Feeling	Thinking
Sensing	Sensing	iNtuition	iNtuition
iNtuition	iNtuition	Sensing	Sensing
Feeling	Thinking	Thinking	Feeling

provides us with a normative decision-making model (Figure 10.3), which suggests that the best approach to important decisions and complex problems is to ensure that all four bases are covered in the S to N, then T to F zig-zag sequence, in a balanced way. This is likely to happen best in teams composed of different types, where team members respect and make constructive use of the strengths and values of their opposites.

Many interactive variant exercises are possible with small groups of students. You can think of creative ways for them to experience type. One option is to print in large font the brief descriptions of S–N, T–F (as below) on different coloured A4 sheets of paper, or even illustrate these differences with pictures. Post them in the four corners of the room and have your students visit each corner individually, covering a given decision topic in the zig-zag sequence. They are likely to feel more comfortable in those corners that represent their main preferences. A variant would be to have them do this in pairs with opposite dominant preferences, and to see whether this helps improve their decision making.

Styles of decision making

The 1960s and 1970s saw a proliferation of theories (e.g. the Tiedeman-O'Hara Model, 1963; Jepsen and Dilley, 1974; Arroba, 1977; Harren, 1978) which concentrated explicitly on decision making, in the sense that they did not just describe talent-matching or developmental approaches, but attempted to focus on **how** individuals deploy these different traits and styles. See if you can make connections between type differences and some of the styles identified by Arroba (1977), as below:

Rational: You dispassionately and logically appraise information pertinent to your decision. You systematically list factors 'for' and 'against'.

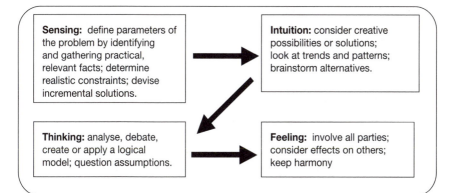

Figure 10.3 The zig-zag model of decision making and problem solving.

Emotional: You are in touch with your inner values and ethics, and your choice is based on what you subjectively feel is right.

Intuitive: You instinctively and somewhat impulsively make a decision based on 'big picture possibilities' rather than on practical considerations, facts and details.

Avoidant: This is the classic ostrich 'head in the sand' attitude, where you refuse to confront the decision, hoping it will go away or somehow resolve itself. You procrastinate and may even defensively avoid relevant information, mentally not taking it on board. This may be because you find change uncomfortable. Your aim is to maintain your short-term psychological comfort, whatever the long-term costs.

Hypervigilant/Hesitant: Here you try too hard, and may want to continue to gather more information and experience indefinitely before you can reach a conclusion. This could indicate lack of confidence, or a desire for security, which cannot be guaranteed. You may perceive the decision as being irreversible or the consequences as doubtful – in any event, your anxiety decreases the efficiency of your decision making. You are likely to miss deadlines and opportunities.

Compliant/Dependent: You conform to what others expect of you, or passively depend on other people's advice and influence.

Regardless of the details, variants and validity of such theoretical models, an important finding was that decision-making style varies not only with both person and situation, but that any given person is likely to use a number of styles in response to a variety of situational factors. There is a good deal of complexity both in our internal make-up and in our environment. Thinking about this, I feel that I have veered from being an unrealistic dreamer to an optimistic seeker to a determined realist at different times in my career. A complex mixture of variables influences responses – psychological, sociological and economic. It is generally accepted a mature adult is able to use styles appropriate to the situation in which the decision has to be made.

Defending one's job-choice in a life-raft game

This game picks up threads from previous work and extends it into both individual and group decision-making experiences. The outcomes can be deconstructed in various ways. You might appoint some students as observers, and brief them to look for specific behaviours and processes during the team presentations and discussions. You could do some of this observation and feedback yourself. Additionally, ask students to analyse the experience and what they learned from it.

Prior to the class session, ask students (for homework) to prepare a three-minute presentation on a job of interest to them (this may be their chosen job from Chapter 8). They will need to persuade others that this job is really interesting or exciting for them and of value to society. You could, of course, substitute in this game any topic of your choice that involves a decision, proposition or solution that students can defend.

When running the session, divide your class into teams of six and present this scenario:

Your team is stranded in a life raft that is too small to hold everyone without sinking. Two people must be thrown overboard (in shark-infested waters, if you prefer the macabre version) – and you must decide who are to be the unfortunate victims. Your decision must be based on the job each person is doing: how successful and useful is the person in his or her contribution to society?

First, each person has strictly three minutes to present reasons why they should stay, using whatever persuasive powers and media are at their disposal (some students like to draw pictures or roleplay, but I suggest keeping this simple). When each person has presented their case, allow 20 minutes for the group to debate the relative values and importance of the job. Within this debate individuals can continue to argue their own cases, but must also balance this with a fair consideration of other cases. You may want to guide the team as to its decision method, or leave it to them to choose between a secret ballot, show of hands, or alternative method of casting their votes.

This game can reveal a number of factors and personality type differences, for example:

- Quality and effect of individual powers of persuasion and negotiation – presentation and oral communication skills.
- How individuals behave and respond to threat and (possible) rejection; are they hard-headed and objective (T) or do they display compassion and empathy (F). What is the reaction of the team members and the victims after the vote?
- Participation and noise levels (E–I differences).
- Constructive, supportive input ('How can we best approach this . . .?') versus negative contributions or avoidance ('This is a stupid game . . .').
- How the group organized itself to manage the difficult discussion and decision process: e.g. how to allow everyone's views to be heard. Was there an awareness of process and consensus principles?
- How different personality types within the group react in different ways to the debating and decision processes – do natural leaders emerge? Natural process checkers or time-keepers? Results-driven players who seek quick clarity and closure? How did the group come to a final agreement – did they reach a consensus? (Should reveal J–P and T–F differences in particular.).

- The different perceptions among team members of the relative values and importance of job-roles. Who made a logical and objective assessment of jobs, and who wanted to subjectively consider how particular people would react to being thrown overboard? (Note T–F differences.)

Aspirations and decisions from the viewpoint of selectors

Students can be motivated if they are made aware of the importance of the 'decision-making skill-set' for both current and future positioning. Thinking about the process involved in arriving at personal decisions is actually a vital bit of self-knowledge and a tool in self-promotion: it provides valuable insights into aspects of your personality and the ways in which you think, perceive and judge. Selectors are understandably interested in discovering how candidates will apply these traits in the work or course they are applying for. Here are some questions (not untypical), taken from application forms:

- Have you ever had to make a major decision in the absence of someone in authority?
- Tell me about making an immediate decision and the consequences.
- Tell me about making a bad decision and what happened.
- Describe a time when you have had to make a decision that you found difficult.

The last one is taken from an application form for the post of patrol constable. The police told me one candidate had simply responded: 'The decision to marry my girlfriend.' Here's another statement taken from a cover letter: 'Please don't misconstrue my 14 jobs as "job-hopping". I have never decided to quit a job.' Do you consider these to be appropriate answers in this context? How would you answer?

An application form exercise

Employer X requests:
Give an example of a time when you used problem-solving and decision-making competencies. Our managers must make decisions about proposals, assess how feasible they would be in practice, and assess the consequences of implementation. Decision making has an impact on the decision maker, on others and on future practice. They need to:
- make decisions following a careful analysis and evaluation of the evidence;
- assess the feasibility of a proposal and identify the results of implementing it;

- make correct decisions quickly when unexpected situations arise;
- draw on others' experience.

How would you rate this sample answer from a candidate?

> 'My job as sales coordinator involved making decisions about which of the team was to work in which area, and what to do if appointments were cancelled. As a retail assistant in charge of a department I had constantly to solve problems as they arose. As an English teacher in Romania I had to decide on the progress of the pupils and how best to stimulate their learning.'

The employer's comments on this response:

> This candidate has had three responsible jobs, all requiring some level of problem solving and decision making. There shouldn't be a problem, therefore, in answering this question. Unfortunately, by trying to cover too much ground, candidates inevitably end up with not enough detail. It would have been better if he or she had concentrated on one example and gone into an appropriate amount of detail regarding the type of problems encountered and the decisions that needed to be made.

In similar vein this employer requests an example for the competency of 'planning and organizing'. They explain that their industry managers use these skills to:

- identify objectives prior to action;
- plan a logical sequence of events or tasks;
- implement a plan by arranging events and directing the use of resources;
- monitor progress, making modifications if necessary.

How would you rate this sample candidate answer?

> 'I believe myself to be a natural planner and organizer. I apply organizational skills to many parts of my life, including academic work, sport, organizing events in my social life and getting my flatmates to take an equal share in the domestic jobs in the house. I can do all this without being rude and pushy, and people generally respond well to my efforts at organizing them'.

The employer's comments on this response:

> A simple statement that you possess the skills required, even if (as in this
> example) it is done with an impressive certainty, is no more than a starting
> point. We do need to know more. Don't tell us that you have the skills we
> are looking for without also clearly stating how, when, where, with whom
> and to whom you have demonstrated them.

Now that you understand what is required, it's your turn: write your examples,
bearing in mind the STAR formula and previous tips given for completing effective
applications.

Planning, implementing and managing action

When you are thinking of success factors in HE – and life generally – the ability
to set clear, achievable goals and plan out the steps to achieve them within a
realistic timeframe is as important as intellectual ability. Some students are apt
to be natural 'action planners' whereas others may be left cold and bored at the
mere idea of having to produce a formal written plan. However, this can in principle
be anything from:

1   a simple list in your diary, setting out the tasks for a particular day;
2   a weekly planner, where you can see your study timetable or working week
     at a glance;
3   a strategic and complex annual business plan, incorporating goals and
     objectives for a company to achieve in the longer term.

The process skills of goal setting, time management and logical planning are all
forward-looking: they set out tasks or goals to be achieved, and involve varying
timescales for achieving them. At some point within this timescale, however, you
will look back and probably review your tasks, and may need to adjust them in
the light of changing circumstances, and the information and experience you
accumulate as you proceed. This stage of review and adjustment makes the process continuous and cyclical. So those of us who are allergic to rigid action plans
need to remember that they really should be viewed as flexible documents – life-
jackets rather than strait-jackets.

Self-audit: planning and managing study and work

Students can allocate ratings to each statement along a four-point scale, as follows
(see box on facing page).

1 = never, 2 = rarely, 3 = frequently, 4 = very frequently.	
To what extent do I plan and manage my priorities, to achieve my goals?	**Ratings 1–4**
I focus on my goals, and what I need to do in order to achieve them – in the short, medium and longer term.	
I break down complex end-goals into shorter, simpler, more manageable tasks and action steps.	
I clarify precisely what type of action I need to take at each stage, at an appropriate level of detail, to meet critical deadlines.	
I prioritize and set out a plan for managing my task objectives, on a daily, weekly and longer-term basis – so that urgent and important tasks are completed on time.	
I identify and use various sources of information appropriate to my tasks at each stage.	
I organize in advance the help and resources I need to complete my tasks.	
I organize my study/work environment systematically.	
I manage routine distractions effectively (e.g. I respond to e-mail, phonecalls and requests promptly).	
I balance and schedule my study, work and leisure activities to make the best use of my time and resources.	
I recognize my progress towards my goal(s) and reward myself for keeping on track with difficult and complex tasks.	
I anticipate barriers to achieving important goals and plan for contingencies.	
I flex priorities according to changing needs and opportunities.	

What stops you from achieving?

Having a plan on paper is very useful, but why do so many people miss deadlines and fail to follow through? It may help you (and others) at this point if you can think individually, then share your experience of tackling tasks.

1 Think of two fairly extensive tasks that you have seen through to the end. Describe these in detail and try to work out why you persevered with them.
2 Next think of something you are finding difficult to finish. What are your reasons, and what can you do about them?

In debriefing, ask students to reflect on the internal traits and external obstacles that prevent them from planning and achieving in the ways indicated by these behavioural items. For instance my students often mention:

- fear or unwillingness to make a change;
- fear of proving to be 'wrong' or making an incorrect decision;
- lack of confidence;
- feeling disadvantaged – e.g. too young or too old;
- feeling overwhelmed by too many perceived occupational options;
- insufficient preparation or experience to do something;
- self-limiting expectations, such as having to make a lot of money or enter an occupation with status.

External obstacles arise from the outside, for example:

- financial responsibilities, paying bills and mortgages, having to pay off debts;
- having to look after someone;
- exposure to a threatening or demanding environment;
- meeting the expectations of others;
- social stereotypes – e.g. age, race, gender, sexuality, disability.

Individuals may see their experience reflected in their list, and progress through discussion to explore what they might do to overcome such barriers. They may already have identified the significant influences in their lives (both positive and negative) through the Lifeline and Community Interaction exercises. Use students' stories as case studies if they are willing to share them. You might get them to 'interview' each other to find out what internal and external sources of influence and help they can discern in their decisions and plans. Is any particular personal style predominant?

> One student commented in a reflective piece after the latter:
> 'I have just realized that I've been blaming my boyfriend for holding me back, not being able to apply for graduate management training schemes. The real problem is that so far I've been too lazy and scared to even try and get any work experience.'

In fact it's not uncommon to use a so-called external obstacle as an excuse for internal anxieties in making decisions, but this particular student showed courage in confronting this. She was then able to move on to positive action.

Get students to address such reasons – maybe change one thing at a time. It helps to set personal goals that are sensitively in tune with your own body clock or you may have it ticking like a time-bomb and setting off alarms you could do without. When you have thrown down lists of tasks to achieve in your wild enthusiasm, stand back and ask yourself how they fit in with other things going on in your life. One person's 'overload' will seem like another's 'picnic'. Sort out your tasks in order of importance and in terms of the deadlines you will have to meet. Allow yourself time for reflection, and for unexpected events that might make demands on you.

What makes an action plan 'good' or 'bad'?

Is it SMART? If your plan is to serve a really useful purpose, your goals and action steps or tasks should be **SMART**: i.e. Specific, Measurable, Attractive, Realistic and Time-bound. You can use this mnemonic as a checklist of criteria to assess your plans. Ask yourself the following questions:

Am I specific and clear in expressing what I need to do and how I will do it?
For example, 'I plan to work as a primary school teacher' is a laudable end-goal, but you need to turn this into specific objectives:

1   By the end of this week I will visit the Careers Service to find out what types of work experience are available relevant to becoming a primary school teacher.

This should result in further specific action steps, such as:

2   Read the occupational profiles for teaching in schools in England and Wales.
3   Complete application form for the 'Students as Tutors' scheme, for voluntary work experience in a Primary School. Deadline for this is 30 September.
4   Write draft of Personal Statement for the PGCE application form.
5   Book interview appointment in August to discuss my draft with a Careers Adviser.
6   Complete and post PGCE application by middle of September.
7   Keep abreast of current affairs in education by regularly reading the *Times Educational Supplement* in the university library.

Am I able to measure my achievement of targets?
Your action steps need to be expressed so that you can see for yourself how you are making progress towards your final goal. The goals above are specific enough for you to know how you will achieve them, and to measure your progress as you cross them off your 'list'.

Are my goals attractive, realistic and time-bound?
Have you set yourself goals and tasks at a level and within a timeframe that is genuinely feasible, motivating and interesting *for you* to achieve? For example, 'Get onto a trainee scheme as a local newspaper reporter' is more realistic as an initial target than 'Become the editor of a national newspaper'. The latter may be your ultimate long-term aim, but you will need to break that down into sub-goals and many interim action steps in order of priority – what needs to be done before what?

Have you set out and prioritized specific tasks within your timescale, to meet critical deadlines? Your plan will inevitably be constrained by the timetable and deadlines set by others. If the second semester starts on 15 February you obviously should not book a holiday in the Bahamas (or anywhere else) that week. If you are applying for the Bar Vocational Course, you will have to take account of their early November deadline (for entry the following September), or you may end up in a very different kind of bar. This may seem like an obvious and patronizing point – but I make the point because closing dates are often missed, and we are all capable of postponing difficult or unpleasant tasks.

A suggested format

Here is a suggested simple format into which you can fit your personal SMART action plan, adding all the specific details *you* will need to consider. Think first about your long-term career goal, then break it down into the medium-term and short-term goals you will need to achieve as steps towards your ultimate aim (if appropriate). Then fill in the specific actions, tasks and stages you intend to go through in order to reach your immediate, short-term goal – i.e. your initial target after completing your current course. Alternatively, some people find it easier to represent their plans as mind-maps, and even to draw up two or three plans as safety nets to fall back to in case the first one fails.

Table 10.2 A suggested action plan format

Your main long-term goal	to be achieved by:
Short-term goals	to be achieved by:
Action steps: How am I going to achieve this?	

Tasks/stages involved	Resources/people who can help	Time-scale
1		
2		
3 ... and so on ...		

Remind students about the sources of support available to them at your HEI – e.g. personal tutors, counsellors and careers advisers. It can help to discuss and review whether one's goals are achievable within a set timeframe, to revise them if necessary and consider alternatives, to be aware of critical closing dates. Whatever your circumstances and capacity, I believe firmly you should celebrate your achievements as you progress. Personally though, I reward myself with chocolate on just two occasions: when the sun is shining, and when it is not.

Chapter 10: Summary of main points

- In the SOAR process model, Aspirations are formed, tested, implemented and adjusted, largely as a result of the dynamic interactions between Self and Opportunity. The quality of our experience and 'success' is determined by the quality of our decision-making, problem-solving, information-evaluation and action-planning skills – and this complex, important skill-set can be learned and improved.

- Decision making and action planning are important features of career transitions, and a variety of theories attempt to explain the process of individual choice, from both normative and empirical perspectives. For example, Law's 'career decision learning theory' synthesizes previous psychological and sociological theories within a developmental approach. Betz and Hackett posit strong correlations between self-efficacy and career decisions. Greenhaus connects career decidedness with goal setting.

- A philosophical view we might identify with is that decisions have inevitably to be made with imperfect and limited information and judgement, because every decision is future focused and involves some risk. The process involves defining the parameters of the particular issues, gathering information, weighing up the pros, cons, risks and consequences – and the outcomes of all this can only be understood as 'good' or 'bad' in retrospect. Given that this is the case, any decision can lead to learning experience, and can be 'good' if the decision-maker commits to achieving its outcomes.

- Various questions for discussion, an application-form exercise, a group game and a self-audit are given for enabling students to experience the process, pitfalls and complexities of dilemmas in decision making and action planning, to identify their personal preferences and styles, and improve their abilities in this skill-set.

Part 5

Results in the SOAR process

Chapter 11

Demonstrating results

As we reach the **R**esults stage of SOAR this may be paralleled by students moving into their final year, when they will be under increasing pressure to apply the results of their learning from previous years, to get better grades, and also to demonstrate the results of their broader skills-development directly to recruiters. Job applicants are likely to face competitive selection procedures. In principle students should be better prepared for life beyond HE as you will have facilitated them gradually through the SOAR process. All that remains then is to pull these threads together and finally prepare them to move from the stage that is passing to the stage that is emerging – or rather *can* emerge if they make the right moves. This is particularly important for those who aspire to enter graduate-level employ-ment straight after HE, but the skills developed through this chapter are (as ever) useful in all areas of life.

I do not think finalists who are aware of the 'testing' nature of recruitment will be in any doubt that applications, interviews and assessment centres can impose barriers between their aspirations and actual implementation. Careers Advisers see many graduates in crisis conditions when they seek guidance, sometimes after they have applied for many jobs and faced rejection. The relevance of the SOAR process kicks in with force at this stage – so the importance of integrating it into curricula is brought home to many through stark reality. This becomes the source of the many comments in publications such as *If Only I'd Known* (Hawkins and Gilleard, 2002) and *Lost in Transition* (Farrer, undated)

Completing the SOAR process in the final year can take place through optional workshops and employer presentations on campus, but it is best ensured through integration with final-year projects, accredited and assessed in some way. In moving from student to graduate identity and employment, students should do further relevant 'labour market research', continue to test and match their strengths and aspirations to suitable 'markets' and apply what they already know. It is challenging for them to present their evidence convincingly – on paper (through CVs, letters and application forms) and in person (through interviews and assess-ment centres). High-level skills and attributes are required, especially clarity and precision in written and oral communications, and 'teaching' these would complement academic development neatly at this stage.

This chapter is about enabling students to:

- demonstrate personal efficacy in high-level skills, for final year study and beyond;
- critically appreciate the recruitment process from the viewpoint of employers as well as applicants;
- promote their 'strengths' on paper, through written application documents, in order to realize their aspirations;
- hone oral communication, social and professional conduct, for effective self-presentation in person at interviews and assessment centres.

Now advice on CVs, interviews, etc. has grown into a veritable industry in its own right, with sufficient material to dominate the Internet or the shelves of any careers library. Rather than add to this body of advice, I use the space here to summarize and show how you can build this into curricula. You can refer students to the information and guidance available in careers services. Videos and DVDs are especially good for learning to cope with interviews and assessment centres, since much depends on body language and impression management.

Although this is a well-documented subject, it is not well researched as to what works and why. It has to be said that many subjective judgements are made by employers (and of course by candidates, too) during the selection process. Much advice is based on anecdotal evidence and personal experience or opinion. Some of it can be conflicting or confusing. Given that there is no single 'right way to promote oneself', students really need to appreciate the defining principles of application and selection so that they use sound judgement in deciding how to present their information convincingly.

Role-play: recruitment and selection from employer and applicant perspectives

The aim of the following exercises is to help students appreciate the recruitment and selection process from both an employer's and a job-seeker's perspective, and to show how employers' needs and concerns are largely mirrored by the needs of applicants during the process. This can help to improve the experience for everyone involved – on both sides of the table.

Imagine this scenario: at any given time, vast numbers of people are concerned about entry to work, applying for promotions or a change of career direction – and on the other hand many employers are concerned about recruiting 'the best workers'. 'Human intellectual capital' is vital to the knowledge economy, and graduate recruiters are prepared to spend massive amounts to appoint those who will rise to new challenges. Poor recruitment decisions can cost the firm dearly – in time, effort and money. But what are the realities and constraints employers face – and what will potential recruits face?

Ask half your class (in small groups) to role play the employer perspective, and give them the instructions in the following box.

> You are a young manager in a small firm that has no specialized HR department. The business is growing and needs to take on an extra person. You have been asked to recruit the right person for the job. What stages do you go through, from first identifying the vacancy to making the job offer? What do you need to know, consider and do? What difficulties do you face at each stage?

Instruct the other half, in their set of small groups, to role-play job-seekers, as shown in the following box.

> You are job-seekers. What steps do you take in your job-search, from identifying suitable job vacancies, through to securing a contract? What stages are involved in preparing for application and selection? What do you need to know and be able to do? What difficulties do you face?

Ideally, a good outcome for both the employer and applicant groups would be to identify that each stage of a typical employer's recruitment process generates a corresponding needed response from an applicant. Knowledge and skills (not to mention a big investment of time, effort and money on the part of the employer) are needed to get the right person into the right job at the right time. The stages in the process may look something like those in Table 11.1.

Students participating in this exercise over the years have made points similar to those given in Table 11.1, but you could add depth through examples and further tasks, as suggested below. At each stage, it should become apparent to students that this process is heavily dependent on the expertise, time and resources available to the recruiter. We hardly need surveys to tell us that the complexity and sophistication of the recruitment process increases with the size and scope of the employer-organization and the level of the job. Large and small firms may equally understand the importance of recruiting the right people, but it is likely to be the ones with resources that can allocate money and trained staff to it.

Large companies with their own personnel departments are generally more capable of tailoring their procedures to different skill levels, and are more demanding in filling their higher level vacancies. Some companies outsource their vacancies to recruitment agencies or consultancies. However, the cost of doing this for SMEs may be prohibitive. As you might expect, the most inexperienced SMEs find it difficult to articulate their skill requirements clearly and in such a way that it is possible to develop effective selection criteria from a job description. Since the stages build on one another, this fundamental lack of expertise leads to

Table 11.1 Recruitment and selection from employer and job-seeker perspectives

Employer perspectives	The job-seeker's perspective
Preparation: Identify what the job entails and provide accurate written information for applicants, via job description, person specification, and job advertisement placed in media most likely to reach the target pool of applicants. Decide on the selection criteria and methods by which they will be applied in order to assess candidates. Provide information on the company, e.g. via brochure, website, annual report or business plan (as appropriate).	**Preparation:** Assess yourself honestly in relation to the job and company information, bearing in mind your talents, energies and priorities. Find sources of vacancy information specific to the occupation/employer organization and industry sector you are targeting. Understand the job *on offer*, not some ideal or stereotypical notion of the job. Assess your level of interest objectively. Think of questions you still want to ask.
Application process: Provide opportunities for a fair assessment of suitability – e.g. via: • Application form (online or paper) or • CV and covering letter • First interview: face-to-face, telephone, one-to-one or panel interview • Second interview and/or assessment centre activities, psychometric tests, personality inventories. • Taking up references. Concerns about applicants – e.g.: • shortfall in requisite skills • unrealistic expectations • lack of motivation and enthusiasm • lack of commitment and loyalty • academic over-qualification • lack of initiative and business skills.	**Application process:** • Expect to demonstrate your suitability: knowledge, skills and experience – on paper, in person, on the telephone – *as specified by the employer.* Prepare, using available resources and services. • Be aware of the importance of 'soft skills' in today's economic climate; give balanced evidence of these from any area of your life: study, work, life experience and leisure interests. • Do not rely on academic qualifications and ability to any great extent (this has been called '*disablement by expertise*') – unless the job predominantly requires your subject knowledge and intellectual skills. • Ask permission from referees to include them and their contact details; give them copies of your applications or CV, keep them informed.
Selection: At the interview and assessment centre: Assessment of 'soft skills': • very high priority • through a variety of indicators/ assessment centre activities Process likely to be: • rigorous and systematic • partly online (e.g. aptitude tests) • multi-faceted • reflective of company ethos 'Providing a fair chance' involves: • time, energy, experience, expertise and resources • awareness of prejudice, knowledge of relevant equal opportunities legislation • genuine cultural awareness, support of equal opportunities, valuing diversity, sensitivity and consideration.	**Selection: At the interview and assessment centre:** • Be responsive and socially aware • Attend to basics (good grooming, a clean shirt helps) • Listening is very important • Be involved and aware of your impact on others • Show interest (above all else!) • Be prepared to demonstrate a range of skills and appropriate attitudes at assessment centre activities • Think about what you really expect from working in this job and organization – and ask your own questions sensibly • Understand your rights and duties • After the experience, record your impressions and what you learned – handy for future reference and re-use.

poor interview procedures and poor recruitment decisions in many cases. (Note that this is a generalization to which there are notable exceptions. SMEs are very diverse, and recruitment expertise is certainly manifest in some.)

Preparation from an employer perspective

First, recruiters need to develop a clear mental picture of the job: its main tasks and responsibilities, how they will be carried out, where the new recruit will be based, what training and salary the firm can offer, etc. These factors should be communicated clearly as they form the basis of the job description and further procedures.

Next, form a mental concept of the person who would fit this job: what knowledge, qualifications, experience, temperament, skills and abilities should be sought, and what would provide the right evidence? (See Table 2.4, p. 25, for a list of the most sought-after graduate skills.) The recruiter also needs to check that applicants possess a certain level of health and fitness, have no criminal convictions, and that their personal or family circumstances would not interfere with reliability in job performance. Some of these considerations are expressed in the written person specification, but others remain hidden expectations.

Then the selection criteria may be subdivided into 'Essential' and 'Desirable' criteria, depending on how important they are in the job. How will these criteria be assessed? Education and training qualifications may give clues about the technical proficiency or creativity needed for the job, but other personal attributes relate more to the social skills of fitting into the culture of the organization and the rest of the team. The ability to get on with colleagues and customers bears no obvious relation to academic credentials. So recruiters need to find ways of discovering whether applicants possess them, but assessing such attributes is more open to subjective judgements.

The next step is to decide **how to invite people to apply**, and explore two options that might best elicit the information required:

- **An application form** designed specifically for the purpose has the advantage of enabling a direct, more objective comparison of applicants, as all are required to supply the same information. A further decision is about making this available online or as a hard copy document.
- **A CV (with a cover letter)** elicits information that the applicant chooses to give but through which recruiters may not learn all the 'facts' they need at this stage. Although CVs have disadvantages, employers (especially in SMEs) might opt for them if they don't have either the expertise or the time to design their own form.

Job-seekers: preparing to find a perfect fit

Your job-seeker group should recognize that they have learned through SOAR processes so far, and especially through the job study assignment (Chapter 8), to assess the extent of fit between their profile and the requirements of specific occupations. They are well placed to check out the:

- job: duties, responsibilities, prospects, salary, etc.;
- organization: location, size, customers, products, services, philosophy, etc.;
- the extent to which they fit the person spec: skills, qualities, qualifications, experience;
- application: how (CV, application form)? where to? by when?

Even so, most students who need to design a CV do so at the eleventh hour and start with the thought that the document is 'about me'. This needs to be reframed to the concept that it is 'about me in relation to the position I am applying for' – and the starting point is to gain a clear idea about the job and company requirements, and then tailor the CV and write an accompanying 'cover letter' to show the 'fit'.

A mirroring exercise: You might reinforce the need for applicants to 'match' the requirements of the position through the following activity.

Get students to sit back-to-back in pairs, naming themselves A and B. Give A in each pair an abstract diagram composed of any juxtaposition of squares, circles and triangles. B should have a blank sheet of paper. Ask A to describe the picture while B tries to draw an identical copy.

Ask students: What did success depend on in this exercise?

(The skills of A to describe accurately, the skills of B to listen, trust and replicate accordingly. If A was the employer and B the applicant, one could think of the diagram as a description or advertisement of the job, and B could design a CV and cover letter, or complete an application form to mirror its requirements as closely as possible.)

What do job-seekers do if there isn't a job description and person specification? Even some large employers do not provide one – perhaps deliberately, because they want applicants to demonstrate research skills in finding out for themselves, or because they do not want to pigeon-hole the job, as it is evolving. They may want applicants to play a key part in growing the job, the company and the profitability of the business. Remind students they should have all the research skills and access to resources they need, to construct their own job description.

Other competency-based initial selection practices are on the increase: 'More than one-third of employers use an online self-selection/pre-qualification exercise to screen their candidates and one-third conduct telephone screenings' (AGR, 2006: 28). Some online questionnaires allow job seekers to self-select themselves into jobs to some extent, or at least to test their competencies against those required (assuming that the tests genuinely simulate these requirements – an assumption that sometimes gets challenged!).

Advertising: transparency, half-truths and ambiguities?

The difficulties of providing accurate but concise descriptions is a key concern for employers and some have deliberately decided not to advertise but to simply respond to speculative approaches, or recruit through work experience and placements. This makes it imperative for applicants to be proactive in increasing their network of contacts, and to seek work placements as stepping stones to permanent contracts. Relevant work experience is a key success factor in gaining entry to the graduate labour market.

For a somewhat different reason the British Army has introduced a new campaign – One Army Recruiting – and is no longer attempting to attract people to specific roles. 'The need to increase numbers enlisting is transforming army recruitment methods,' reports Joe Clancy in *The Guardian* (10 April 2007). Trained life coaches put potential recruits through motivational psychometric and 'pathfinder' tests, and a 'jobs wizard'. They interpret information from these indicators alongside educational qualifications, and discuss the results and options with applicants, matching them to suitable positions from the range of 140 trades that are possible – as diverse as music, catering, engineering, healthcare, administration and finance, etc. The army has taken to coaching, mentoring and nurturing people through the system, starting with this recruitment process.

Writing and reading job advertisements

Most employers do **write a job advertisement** that captures the essence of the job description, person specification and company information, summarizing it in a form that both attracts the attention of suitable applicants as well as screens out those who are unsuitable. Quite a skill, don't you think? You might get students to write an advert for a job they are interested in – it's an exercise in writing clearly, concisely and with a specific purpose and readership in mind. Have them describe any difficulties they experience in doing this.

However carefully one constructs an advert it can never tell the whole story, so you might set up an exercise to **read between the lines of a job advertisement.** What questions are raised for you by this advert from Taylor Nelson Sofres (Figure 11.1, p. 258)? How much access does this recruitment language give you to what you need to know, and what else will you wish to find out?

Here are some thoughts that occur to me:

The advert doesn't give a job title, or offer the chance to get a job description: what tasks and responsibilities will be involved?

TNS appears to be a large, London-based, multinational market research company. What would be the practical and financial implications for me to live in London? What is the company's global reach? Who are their 'blue-chip clients' – and in which countries/market sectors do they operate? Does this mean I might have the opportunity to travel or work abroad – and if so, at what stage of my

Figure 11.1 Reading between the lines of a job advertisement.[1]

working life? On the other hand, would it compel me to move around different locations in the UK or abroad?

How do they judge 'top-class graduates who are creative'? Will they shortlist candidates by class of degree and look further back for consistent academic achievement? How will they assess other qualities such as 'graduates with their wits about them'? How will creativity be needed in the job?

Do I have the ability – and the motivation – to lead a team within three years? Who would my team consist of? Will I be working mainly with other graduates or with people of different ages and backgrounds? Who will I report to, and what support will I have?

Will I have to negotiate my salary? What is reasonable to expect for this type of job in this type of company? I like the idea of benefits and relocation allowance!

What is meant by 'structured training'? How long and hard would I have to work? Would this be on-the-job or sponsored off-site opportunities to gain professional qualifications? How would this be organized, and what extra time, expense and effort would it involve? Would it be required or simply desirable for future progress and promotion prospects?

The right advertising media

Employers must **advertise the vacancy** in appropriate publications, or through avenues where they are likely to attract the type of people identified earlier in the 'person spec'. They need to know (or find) the right media. If their requirements are unusual, they may have to target unusual avenues. Increasingly, organizations use streamlined recruitment processes on the Internet. They might place the advert, job and person specification, application form and instructions as down-loadable documents on their website. This online format is usually complemented by a smaller advert in print media containing far less detail but directing readers to the website for further information. This strategy allows recruiters to reach a wider audience at lower cost. And, of course, some use recruitment agencies, special links with HEIs, campus presentations, careers fairs, etc. AGR employer members' median spend on graduate recruitment marketing (using various promotions) amounted to £53,300; and their spending per vacancy was, on average, £1,600 (figures for 2005: AGR, 2005).

It will be obvious that constraints can be cumulative and occur at any stage. Lack of resources, experience and ability to use a range of methods and media, and to cast the net across a wider geographical area, presents problems in finding the right person. Job-seekers on the other hand need to know where to find vacancies in their field, which media to look at and job-finding methods to use. There's another activity here: you might ask students to look at newspapers, employer directories and brochures, visit recruitment and commercial websites, attend career fairs and employer presentations on- and off-campus, in order to collect adverts of interest to them and to bring in and share with others.

Initial sift of applications or CVs

After the closing date, recruiters scan the CVs received, matching them against the person spec and selection criteria. Those that meet or exceed the criteria are placed in a file 'To interview', others go on the 'Reject' pile – probably synonymous with the bin.

A word of warning: mass CV scanning can bring on headaches for employers. The time given to sorting CVs typically starts with five minutes looking at each one, then goes down to an average scan of 30 seconds as recruiters become busy and careless. Not only are they busy, the vast majority of those CVs are deadly dull and irrelevant. Either that or they contain many careless errors, exaggerated claims or excuses for poor performance. Employees wish somebody would spring off the page and live for them as a three-dimensional person – a real possibility as a potential employee. They wonder if it wouldn't make more sense to hand over the whole process to a recruitment agency, or to a software package that would scan CVs electronically. What do you think about these constraints and possibilities?

 Exercise: You could include an activity where students bring in their (draft) CVs and cover letters tailored to specific job areas. Have your employer group assess job-seekers' CVs with the authentic purpose of deciding who would be in the running for the job – and if not, why not? What should the job-seekers do to improve their CV and letter?

Have them look at different types and examples of CVs on www.prospects. ac.uk. **Ask**: Which of these would you consider most suitable for your own purposes, and why might you use it as a model for creating your own unique CV? Draw up a list of general criteria you could use for assessing the effectiveness of any CV. How does this compare with the criteria given below? (This marker sheet can be used for both self-assessment and tutor feedback.)

Assessing a Curriculum Vitae

CV and CL Assignment marker sheet. Name of student: _____

A Excellent CV very likely to be selected for interview even in competitive field.

B Likely to be shortlisted for interview.

C Could be selected for interview in an uncompetitive field but otherwise unconvincing.

D Could reach 'maybe' pile in an uncompetitive field but unlikely in an area of stiff competition.

E Very unlikely to be selected even in an uncompetitive field.

F Destined for the 'reject' pile.

Note: One or two 'E' or 'F' marks may not result in rejection if the majority of important fields are graded 'A' and 'B'. More detailed feedback will be given in the comments on the CV itself.

A: Outstanding   B: Very Good   C: Good   D: Satisfactory
E: Further work needed   F: Unsatisfactory/weak

Excellent	A	B	C	D	E	F	Inadequate attempt
APPEARANCE – 30%							
Attractive, neat appearance							Messy, unbalanced
Clear, easy to read lay-out							Not easy to read
Word-processed							Structure not obvious
Appropriate length (no more than two sides of A4 paper)							Too long or too short
CONTENT – 70%							
Format appropriate for occupation/type of employer/ personal circumstances							Poor choice of format
Appropriate amount of information/examples/evidence of suitability							Too much or too little information given
Relevant strengths, interests, experience highlighted							No attempt to draw out relevance
Good use of active language and focus on positive points							Negative language
Gives truthful, authentic impression							Appears clichéd
Free of errors of spelling, typing, grammar, syntax . . .							Many errors
Covering letter provides useful extra information							Adds nothing useful

Comments on CV and covering letter

Overall Grade:

A word (or several!) about bad spelling and grammar. They are a common reason selectors give for rejecting people who otherwise meet the job and person spec. So it really is worth using a dictionary, and asking a reliable friend or family member to proofread your document, to check for errors and also give you objective feedback.

But tell me where does spelling lie: in the brain or in the eye? Many people say they have to write down a word or visualize it before they can decide if it 'looks right'. Others submit their applications and CVs to a spellchecker, but witness the folly of relying on that, evident in this clever poem:

> **The Spelling Chequer**
> (or poet tree with out miss stakes)
>
> I have a spelling chequer
> It came with my pea sea
> It plainly marks for my revue
> Miss Steaks eye cannot sea.
>
> Each thyme when eye have struck the quays
> I weight for it two say
> If watt eye wrote is wrong or rite
> It shows me strait a weigh.
>
> As soon as a mist ache is maid
> It nose bee fore two late
> And eye can put the error rite
> No, I shall find it grate!
>
> I've run this poem threw it
> I'm shore yore policed two no
> Its letter perfect in its weigh -
> My chequer tolled me sew.

(Anon., 1998)

Points to reinforce about CVs, application forms and covering letters

Curriculum Vitae means 'the course of life' in Latin, but you are not about to write your autobiography. The defining principle for applications and CVs is to remember to assess your document from the selector's side of the table. What sort of application would you want to see if you were a busy employer – a handwritten, illegible scrawl running into an entire life history, or a concise, word-processed, easy-to-read summary which proves that the writer has analysed the job and taken pains to provide selective evidence which meets your requirements? Who would you want to invite for an interview?

An effective CV and covering letter should act together to advertise your actual and potential ability to do the job successfully, or to benefit from the opportunity you are seeking. The emphasis should be on what the selector will find important, not what you think is important. So, make the right impression on a recruiter – whether this is a personnel officer in a large company, an admissions tutor for a course, the owner of a small firm, or the manager of a volunteer bureau.

Given that written communication skills are very important in the workplace, this is the first piece of evidence you are providing to an employer that you possess (or lack) this skill. If you are sending in a CV when an application form was requested (or vice versa), you are saying in effect that you cannot follow instructions or pay attention to detail. If you haven't taken the trouble to present a neat and tidy, easily accessible document, then an employer will assume you are careless, lazy and inconsiderate in other areas of your life too.

Since CVs and 'personal statements' on application forms are meant to be uniquely about you – to capture the synergy inherent in your personal mix of circumstances, experience, skills and qualities – you need to understand the basic principles of tailoring CVs to show that 'fit' between your profile and the requirements of the position you are applying for. There are several Internet formats available, but the most convincing CVs are those designed to uniquely present your strengths and circumstances in the best possible light. It can help to look analytically at various CV examples, but there would be little point in slavishly copying any of them without understanding why.

Whatever format you decide to use, the bottom line is that your CV should enable a selector to easily identify what skills and attributes you possess, where you developed these, and how you are likely to apply them. Your covering letter can then make even more specific links between you, the job and the company. Requirements for this type of specificity for purpose has led to specialist advice about – for example – a legal CV, a social work CV, a design CV, etc.

How you present your evidence will depend largely on the format specified by the employer, and the type of job you are applying for. If you are asked to send in a CV, or to apply 'in writing', then you have the chance to design a document that expresses your individuality, with slightly more freedom than the application form would allow. However, even with the latter, you usually have to write a 'personal statement' or answer some very open questions. These are like pegs on which you can hang a great deal of personal 'marketing information'. So again they allow you scope for promoting yourself for the post.

Employers know you will present yourself on a CV in the best possible light, omitting any negative details. However impressive, you will not be offered a job on the strength of the CV alone. They will want to see you in person and check out whether you live up to the expectations you have created on paper. Every CV needs to strike the right balance between:

a   optimistic self-promotion – and being truthful and authentic;
b   appearing professional – and making an impact;
c   brevity (saying too little) – and substance (saying too much).

In various self-appraisal exercises and e-portfolio or Progress File records, you should already have the content for your applications and CVs. Take stock of these experiences and achievements, analysing them for the benefits gained and the skills developed. Remember you are now aiming to be selective – so you can look back at this complete inventory of all your characteristics and pull out the ones that make you right for the job. Consider carefully every item that you can link to the vacancy, and everything which gives evidence that you possess both the specific and soft skills required. Highlight those that will contribute positively to your application or CV, and use them to demonstrate you have the necessary qualities.

Giving enough relevant information to persuade and impress is crucial, so that you are invited to an interview. It is expected that you will provide certain personal, educational and employment details, at the very least, on any application, but exactly what you include, and how you present it, is what stretches the minds of most people. We have been through many application form exercises earlier in this book, and now – since students are coming up to a major transition point where their capacity to deal with change will be tested – we might usefully engage them with a related exercise.

The ability to cope flexibly with change: an application form exercise

Generically the ability to cope with change has become very important in modern times (see Chapter 9), and employers seek flexibility and adaptability in candidates. As Employer X explains, managers in their company need to work flexibly with a wide variety of tasks and adapt quickly to unplanned events. This requires an innovative approach to develop new ways of working and achieving objectives. They need to:

* generate new ideas to solve problems and overcome obstacles;
* develop new ways of working, or new approaches to research, and to obtaining information;
* work effectively with a variety of tasks;
* respond quickly to unplanned problems that require immediate attention.

The following is a sample candidate answer that you can ask students to assess in relation to the usual criteria, which they should by now appreciate without prompting.

When students have commented on this, share with them what the employer's feedback was:

> There is evidence of some flexibility here, although it could be argued that it is fairly normal to have to choose from a range of options in your final year. There is little evidence of innovation or skill in managing change. This is not a rank bad answer as such, but its ordinariness is not going to make it leap from the page and demand to be noticed. Don't go over the top in

describing the interesting parts of your life, but do avoid sounding dull, unimaginative and ordinary.

Now it's the turn of students to write their example, bearing in mind the main message from the employer's comment: *you need to stand out from the crowd.* At this stage students should demonstrate better results, through understanding all the criteria for effective application responses.

Interviews: the employer's perspective

In today's 'global economy' employers increasingly recruit for overseas branches or markets, and their candidates may be anywhere in the world. An initial telephone interview is a sensible way of making contact with them, and may be used to screen-out unsuitable candidates. Those selected may be invited for a first face-to-face interview. It is good practice for employers to reimburse travel expenses incurred, but this may prevent them from casting their net wide to attract talent from overseas.

Interviews can cause more headaches! They may be one-to-one or conducted by a panel, and each type has its pros and cons. The board or panel interview is often justified in that it:

- reduces the chance of bias, which can reign unchecked in an individual interview. Policies on this subject usually stipulate the panel should be composed of three to five members as appropriate, allowing for a fair spread in terms of interest, race, sex and age, etc.;
- enables the different interests of departments or managers involved to be represented, so that the candidate gets an all-round hearing, and is viewed from several angles;
- gives each interviewer on the panel a chance to concentrate wholly on listening to the candidate while others are asking questions (and even to make some notes);
- makes a more impressive occasion for senior appointments;
- acts as something of a training ground for inexperienced interviewers to learn from experienced ones.

On the down side, panel interviews are more time-consuming and expensive to organize and manage. A panel needs a chairperson who greets candidates, makes introductions, coordinates the sequence of questioning and controls the situation. All this creates a more formal atmosphere, which inhibits some candidates. Sometimes it is difficult for the panel members to reach agreement on who to appoint – in which case it is often the chairperson who casts the deciding vote.

It is very important to create a comfortable space, with a seating plan that conveys a businesslike but friendly approach. Attention to detail can make all the difference, such as having chairs all at the same height, ensuring there are no interruptions or distractions, diverting telephones and putting a 'do not disturb sign' on the door. (I have horrendous memories of an interview in a room next to a building site where a pneumatic drill was in use. On another occasion I arrived sweating in my interview suit on a sweltering July day, only to find myself in an airless, windowless room that reeked of fishy food.)

The social and communication skills of all involved are tested to the limit on the day. When I say 'all', that includes reception, administration and security staff. They need to welcome candidates, show them where the cloakrooms are, and generally 'look after' them between interviews. Common sense? Yes . . . but all too often common sense is not all that common. 'You never get a second chance to make a first impression' says the platitude, and it applies to both employer and applicant. The human factors are perhaps even more important than the physical factors. The panel members must rid themselves of preconceptions, listen with an open mind and an interested, positive approach – putting each candidate at ease and allowing all of them to demonstrate their attributes at their best.

The selection interview is a skill and an art rolled into one of the most complex and fallible of human interactions (correct me if I'm wrong). It is the most widely used selection method of personality assessment, a means of eliciting from the candidate a report of past, present and anticipated future responses. Experienced and sensitive interviewers are perceptive and responsive to all sort of signals – not only what is said, but body language, i.e. non-verbal cues such as facial expressions and posture. The main instruments (and they should not be used as instruments of torture!) for successful interviews are different types of questions (e.g. open, probing, closed, checking), statements, summaries, listening and observing skills.

Have your students recognize the difference between dead-end questions and those that will elicit relevant information. They could compile a list of tough questions and consider the potential pitfalls in answering these. Have them set up an interview situation as above, and practise in groups of three, taking turns to ask questions, answer, and observe, using the **Observer Evaluation Form** (p. 267). Give them a chance to prepare – mentally, physically, emotionally – to focus on positives and share tips on what works well. Remember you are raising the game now and expecting them to demonstrate results, in the sense of building on previous skills-development. If possible, set up video and playback facilities so that students can see their own performance and self-evaluate it. This is usually most effective.

Take time to familiarize yourself with this checklist, and use it as the basis for giving feedback and helping the interviewee to improve. See guidelines for 'giving feedback' (see Chapter 3, pp. 69–70). Try to rate the behaviours and answers you observe along a scale from 1 to 4, where 1 = effective and 4 = poor.

Physical self-presentation/non-verbal communication	Ratings 1–4
Posture (upright and alert but relaxed)	
Facial expressions (smile occasionally, friendly and interested)	
Hand gestures (under control, no fidgeting)	
Eye contact (conveys engagement with the interviewers)	
Suitable attire and grooming (appropriate dress and accessories, etc.)	
Attitude	
Confident and enthusiastic (evidence of positive motivation)	
Friendly and approachable (employers are thinking: 'do I like you'?)	
Professional conduct (with everyone, including receptionists . . .)	
Voice	
Speed (pause for thought; do not speak too fast or too slow)	
Pronunciation (clear speech, comprehensible answers)	
Casual or formal? (not as you would speak to your friends in the bar!)	
Content of answers	
Relevant to the questions asked (don't go off at a tangent and ramble)	
Appropriate length (short sentences, no fancy words needed)	
Credible examples given from real life experience and achievements	

What did the interviewee do best? _____

What one thing should s/he improve? _____

Before you give feedback, ask: What worked well for you?

In a real interview candidates are judged on additional factors such as punctuality, suitability for the position and knowledge of what it entails, etc. Prepare well prior to the event – e.g. further research on the position and the company. On the day, arrive well in time and remember it's easier to perform at your best if you are not too hot or cold, hungry or thirsty. Approach the event as an opportunity to gather 'insider' information about the job and the company. 'Other-focus' works better than 'self-focus' now – forget yourself and focus on the employer's needs – this will help to control nerves. It's important to interact but not to compare yourself with other candidates during the process. Use your CV as a carousel of achievements that point to your suitability for the position, and to future successful performance.

Assessment centres (ACs)

According to recent research (AGR, 2006) 83 per cent of employers use AC tests and activities at some stage during recruitment – not just for graduate vacancies but also for sub-degree-level jobs. Some IT companies require computing aptitude tests to be taken even before the written application stage. Usually at the first or second interview, organizations add activities that simulate the actual job tasks (see Figure 11.2), all of which are collectively referred to as 'the assessment centre' in recruitment jargon. Since these methods are increasingly used, it is important for job-seekers to prepare for them.

> The assessment centre is an integrated process of simulations designed to generate behaviour similar to that required for success in a target job or job level. It enables candidates' performance to be measured objectively against specific key criteria.
>
> (AGR, 2001)

What similarities do you see between the typical assessment tasks in Figure 11.2 and the formative assessment opportunities you provide for students? What

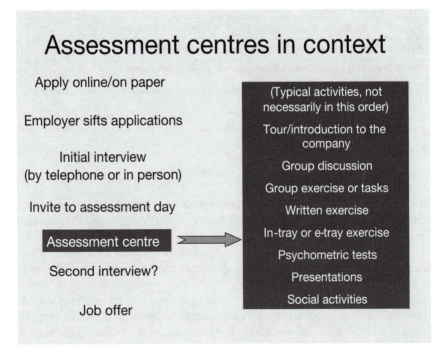

Figure 11.2 Assessment centres in context.

is the common ground between the 'behavioural competencies' that employers seek and the ideal attributes you seek in a student? My contention here is that we can use assessment centres as an additional motivator and rationale for having students practise and demonstrate these behaviours and attributes.

The SOAR process should already have answered such questions, and given students formative learning opportunities to practise such tasks. In the final year there may be a variety of ways in which this could be refreshed, revisited and lifted to higher standards. As a summative assessment challenge, students can demonstrate their skills and have them accredited as part of a final-year project, or certificated, recognized and rewarded in some way as a co-curriculum offering. Allocating a professional skills day (or week) would enable a concentrated focus on such matters, where finalists might set up activities working with and for each other, especially to provide observation and feedback on group discussions, presentations and interviews (the most frequently used selection events).

Psychometric tests

These tests claim to be objective and standardized, developed by occupational psychologists using specialist skills and procedures consisting of carefully prescribed content, methods of administration, and interpretation. The tests have known properties of reliability and validity, and norms for a particular 'population' so that you can reliably compare an individual's results with a similar group of people. For example, you could compare a candidate's Verbal Reasoning with that of a general population of 'all graduates' or with a more specific sample of graduates with English or Language degrees.

Tests are of three main types:

1   Personality tests and inventories that measure some aspect of human behaviour.
2   General intelligence tests.
3   Aptitude tests that measure specific types of skills or intelligence, e.g. verbal reasoning, numerical ability, spatial judgement, mechanical ability, scientific and technical skills, reading, spelling and administrative or clerical abilities, creative aptitudes, computing ability, etc. These can be taken as a battery to test different skills, resulting in an individual profile of strengths and limitations.

I have mentioned psychological testing in connection with self-awareness, careers guidance and self-development in previous chapters. Psychological career theories resulted in the widespread use of tests in the US and the UK, especially during the 1950s and 1960s, but tests have been used for selection purposes for nearly 100 years. In all that time they have been dogged by controversy. Major objections stem from two interrelated issues: technical shortcomings in test design; and ethical problems in the way they are interpreted and applied. The relative significance of differences in intelligence, personality and skills in relation to different types of work is hotly debated. Recently much of this criticism has come to a head, driven by changes in work and society:

> Traditional tests do not measure a person's ability to adapt to the environment, to learn and to change. Test publishers in the USA stick to the formula that they have been using for almost a century.
>
> (Sternberg, 1997)

It has been argued that the tests currently in use do not test the type of streetwise, practical talent needed in the dynamic modern world, the attributes that can innovate and move an organization forward. Attempts to increase correlations between test results and successful work performance are ongoing – they only measure a small amount of some personal qualities, such as flexibility and adaptability, motivation and willingness/ability to learn and innovate, enthusiasm and interpersonal skills. A new generation of tests has therefore recently been developed, but it may be too soon to judge their usefulness.

As an employer you would have to make a judgement about whether and what tests to use, and how much reliance to place on their results. Even most psychologists would agree that it is unethical to use test results alone to bar people from educational and employment opportunities. They should at best be used as only one source and type of information about an individual. Job-seekers would do well to familiarize themselves with practice tests. Some are available on www. shl.com/shl/en-int/candidatehelpline.

Legislation and equal opportunities

Recruiters should know at least the basics of employment legislation so that they define suitable criteria, use methods and ask questions that are legally and 'politically correct'. There are several Acts in force that make it unlawful to discriminate in certain ways: on grounds of gender, race, age, etc. – and many companies have policies on the subject.

Genuinely supporting equal opportunities is of course much more than worrying about falling foul of the law. One can legislate against discrimination but not against prejudice and stereotypical views or assumptions. The mission of bodies such as the UK's Commission for Equalities and Human Rights is to work towards a just society which gives everyone an equal chance to learn, work and live free from fear and harassment. As an employer, ideally you would see that it makes for good public relations and excellent business sense to employ talent on merit. In the caring and politically correct twenty-first century, we increasingly see statements in recruitment literature that show commitment to equal opportunity issues and also value diversity, for example:

> The BBC is committed to equal opportunities for all, irrespective of race, colour, creed, ethnic or national origins, gender, marital status, sexuality, disability or age. We are committed to taking positive action to promote such equality of opportunity and our recruitment, training and promotion procedures are based on the requirements of a job.

Such statements may be supported in some instances by policies that offer a 'guaranteed interview' to all applicants with disabilities, or those from under-represented minority ethnic groups.

Many employers monitor such policies and 'positive action' by requesting additional information from applicants on their ethnic origin, age, gender, any disability, etc. – and this is only for monitoring and not for selection purposes. The issues and implications involved in all areas of equal opportunities are vast, and a body of literature has sprung up to deal with them, together with many sources of help and advice.

If you and your students are so inclined you could set up a debate on these matters – I have on occasion projected a picture of Noah's Ark with different pairs of animals such as lions, snakes, giraffes, etc. – with the caption: 'This is an equal opportunities ark: all animals will eat straw. Discuss.' Students see the anomaly in treating everybody alike and the difficulties in making genuine exceptions. In fact it may even be culturally biased for me to use Noah's Ark!

This topic may be highly relevant in mixed classrooms where many students fear they might get a raw deal in the labour market. My own view is that assessment centres and interviews are daunting enough in themselves, and approaching them with any sort of negativity will not help! It is not only important to have an optimistic belief in one's capabilities but also to remain positive in one's aspirations, and trust that the environment you are striving for will be fair and just.

Personality type and job-search strengths

Finally, it may really personalize the process of job-search if you have students revisit their personality-type concepts (Chapters 7 and 10), to identify their strengths and preferences in relation to job-search and selection processes. For example, those with E in their type code usually find it easier to make a network of contacts, appear confident and outgoing in social interactions (including interviews and assessment centres), but the potential pitfall would be talking too much or dominating the proceedings. Those with I in their type code tend to be more thoughtful and careful in giving a favourable CV representation, focusing on the most important objectives.

In terms of one's natural response to change: those with P in their type code are generally more resilient in the face of imposed change, and may even welcome it – while 'J' may feel more unsettled by it. However, these are indicators, and each student should use them as a tool to become aware of pitfalls to avoid. Understanding the approaches of others in group activities can also make the difference between landing that vital job offer and the fatal r-word in that letter of rejection.

Chapter 11: Summary of main points

- Demonstrating Results (the R of SOAR) can be oriented towards developing skills for upcoming transition points, and having finalists develop and demonstrate job-search and self-promotion skills that neatly complement the need for high-level academic development at this stage.
- Critically appreciating the needs, concerns and processes involved in recruitment and selection, through role-playing from an employer perspective, helps to generate the requisite attitudes, responses and skills-development in students as job-seekers.
- The stages and steps involved in preparation, application and selection for jobs can be replicated through curriculum activities and assessments. Examples are given for tasks such as 'reading between the lines of a job advert', tailoring one's CV, completing effective applications, preparing for success at interviews and assessment centres.
- Students should recognize that much of this preparation will have taken place through the SOAR process so far, and that it has applications wider than just competing for jobs.

Chapter 12

Evaluating results

Funny, isn't it – we are approaching a sort of ending, and I'm writing a final chapter under pressure, as the publisher's deadline looms large. For people with a 'Perceiving type preference', without that 'last minute' nothing would ever get done! But, by now, you know I believe in cycles and spirals, and we have come full circle with the SOAR process. It is time to review, take stock of results achieved, and identify next steps for further development. You and your students may have assembled your Self-MAP for use in various contexts – both as a map and a compass to find direction. Job-seekers may even have landed that dream job which they barely glimpsed at the start of the process. If they have, they are exceptional, because all the evidence shows that many graduates leave university without a firm destination lined up.

What Results should we evaluate?

But how exactly should we evaluate Results (the **R** of SOA**R**), and what concept of 'success' are we advocating? Personally I identify with these words of Mahatma Gandhi:

> It's the action, not the fruit of the action, that's important. You have to do the right thing. It may not be in your power, may not be in your time, that there will be any fruit. But that doesn't mean you stop doing the right thing. You may never know the results from your action. But if you do nothing there will be no result.
>
> (Mahatma Gandhi, quoted in Exley, 2002)

If you review your own progress through SOAR, you might ask questions such as: What have I learned about SOAR as a whole through reading this book, at both an intellectual and functional level? What have I discovered and developed about myself? . . . about my personal Self-MAP? . . . about my preferred learning, teaching and assessment methods and materials, in real and virtual environments? How have I engaged with this Opportunity, and has it changed my Aspirations in any way? What Results have I achieved: what works well that I can share with others, or replicate elsewhere? What might I do differently?

For students, the SOAR model has not just been about finding 'graduate-level employment' with high status and salary, or even narrowly about entry to work, although to an extent that has been central because it is the aim of the vast majority of students in HE. It has been central also because it provides a relevant and important trigger for developing both generic and specific skills and attitudes that serve personal and career development, and also motivate good academic learning. It makes for the best investment in students' current capacities and identities – linked with their potential futures. For SOAR to empower individuals to take control of their life-careers in twenty-first-century conditions, we equated 'career' with lifelong and life-wide learning along a personal pathway through life.

We should remember that SOAR is essentially a model for development that is intended to broaden the frames of reference for 'learning' (and evaluate it as such):

- learning that integrates personal, professional and academic development;
- learning that is relevant for present and future purposes;
- learning that is the responsibility of the learner and is facilitated by various learning enablers and opportunities;
- learning that is recognized (accredited and valued) wherever it takes place – both within a formal structured curriculum or work environment, and outside through informal activities and life experiences;
- learning attitudes and abilities that lead to the willingness and ability to engage in lifelong learning.

How may we evaluate?

SOAR has been presented here as a vehicle for the PDP agenda in the UK, which requires students to record learning outcomes in paper-based or computer-based formats. Such records, when structured through a SOAR model, would in themselves provide evidence of the results and benefits for individuals. SOAR can enhance four main types of PDP records:

a   Learners may be encouraged to record the process of their learning, development and achievement for their own purposes, using writing as an aid to personal reflection and self-assessment. The responsibility and ownership would then rest with them.

b   They may be required to produce more formal records, which can be used for the purposes of assessment or selection – usually word-processed documents such as CVs or e-portfolios.

c   These documents may build up as records in respect of the HE Progress File as a whole, taking participants through all levels of programmes of study.

d   E-recording can be carried across sectors flexibly, travelling with the learner from sub-degree level through HE and beyond.

Practices related to recording achievement vary enormously across the UK HE sector, and even within institutions. Many HEIs are prioritizing the PDP element – providing opportunities to incorporate the *process* rather than the product(s) or records. Employers, too, do not wish to see extensive paper-based records during recruitment – they are more interested in the benefits that derive from the PDP process. However, records are important focal points for students and writing is an aid to reflective learning. HEFCE's e-Learning Strategy (2005) includes encouragement for e-based systems to be used and developed in order to meet Progress File requirements – see www.hefce.ac.uk/pubs/hefce/2005/05_12/05_12.doc.

The intangible and long-term results of engaging in the processes of SOAR are inevitably more difficult to identify and evaluate than its immediately demonstrable outcomes. In our model for SOARing to future success, entry to work is a central emphasis but not an exclusive option – and Aspirations will translate into different personal outcomes for each individual. We will return to this later but, if you have an accredited SOAR module, for now the results of students' immediate learning may be apparent in their verbal presentations week-by-week, in actions, reflections, questions, discussions and written records. The assignments will usually provide the best evidence of what students have learned.

You should have them return to the self-audit 'It's *My* Journey Through Life' (see Chapter 2, p. 37) and rate themselves again on that questionnaire. They might do the same for other audits given in this book, which all have diagnostic as well as evaluative potential. Their improved ratings will indicate the extent to which they have progressed, and what they still need to do to develop the requisite skills and attitudes.

In asking these questions we are continuing the emphasis on self-assessment of results, and maintaining the positive focus on 'distance travelled' or 'value added' by engaging with a learning opportunity. The same method of evaluation could be applied to reviewing achievement on other modules or units, a course, a whole programme of study – or even work and life experience generally. It is in keeping with the principles of Appreciative Inquiry that, by asking 'what have you achieved', 'what has worked well – in what context, and with what methods and mechanisms?', we maintain motivation to use our strengths and replicate them in other contexts.

This also reinforces students' responsibility for participation in their learning journey throughout. They are now not only judging what we provide as a one-way intervention, but also implicitly judging how they have engaged with our offerings. The review serves the dual purpose of looking back to look forward. How have I benefited? What still needs to be done?

This is different from treating HE as a commodity that students have 'bought', and viewing them as consumers – in which case evaluating results is all about getting them to assess whether a particular intervention has given them what they want, and invites them to criticize what is wanting. The SOAR philosophy on the other hand creates 'self as hero in the journey of life', travelling with tutors as a partner, researcher and curious explorer – responsible for knowledge creation, critical and creative thinking, and with freedom to discover and build a personal Self-MAP, leading to personally defined aspirations and choices for the future.

Evaluation questionnaire for a SOAR-based module

If you have delivered a structured module (as in Tables 3.1 and 3.2, pp. 50–3), you may wish to adapt and evaluate it with the questionnaire below. I have used similar proformas to recover student feedback on both generic and subject-tailored modules at the University of Bedfordshire. The rating scales are structured to elicit students' perceptions of their development ('distance travelled') on specific skills and knowledge elements, but also to prompt free text responses. It is delivered to all students present at the last session of the module.

Note that this is addressed to students:
It would greatly help the module team if we could have an evaluation of your experience of the module in order to assess if it is meeting the learning outcomes. It will also help you to review the extent to which you have benefited as a result of doing this module. Please complete this questionnaire using the scale 1 to 4, where 1 = greatly improved, 4 = not improved.

I To what extent has the module developed your skills in . . .	Ratings 1–4
a) identifying your strengths, interests and priorities?	
b) retrieving information from a variety of sources?	
c) learning effectively from a variety of learning opportunities?	
d) group/teamwork and interpersonal effectiveness?	
e) designing a tailored CV?	
f) completing an effective application form?	
g) applying for jobs and courses?	
h) producing an action plan?	
i) decision making and problem solving?	
j) communication and self-presentation (especially in interviews and assessment centres?)	
k) analysing and evaluating yourself against desired results?	

2 How far has the module given you the knowledge to:	Ratings 1–4
a) identify your actual and potential strengths (your skills, interests, abilities, priorities)?	
b) identify and address your development needs?	
c) understand changes in the world of work?	
d) research a chosen job/occupation?	
e) make realistic further study and/or employment choices?	
f) analyse job vacancies in relation to a) above?	
g) differentiate between employer organizations and sectors, e.g. public, private and voluntary sectors; large, and small and medium-sized enterprises?	
h) appreciate the recruitment and selection process from an employer's viewpoint?	
3 Using the 1 to 4 scale please indicate to what extent the following resources and methods supported your learning on this module [Here you might list the main resources you used in support of your module – e.g. we had web-based tutorial materials and used the Blackboard VLE. Students can tell you to what extent they found these relevant and useful, and the extent to which they used them. They can also identify what learning methods worked best for them in this module.]	
4 Please complete the following statements in whatever way is most appropriate to you The course made me feel . . . I was surprised by . . . I liked . . . I'll use . . . Now I can . . . I didn't like . . . I wish we'd had time to . . . I want to know more about . . . I'd also like to say . . .	

Student feedback from using the above questionnaire

The results are broadly and generally very positive, particularly grouped around the novel nature of the material, the development of skills and the idea of planning for the future. The negative aspects have on occasion grouped around the 'administrative aspects': students complain that a two-hour session without a break is too long. A few find the theoretical aspects unnecessary, which suggests that careers theories, although relevant, should be linked more closely to the student activities and real-life relevance. The feedback shows that they find the methods and materials challenging and useful. Many comment on the usefulness of being pressed to consider their careers – which they would not have done otherwise.

For example, on the module *Accounting for the Future* that Rob and I customized for Accounting and Finance students and co-delivered for the first time, the scaled ratings of knowledge and skills outcomes produced a very positive view of the module: each question produced a mean average in the range 1.25–2.1. The weakest results tended to group around issues associated with knowledge of the world of work (2.05) and recruitment issues (2.1), while the strongest responses were grouped around skills-development, especially self-knowledge of their own strengths and development needs. Rob and I felt this represented a considerable success, as this was the first such attempt aiming to develop skills for personal and career development in this subject field.

The free text method elicited many positive comments – for example:

- about the way the course made them feel ('confident, secure, comfortable, good, happy with my decisions');
- about what they liked ('the way the course was taught', 'related to me, to the job – and I found the path!', 'the topics of lectures', 'the group work; the idea of working in mixed groups', 'the job researches we made during the course');
- about what they could now do ('understand what job is suitable for me', 'develop my skills and target my weaknesses – to improve', 'assess my situation' 'develop these skills on my own', 'do something about planning my career', 'research and apply for jobs' – and many comments about enhanced ability to design and use CV, CL and application forms);
- about what they would use ('CV, CL and SAF in my future when I apply for jobs', 'my action plan', 'all the knowledge you gave me', 'the feedback from group work in the future and now', 'the website CMS regularly', 'the techniques I learned to make CVs', etc.).

The stem 'I'd also like to say . . .' produced many expressions of thanks to us, which were all immensely encouraging, including one heartfelt comment thanking someone else: 'There must be a God out there, for God knows I really needed this module!'

SOAR and DOTS

To a large extent it is relevant to look at feedback from modules based on the DOTS model because of the similarity of context and approaches between SOAR and DOTS (see Chapter 1). DOTS is generally used as a basic framework for CMS/CDL interventions in the UK, and various approaches have been developed to suit different student groups and institutional contexts. It is widely reported by careers educators who evaluate these that student feedback is overwhelmingly positive on the real-life relevance and usefulness of the process. However, there is a dearth of formal longitudinal research to evaluate how the model's benefits transfer to graduates' futures.

The long-term results of SOAR may not be apparent, not until students transfer their learning beyond HE. The structured SOAR process spans across transitions – it is one that they can use in lifelong learning, in future job performance appraisals, continuing professional development, further study, training and promotion opportunities, and in deciding changes of career direction. In this respect I know of only one small-scale study by Julie Blant, which tracked graduates to look at the influence of careers education on employability.[1] I asked her to summarize her findings for this book:

> During the final stages of a Masters programme I researched the impact of careers education on graduate employability and explored how a contemporary approach to careers education could enhance this impact. Research was conducted with a small number of Combined Studies graduates, from a post-92 institution, who had undertaken an optional accredited careers education module in the second year of their degree programmes. The module was based on the Decision learning, Opportunity-awareness, Transition skills, Self-awareness (DOTS) model.[2]

> The aim of my research was to review the relevance and efficacy of a conventional careers programme post-graduation. Using survey methods I incorporated the institution's definition of employability alongside the learning outcomes of the module to learn about the graduates' experiences of the module and their subsequent career trajectories.

> Findings indicated that the module had contributed to graduate employability by giving graduates the tools and confidence to navigate the labour market. Their views, overall, were very positive and comments suggested that practical skills such as self-reflection, researching careers, job search and self-presentation were the major benefits of the module. However, whilst initial employment levels were high, frequent job movements were explained as 'experimentation' suggesting that neither the module, nor their degree programme, had resulted in definitive career decision making for this cohort. On further exploration of their career decisions it was clear that the graduates saw little connection between their degree and the workplace and felt that experimenting was necessary in order to find the links.

To build on the effectiveness of the module a contemporary model was examined as a possible way of strengthening employability and careers work within the curriculum. My conclusions indicated scope for piloting Bill Law's new Coverage Process and Influence (CPI) model[3] within the higher education curriculum in order to facilitate career learning through deeper links with academic activities.

Evaluating the effectiveness of SOAR through data on entry to 'graduate jobs'

In the UK one of the performance indicators by which HE is judged is through the annual collection of graduate destinations data. Of particular interest are the statistics for those in full-time employment. The results are influential in a number of ways: they are used to compile national league tables, which receive a fair amount of press and Internet publicity. They can help us understand where graduates from different courses have gone, and how best to support future students and alumni.

People who want SOAR to justify its existence within HE curricula may wish to judge its 'employability advantage' by placing inordinate emphasis on numbers actually entering 'graduate-level employment'. There are several reasons why we should qualify the validity of such judgements.

'Career' – as defined in Chapter 2 – is no longer equated with 'graduate-level employment' but defined broadly as a 'pathway through life'. Accordingly we have engaged students in a process of progressive empowerment, with staged outcomes, developing the knowledge, skills, attributes, experience and networking ability they will need to become employable. It is right to judge the SOAR process and its methods of delivery on the extent to which it enhances the capacity of students as a process of development.

However, whether a career decision was right or wrong can only be judged in retrospect. The process of self-assessment and career research we encourage can result in students realizing that their chosen occupation is not suitable after all and needs to be reconsidered, or is actually very competitive to enter. They may therefore decide to gain work experience or embark on further study or specific training to improve their chances. This may not look so positive on the DLHE survey (Destinations of Leavers from HE), but would be the better choice for the individual.

Successful entry to work depends on two sides of the equation: the aspirations, abilities and priorities of the job-seeker on the one hand, and the capacity of the labour market to absorb that individual on the other. In HEIs most of us have limited access to and impact on the power structures that determine the social, economic, educational and training environments in which our graduates will seek to survive. We tend to influence the person, and have less influence on the environment and the larger context. Since we are working with just one side of this equation (empowering students), evaluating SOAR interventions and its supporting resources on the evidence of 'first destinations' is not wholly valid.

The value of collecting first destinations data to represent a snapshot in time of what graduates are doing six months after leaving HE has been questioned. Entry to a first job may be determined by factors such as student debt and the need to repay loans, or earn money immediately in whatever job is currently available. A high proportion of students have part-time jobs while studying, and some continue in these lower-level positions due to financial constraints for quite some time after graduating.

Widespread discontent with the limitations of currently available data has led to various research projects to follow up graduates more longitudinally, thereby providing valuable evidence and intelligence about the graduate labour market. More longitudinal research reveals that the labour market is very fluid and flexible for the first few years after graduation (Purcell et al., 1999), and many graduates do progress into better jobs within two to three years (Elias and Purcell, 2004).

The definition of 'graduate jobs' is itself in question, as discussed in Chapter 9. There are now many more graduates than traditional graduate schemes and positions to absorb them, and not all graduates aspire to the latter, anyway. Students are part of a wider culture and society, with widely differing assets and constraints in their backgrounds and circumstances – therefore choice is differentially available to each. Moreover, we should recognize we are not the sole or even primary education and guidance providers for many students; we might actively encourage them to use other sources of help, influence and guidance. We cannot then isolate our impact from those other sources – and claim either all the success or all the failure for their transition beyond university and the jobs they enter.

A number of external variables affect the career decisions and life chances of an individual. Despite legislation and equal opportunities policies, discrimination in graduate recruitment still exists against older, disabled, female and ethnic minority graduates, and those from social classes C and D. At HEIs that pursue 'widening participation' strategies, many students present in one or more of the non-traditional categories – indeed many suffer from multiple disadvantage, marginalized by poverty, lack of family or social support.

In addition, many graduate recruiters continue to demand high academic grades at sub-degree level as a precondition of selection – which means that students cannot compensate with good degree results alone. A SOAR model can build self-awareness of strengths and self-efficacy beliefs, but it also makes students aware of constraints, diversity issues and the competitive nature of entry to many jobs at this level. SOAR cannot fully overcome obstacles such as employer attitudes.

Having said all this, the process in which SOAR engages students should be thoroughly evaluated in relation to well-defined knowledge and skills outcomes. We have done this in the past through standard university forms, our own more specifically designed evaluation forms, and focus groups organized by students. All the evidence points to the fact that we do add value to our students, developing attributes like confidence and motivation as well as skills and understanding. However, there is a great need to follow graduates' stories longitudinally to evaluate the impact of SOAR through qualitative and descriptive research – possibly something for you to undertake with your students and alumni! These stories can provide real-life exemplar material to enrich further work.

However important it might be to use robust research methodology, it is important to ask the right questions when we elicit feedback from learners: since SOAR is student-centred and emphasizes ownership by the individual, we should be asking students to assess the extent of their own engagement with the structured processes we provide, and the 'distance they have travelled' as a result – the skills developed and benefits gained. This type of ipsative evaluation further develops their skills of review and development in a way that should be useful for their future performance appraisals at work and in continuing professional development.

We will also need to elicit feedback from employers who recruit our students. The results of such reviews should then enable us to see whether our processes are useful from an employability perspective, and to improve our strategies for empowering students and better meeting the priorities of employers. And so we will close the feedback loop. . . . In yet another way then, this is not an ending. I leave you with two thoughts (only one of them in my words).

Feeding yourself (as in your Self-MAP)

> One evening an old Cherokee told his grandson about a battle that was going on inside himself. He said, 'My son, it is between 2 wolves. One is evil: anger, envy, sorrow, regret, greed, arrogance, self-pity, guilt, resentment, inferiority, lies, false pride, sloth and ego.
>
> The other is good: joy, peace, love, hope, serenity, humility, kindness, benevolence, empathy, generosity, truth, compassion, charity, trust and faith.'
>
> The grandson thought about it for a minute and then asked his grandfather 'Which wolf wins?'
>
> The old Cherokee simply replied, 'The one I feed.'
>
> (Author unknown)

A new beginning, then: as you stand on the verge of your future, I share with you the thought that this is 'the millennium of the mind' – as gurus like Tony Buzan (1988a) and Charles Handy (1995) have pointed out. Lifelong learning and 'intellectual capital' are the order of the day, the new wealth of nations. You are in the business of getting students to consider their HE knowledge, transferable skills and 'intelligences' as the currencies with which they open doors to new opportunities. It is my hope that this book will have opened doors to some new ideas and possibilities for you as well, in your personal and professional life. If that has been the case your story would be immensely interesting – drop me a line and share it with others!

Notes

Foreword

1   Barnett, R. (2000) Supercomplexity and the curriculum. In Tight, M. (ed.) *Curriculum in Higher Education*. Buckingham, SRHE and Open University Press.
2   Barnett, R. and Coat, K. (2005) *Engaging the Curriculum in Higher Education*. Buckingham, SRHE and Open University Press.
3   Compexworld wiki, http://complexworld.pbwiki.com/ 'Supercomplexity page'.
4   Progress Files for Higher Education, www.qaa.ac.uk/academicinfrastructure/ progressFiles/default.asp.
5   Covey, S. (2004) *The Eighth Habit: from Effectiveness to Greatness*. London and New York, Simon and Schuster.

2 Defining key concepts and principles

1   A range of project papers can be found at www.open.ac.uk/vqportal/SkillsPlus/home. htm.
2   USEM, discussed by Knight and Yorke (2004).
3   Figure 2.4 has been previously published in Kumar, A. (2004) *A Resources Guide to PDP and the Progress File*, available on the HE Academy webiste, www.heacademy.ac. uk/hlst/resources/guides/guides/guides_techingandlearning.
4   Figure 2.5 has been previously published in Kumar, A. (2004) *A Resources Guide*, details as in note 3.
5   Based on ideas by Peter Hawkins, from *The Art of Building Windmills* (1999).

3 Realizing the potential of SOAR

1   My thanks to Rob Carman for agreeing to the inclusion of extracts from this report, 'Learning Lessons from co-delivering a PDP module' which we co-presented at the annual Teaching and Learning Conference on 17 June 2005 at Luton, and also as a discussion paper entitled 'Personal and Career Development for Accounting and Finance Students' at the annual conference of the Subject Network for Business, Management, Accounting and Finance on 6 April 2005 in London.
2   MBTI® and Introduction to Type are registered trade marks of the Myers-Briggs Type Indicator Trust. (See Chapter 7.)

4 Building a 'Self-MAP'

1   www.recordingachievement.org.uk/.
2   Dorothy Spry is a business psychologist and co-author of *The Psychometric Testing Management Pocketbook* (Spry and Cripps, 2007) email: Dorothy@career performance.co.uk.

3   www.teamfocus.co.uk.
4   Prospects Planner is freely available via www.prospects.ac.uk and is jointly developed
     and owned by AGCAS and Graduate Prospects, UK.
5   (UK – CASCAID), www.careersmatch.co.uk.
6   Theories, as presented here, are adapted from AGCAS Diploma papers and my own
     readings from various sources. My thanks to Bill Law for allowing me to reproduce
     theory-related Figures 2.1, 10.1 and 10.2, and Table 8.1 – and to interpret his concepts
     in my own way.

5 Motivation in the Self-MAP

1   My thanks to this employer (who wishes to remain anonymous) for permission to use
     this material, also included in later exercises.
2   Sponsored by various organizations.
3   See LMI on Graduate Prospects website, www.prospects.ac.uk/.

6 Ability in the Self-MAP

1   Project supported by ESECT, CIHE and 12 HEA–LTSN Subject Centres at the time
     of writing; cf. HEA, 2006.
2   My thanks to Helfried Waleczek.

7 Personality in the Self-MAP

1   ®Myers-Briggs Type Indicator, MBTI, the MBTI logo and *Introduction to Type* are
     registered trademarks of the Myers-Briggs Type Indicator Turst.
2   See Kroeger and Thuesen, 1988a, 1988b.
3   For example, CPP publishes a series of *Introduction to Type*® booklets covering a
     range of topics, including leadership development, teams and change.
4   Gordon D. Lawrence (1993: 2–5).
5   Based on Bayne, 2005.
6   Based on Kummerow, 2002.
7   Reproduced with thanks to Linda Ernst *et al.*

8 Researching and engaging with 'Opportunity'

1   Reproduced with thanks to Linda Ernst *et al.*
2   Thanks to Jo Myhill, Academic Liaison Librarian, University of Bedfordshire.

9 Understanding the changing world

1   With thanks to Dharmendra Pokhariya. This is an Internet circular, which goes back
     to at least 2003, but doesn't seem to have a clear origin.
2   C. Gilleard, CE of the AGR in conference presentation 2005.
3   My thanks to Maggie Summers. The paper was delivered at the European Distance
     and E-Learning Workshop 4th Research Workshop, 25–8 October 2006, Barcelona,
     Spain. The workshop proceedings are available via the EDEN website: www.eden-
     online.org. For further information contact Dr Helen Jones, Principal Lecturer in
     Criminology, Manchester Metropolitan University (H.Jones@mmu.ac.uk).

10 Aspirations, decisions, plans

1   Quenk, N. L. (1996).

11 Demonstrating results

1   Thanks to TNS for providing their advertisement with permission for me to use it as the basis for an exercise.

12 Evaluating results

1   Julie Blant presented her Masters research findings at a Guidance Research Network Event in June 2005 hosted by the Centre for Guidance Studies (CeGS), University of Derby. Julie is currently a CeGS Associate and Deputy Director of the Postgraduate Careers Service at Nottingham University Business School.
2   Law and Watts, 'Decision Learning, Opportunity Awareness, Transition Learning, Self Awareness' in Law and Watts (1977).
3   Law, B. (2005).

Bibliography

Adler, C. (2006) 'Mix and match'. *The Guardian*. London. 4 November. Available at http://jobsadvice.guardian.co.uk/graduate/story/0,,1939033,00.html .

AGCAS (2000) *Assessment Centres* (DVD). Sheffield, Association of Graduate Careers Advisory Services.

AGCAS (2005) *Careers Education Benchmark Statement*. Sheffield, Careers Education Task Group, Association of Graduate Careers Advisory Services.

AGCAS (2006) Phoenix 117, Sheffield, Association of Graduate Careers Advisory Services.

AGR (2001) *Assessment Centres: AGR Briefing Paper*. Warwick, Association of Graduate Recruiters.

AGR (2005) *The AGR Graduate Recruitment Survey 2005 Winter Review*. London, Association of Graduate Recruiters.

AGR (2006) *The AGR Graduate Recruitment Survey 2006 Summer Review*. London, Association of Graduate Recruiters.

Allan, R. (2006) *A Wider Perspective and More Options: investigating the longer term employability of humanities graduates*. Southampton, Subject Centre for Languages, Linguistics and Area Studies, University of Southampton.

Angelo, T. A. (1994) 'From faculty development to academic development'. *American Association for Higher Education Bulletin*, 46, 3–7.

Angelo, T. A. and Cross, K. P. (1993) *Classroom Assessment Techniques: A handbook for college teachers*, San Francisco, CA, Jossey-Bass.

Anon (1998) The Spelling Chequer. *Professional Manager*, July 1998.

Argyris, C. and Schon, D. A. (1991) 'Participatory Action Research and Action Science Compared'. In Whyte, W. F. (ed.) *Participatory Action Research*. Newbury Park, CA, Sage.

Arnold, J. (1997) *Managing Careers into the 21st Century*, London, Sage Publications.

Arroba, T. (1977) Styles of decision making and their use: an empirical study. *British Journal of Guidance and Counselling*, 5, 149–58.

Arthur, M. B. (2003) *New Careers, New Relationships: understanding and supporting the contemporary worker*, Derby, CeGS.

Ball, B. and Butcher, V. (1993) *Developing Students' Career Planning Skills: the impact of the Enterprise in Higher Education initiative*. Sheffield, Employment Department.

Bandura, A. (1995a) 'Exercise of personal and collective efficacy in changing societies'. In Bandura, A. (ed.) *Self-Efficacy in Changing Societies*. Cambridge, Cambridge University Press.

Bandura, A. (1995b) *Self-efficacy in Changing Societies*, Cambridge, Cambridge University Press.

Bandura, A. (1997) *Self-efficacy: the exercise of control*, New York, W. H. Freeman.

Barger, N. J. and Kirby, L. K. (2006) 'The MBTI® instrument: Relevant for the future?' *MBTI European Conference*. London.

Barnett, R. (1999) Realizing the University in an Age of Supercomplexity, Buckingham, SRHE and Open University Press.

Baume, D. (2001) *Assessing Portfolios,* York, The LTSN Generic Centre.

Bayne, R. (2004) Psychological Types at Work – an MBTI® perspective, London, Thomson.

Bayne, R. (2005) *Ideas and Evidence: critical reflections on MBTI theory and practice CAPT, Florida*, Gainesville, FL, Center for Applications of Psychological Type, Inc.

Bazerman, M. H. (1986) *Judgment in Managerial Decision Making*, New York, John Wiley & Sons.

Belbin, R. M. (1981, 2004) *Management Teams: why they succeed or fail*, Burlington, MA, Elsevier Butterworth-Heinemann.

Belbin, R. M. (2003) *Team Roles at Work*, Burlington, MA, Elsevier Butterworth-Heinemann.

Bennett, N., Dunne, E. and Carré, C. (2000) *Skills Development in Higher Education and Employment*, Buckingham, Society for Research into Higher Education/Open University Press.

Bereiter, C. and Scardamalia, M. (1989) 'Intentional learning as a goal of instruction'. In Resnick, L. (ed.) *Knowing, Learning and Instruction: essays in honor of Robert Glaser/not listed.* Hillsdale, NJ, Lawrence Erlbaum Associates.

Berens, L. V., Ernst, L. and Smith, M. (2004) *Quick Guide to the 16 Personality Types and Teams: applying team essentials™ to create effective teams*, Huntington Beach, CA, Telos Publications.

Berger, P. and Luckman, T. (1966) The Social Construction of Reality: A treatise in the sociology of knowledge, New York, Anchor Books.

Betz, N. E. and Hackett, G. (1981) 'The relationship of career-related self-efficacy expectations to perceived career options in college men and women'. *Journal of Counseling Psychology*, 28, 399–410.

Betz, N. E. and Hackett, G. (1983) 'Career self-efficacy theory: back to the future'. *Journal of Career Assessment*, 14, 3–11.

Betz, N. E. and Luzzo, D. (1996) 'Career assessment and the career decision self-efficacy scale'. *Journal of Career Assessment*, 4, 313–28.

Biggs, J. (2003) *Teaching for Quality Learning at University*, Buckingham, SRHE/Open University Press.

Black, P. and Wiliam, D. (1998) 'Assessment and classroom learning'. *Assessment in Education*, 5, 7–74.

Bloom, B. S. (1956) Taxonomy of Educational Objectives: the classification of educational goals: handbook 1, cognitive domain, New York, Toronto, Longmans, Green.

Boud, D. (1989) 'The role of self-assessment in student grading'. *Assessment and Evaluation in Higher Education*, 14, 20–30.

Boud, D. (1995, reprinted 2003) *Enhancing Learning through Self Assessment*, London, Kogan Page.

Branden, N. (2001) *The Six Pillars of Self Esteem*, New York, Bantam.

Brennan, C. (2006) *Making your Job Work for You*. Readers Digest (UK). London, Readers Digest.

Bridges, D. (1993) 'Transferable skills: a philosophical perspective'. *Studies in Higher Education*, 18, 43–51.

Brockbank, A. and McGill, I. (2003) *Facilitating Reflective Learning in HE*, London, SRHE and Open University Press.

Brown, D., Brooks, L. *et al.* (eds) (1990) *Career Choice and Development*, San Francisco, CA, Jossey-Bass.

Brown, G., Bull, J. and Pendlebury, M. (1997) *Assessing Student Learning in Higher Education*, London, Routledge.

Brown, S. and Dove, P. (1993) 'Self and peer assessment: learning from experience'. *Natfhe Journal of Further and Higher Education*.

Buckingham, M. (2005) *The One Thing You Need to Know*, New York, Free Press.

Buckingham, M. and Clifton, D. (2001) *Now, Discover Your Strengths*, New York, Free Press.

Burchall, M. (2006) *UK Graduate Careers Survey*, 2006. London, High Fliers Research.

Burgess, R. (2004) *Measuring and Recording Student Achievement: report of the Scoping Group*. London, Universities UK and SCOP.

Butcher, D. and Harvey, P. (1998) 'Meta-ability development: a new concept for career management'. *Career Development International*, 3, 75–8.

Buzan, T. (1988a) 'Intellectual Capital: the New Wealth of Nations'. *Open Saturday*. Buckingham, Open University.

Buzan, T. (1988b) *Make the Most of Your Mind*, London, Pan Macmillan.

Cameron, D. (2006) David Cameron's speech to Google Zeitgeist Europe 2006. *Guardian Unlimited*. 22 May. Accessed: 7 March 2007. Available at http://politics.guardian.co.uk/conservatives/story/0,,1780585,00.html.

Campbell, L. and Campbell, B. (1999) *From Success Stories from Six Schools*, Alexandria, VA, Association for Supervision and Curriculum Development (ASCD).

Carr, S. (1997, 2003) Finding the Fit: helping clients clarify MBTI® Type, Palo Alto, CA, CPP, Inc.

Chabon-Berger, T. (2006) 'Find out what employers are looking for – You don't need a crystal ball, just common sense'. *Palmbeach Post*. 9 August. Accessed: 6 September 2006. Available at www.palmbeachpost.com/jobs/content/jobs/resources/stories/jobs_empseek_main.html.

Chandler, R. (undated) *Raymond Chandler Quotes*. Available at www.brainyquote.com/quotes/quotes/r/raymondcha120415.html.

Chaney, G. (2000) 'The uses of portfolios for learning and assessment'. *CGCHE Journal of Learning and Teaching*, 5.

Checkley, K. (1997) 'The first seven . . . and the eighth: a conversation with Howard Gardner'. *Educational Leadership*, 55, 8–13.

CIHE (1996) Helping Students Towards Success at Work: declaration of intent. London, Council for Industry and Higher Education.

CILIP (2006) Information Literacy: definition. London, Chartered Institute of Library & Information Professionals. Last edited 13 December 2006. Available at www.cilip.org.uk/professionalguidance/informationliteracy/definition/.

Clancy, J. (2007) 'The army understands you'. *The Guardian*. London. 10 April. Available at http://education.guardian.co.uk/egweekly/story/0,,2053154,00.html.

Connor, H., Burton, R., Pearson, R., Pollard, E. and Regan, J. (1999) *Making the Right Choice: how students choose universities and colleges*. London, Committee of Vice-Chancellors and Principals.

Cook, M. and Cripps, B. (2005) *Psychological Assessment in the Workplace: a manager's guide*, Chichester, John Wiley & Sons.

Cooperrider, D. L. and Srivastva, S. (1987) 'Appreciative Inquiry'. *Research in Organizational Change and Development*, 1, 129–69.

Coopers and Lybrand (1998) 'Skills Development in Higher Education'. London, Coopers and Lybrand Report for Committee of Vice-Chancellors and Principals/Department for Education and Employment.

Cottrell, S. (1999) *The Study Skills Handbook*, Basingstoke, Palgrave Macmillan.

Cottrell, S. (2003) Skills for Success: The personal development planning handbook, Basingstoke, Palgrave Macmillan.

Covey, S. (1989, 2004) *The Seven Habits of Highly Effective People*, New York, Free Press.

Cranmer, S. (2006) 'Enhancing graduate employability: best intentions and mixed outcomes'. *Studies in Higher Education*, 31: 169–84.

Crook, C., Gross, H. and Dymot, R. (2006) 'Assessment relationships in higher education: the tension of process and practice'. *British Educational Research Journal,* 32, 95–114.

Daly, H. E. and Cobb, J. B., JR. (1994) For the Common Good: redirecting the economy toward community, the environment and a sustainable future, Boston, MA, Beacon Press.

Dearing, R. (1997) *Higher Education in the Learning Society* ('The Dearing Report'). London, National Committee of Inquiry in Higher Education (NCIHE).

Dilts, R. (undated) Shared Values of the NLP Community. Available at http://education.guardian.co.uk/egweekly/story/0,,2053154,00.html.

DoctorJob (annual) *Fresher Futures*, Wallingford, Oxfordshire, GTI Specialist Publishers.

Donovan, N. and Halpern, D. (2002) *Life Satisfaction: the state of knowledge and implications for government cabinet office strategy unit. London, Cabinet Office Strategy Unit* (UK Government).

Dweck, C. S. (2000) Self-theories: their role in motivation, personality and development, Philadelphia, PA, Taylor and Francis.

Einhorn, H. J. (1989) *Professional Judgement and Decision Making*. Buckingham, Open University.

Elias, P. and Purcell, K. (2004) *Seven Years On: graduate careers in a changing labour market*. Manchester, HECSU, ESRC, IER and ESRU.

Elliot, A. J. and Dweck, C. S. (eds.) (2005) *Handbook of Competence and Motivation*, New York, Guildford Press.

Entwistle, N. J. (1988) *Styles of Learning and Teaching*, London, Fulton.

Entwistle, N. J. and Ramsden, P. (1983) *Understanding Student Learning*, London, Croom Helm.

Evans, C. (2006) *Developing employability and career management skills within the HE curriculum: a review and evaluation of different approaches*. School of Business and Social Sciences, Roehampton University.

Exley, H. (ed.) (2002) *Timeless Values*, Watford, Exley Publications.

Farrer, P. (undated) *Lost in Transition*. London, The Graduate Recruitment Company. (Also available at www.graduate-recruitment.co.uk/grc_report.pdf).

Fleming, N. D. and Bonwell, C. C. (2006) VARK. Version 7.0. Available at www.vark-learn.com/english/index.asp.

Foltz, B. M. and Luzzo, D. A. (1998) 'Increasing the career decision-making self-efficacy of nontraditional college students'. *Journal of College Counseling*, 1, 35–44.

Friedman, T. L. (2000) *The Lexus and the Olive Tree Anchor Books*, New York, Random House.

Friedman, T. L. (2005) *The World is Flat: a brief history of the globalized world in the twenty-first century*, London, Allen Lane.

FSSC (2006) *Graduate Skills and Recruitment in the City*, London, Financial Services Skills Council.

Gardner, H. (1983) *Multiple Intelligences: the theory and practice*, New York, Basic Books.

Gardner, H. (1999) *Intelligence Reframed: multiple intelligences for the 21st century*, New York, Basic Books.

Gibbs, G. and Simpson, C. (2004) 'Conditions under which assessment supports students' learning'. *Learning and Teaching in Higher Education*, 1, 3–31.

Gilleard, C. (2006) Personal communication email, 21 August.

Goleman, D. (1996) *Emotional Intelligence: why it can matter more than IQ*, London, Bloomsbury.

Graduate Prospects (2005–6) *Prospects Directory Salary and Vacancy Survey. Graduate Market Trends*, Manchester, Graduate Prospects.

Graduate Prospects (2006, 2007) *What Do Graduates Do? (annual)*. Manchester, Graduate Prospects.

Greenhaus, J. H., Callanan, G. A. and Kaplan, E. (1995) 'The role of goal setting in career management'. *The International Journal of Career Management*, 7, 3–12.

Gubbay, J. (1994) 'A critique of conventional justifications for transferable skills'. In Bridges, D. (ed.) *Transferable Skills in Higher Education*. Norwich, University of East Anglia.

Hall, D. T. and Richter, J. (1990) 'Career gridlock: baby boomers hit the wall'. *Academy of Management Executive*, 4, 7–22.

Hammond, K. R., McCleeland, G. H. and Mumpower, J. (1980) *Human Judgment and Decision Making. Theories, methods and procedures*, New York, Praeger.

Handy, C. B. (1994) *The Empty Raincoat*, London, Hutchinson Business.

Handy, C. B. (1995) *The Age of Unreason*, London, Random House Business Books.

Harré, R. and Gillett, G. (1994) *The Discursive Mind*, London, Sage Publications.

Harren, V. A. (1978) 'A model of career decision making for college students'. *Journal of Guidance and Counselling*, 4, 195–233.

Harris, B. (undated) *The Holosync Solution™ Nine Principles for Happiness and Healing*. Beaverton, Oregon, Centerpointe Research Institute. Accessed 8 April 2007. Available at www.trans4mind.com/holosync/principle4.html.

Harris Committee (2001) Developing Modern Higher Education Careers Services. In Review Chaired by Sir Martin Harris (Ed.) London, Department for Education and Employment.

Harvey, L. (2001) 'Defining and measuring employability'. *Quality in Higher Education*, 7, 97–109.

Harvey, L. (2003) *On Employability*, York, Higher Education Academy.

Harvey, L. and Bowers-Brown, T. (2004) 'Employability cross-country comparisons: graduate market trends' Manchester, Graduate Prospects. Winter 2004/5.

Harvey, L., Moon, S., Geall, V. and Bower, R. (1997) *Graduates' Work: organisational change and students' attributes*, Birmingham, Centre for Research into Quality, University of Central England in Birmingham and Association of Graduate Recruiters.

Harvey, L., Geall, V. and Moon, S. (1998) *Work Experience: expanding opportunities for undergraduates*. Birmingham, Centre for Research into Quality, University of Central England in Birmingham.

Harvey, L., Locke, W. and Morey, A. (2002) *Enhancing Employability, Recognising Diversity: making links between higher education and the world of work*. London, Universities UK/Careers Services Unit.

Hawkins, P. (1999) *The Art of Building Windmills*: *career tactics for the 21st century*, Liverpool, Graduate into Employment Unit.

Hawkins, P. and Winter, J. (1995) *Skills for Graduates in the 21st Century*, Cambridge, Association of Graduate Recruiters.

Hawkins, P. and Gilleard, C. (2002) *If Only I'd Known: making the most of higher education*, Warwick, Association of Graduate Recruiters.

Hayes, J., Hopson, B. and Daws, P. P. (1972) *Careers Guidance: the role of the school in vocational development*, London, Heinemann Educational Secondary Division.

HEA (2003) *White Paper on the Future of Higher Education*, York, Higher Education Academy.

HEA (2006) *Student Employability Profiles: a guide for higher education practitioners*. Manchester, Graduate Prospects, Council for Industry and Higher Education, Higher Education Academy.

HEFCE (2005) *HEFCE strategy for e-learning*. London, Higher Education Funding Council for England/Joint Information Systems Committee/Higher Education Academy.

Heron, J. (1981) 'Assessment revisited'. In Boud, D. (ed.) *Developing Student Autonomy in Learning*. London, Kogan Page.

Herzberg, F., Mausner, B. and Snyderman, B. (1959) *The Motivation to Work*, New York, John Wiley & Sons.

HESA (2005) *DLHE – development of longitudinal stage*, Cheltenham, Higher Education Statistics Agency.

Hillage, J. and Pollard, E. (1998) Employability: developing a framework for policy analysis, London, Department for Education and Employment.

Hogarth, R. M. (1987) Judgement and Choice: the psychology of decision, 2nd edn, Chichester, John Wiley & Sons.

Holland, J. L. (1966) *The Psychology of Vocational Choice*, Waltham, MA, Blaisdell Publishing Company.

Holland, J. L. (1973) *Making Vocational Choices: a theory of careers*, Englewood Cliffs, NJ, Prentice-Hall.

Holland, J. L. (1985) *Making Vocational Choices*: a *theory of vocational personalities and work environments*, Englewood Cliffs, NJ, Prentice Hall.

Holmes, L. (2001) 'Reconsidering graduate employability: the "graduate identity" approach'. *Quality in Higher Education*, 7, 111–19.

Honey, P. and Mumford, A. (1992) *The Manual of Learning Styles*, Maidenhead, Peter Honey.

Honey, P. and Mumford, A. (1995) *Using Your Learning Styles*, Maidenhead, Peter Honey.

Huber (1980) *Managerial Decision Making*, Glenview, IL, Scott Foresman.

Huws, U., Jagger, N. and O'Regan, S. (1999) *Teleworking and Globalisation: IES Report 358*, Brighton, Institute for Employment Studies.

Hyland, T. (1997) 'The skills that fail to travel'. *Times Higher Education Supplement* 2 May 1997. London.

Jackson, N. (1999) 'Modelling change in a national HE system using the concept of unification'. *Journal of Education Policy*, 14, 411–34.

Jarvis, M. (2005) *The Psychology of Effective Learning and Teaching*, Cheltenham, Nelson Thornes.

Jarvis, P. (2002) *Career Management Paradigm Shift: prosperity for citizens, windfall for governments*. Ottawa, National Life/Work Centre.

Jeffers, S. (1987) *Feel the Fear and Do it Anyway*, London, Arrow Books.

Jepsen, D. A. and Dilley, J. S. (1974) 'Vocational decision-making models: a review and comparative analysis'. *Review of Educational Research*, 44, 331–49.

Jung, C. G. and Baynes, H. G. (1921) *Psychological Types, or The Psychology of Individuation*, London, Kegan Paul Trench Trubner.

Kaplan, M. and Schwartz, S. (1975) *Human Judgement and Decision Processes*, New York, Academic Press.

Kiersey, D. and Bates, M. (1984) *Please Understand Me*, Del Mar, CA, Prometheus Nemesis Book Company.

King, Z. (2004) 'Career self-management: its nature, causes and consequences'. *Journal of Vocational Behavior*, 65, 112–33.

Kirby, L. K., Kendall, E. and Barger, N. J. (2007) *Type and Culture: using the MBTI® instrument in international applications*, Mountain View, CA, CPP Inc.

Knight, P. (2001) 'Employability and Assessment'. Skills Plus – a paper prepared for the fourth colloquium. Lancaster, Lancaster University.

Knight, P. and Yorke, M. (2000) 'Skills plus: Tuning the Undergraduate Curriculum'. Buckingham, Skills plus Project Report, Open University.

Knight, P. and Yorke, M. (2003a) 'Employability and good learning in higher education'. *Teaching in Higher Education*, 8, 3–16.

Knight, P. and Yorke, M. (2003b) *Assessment, Learning and Employability*, Maidenhead, Society for Research into Higher Education and Open University Press.

Knight, P. and Yorke, M. (2004) Learning, Curriculum and Employability in Higher Education, London, Routledge Falmer.

Kolb, D. A. (1984) *Experiential Learning: experience as the source of learning and development*, London, Prentice-Hall.

Kroeger, O. and Thuesen, J. M. (1988a) *Type Talk: the 16 personality types that determine how we live, love, and work*, New York, Delacorte Press.

Kroeger, O. and Thuesen, J. M. (1988b) *Type Talk at Work: how the 16 personality types determine your success on the job*, New York, Delacorte Press.

Kubler, B. and Forbes, P. (2005) *Student Employability Profiles: Guide for Employers*, London, The Council for Industry and Higher Education.

Kumar, A. (2005) 'Developing a quality careers education using ICT'. In Fallows, S. and Bhanot, R. (eds) *Quality Issues in ICT-Based Higher Education*. London, Routledge Falmer.

Kummerow, J. M. (2002) *Talking in Type*, Gainesville, FL, Center for Applications of Psychological Types.

Law, B. (1981a) Careers Theory: a third dimension. In Watts, A. G., Super, D. E. and Kidd, J. M. (eds) *Career Development in Britain*. Cambridge, CRAC, 1981.

Law, B. (1981b) 'Community interaction: a 'mid-range' focus for theories of career development in young adults'. *British Journal of Guidance and Counselling*, 9, 143–57.

Law, B. (2005) 'What are we going to do about careers? Getting to Know CPI'. The Career Learning Network. Available at www.hihohiho.com/underpinning/CPIpdfs/cafcpia.pdf.

Law, B. A. (1996) 'A career learning theory' and 'Careers education in the curriculum'. In Watts, A. G., Law, B. A., Killeen, J., Kidd, J. M. and Hawthorn, R. (eds) *Rethinking Careers Education and Guidance – Theory, Policy and Practice*. London, Routledge.

Law, B. A. and Watts, A. G. (1977) *Schools, Careers and Community*, London, Church Information Office.

Law, B. A., Meijers and Wijers (2002) 'New perspectives on career and identity in the contemporary world'. *British Journal of Guidance and Counselling*, 30, 431–49.

Lawrence, G. D. (1993) *People Types and Tiger Stripes*, Florida, Center for Applications of Psychological Type, Inc.

Learning Skills Council (2006) *Employers Skills Survey 2005: key findings*. Coventry, Learning Skills Council.

Leitch, S. (2006) *Leitch Review of Skills: prosperity for all in the global economy – world class skills*, Norwich, HMSO.

Lent, R. W., Brown, S. B. and Hackett, G. (1994) 'Toward a unifying social cognitive theory of career and academic interest, choice, and performance'. *Journal of Vocational Behavior*, 45, 79–122.

Lent, R. W., Brown, S. B. and Hackett, G. (1996) 'Career development from a social cognitive perspective'. In Brown, D., Brooks, L. and Associates (eds) *Career Choice and Development,* 3rd edn, San Francisco, CA, Jossey-Bass.

Little, B. and ESECT colleagues (2006) *Employability and Work-based Learning*. 'Learning and Employability Series'. York, Higher Education Academy.

Locke, E. A. (2000) *The Prime Movers: traits of the great wealth creators*, New York, AMACOM.

Locke, E. A. and Latham, G. P. (1990) 'Work motivation and satisfaction: light at the end of the tunnel'. *Psychological Science*, 1, 240–6.

Locke, E. A., Latham, G. P., Smith, K. J. and Wood, R. E. (1990) *A Theory of Goal Setting and Task Performance*, Englewood Cliffs, NJ, Prentice Hall.

Luzzo, D. and Taylor, M. (1994) 'The effects of verbal persuasion on the career self-efficacy of college freshmen'. *California Association for Counseling and Development Journal*, 14, 31–4.

McClelland, D. (1988) *Human Motivation*, Cambridge, Cambridge University Press.

McKay, E. G. and Cabrales, D. (1996) *Starting Strong: a guide to pre-service training*, Washington DC, MOSAICA.

McKeachie, W. J. (1979) 'Perspectives from psychology: Financial incentives are ineffective for faculty'. In Lewis, D. R. and Becker, W. E. (eds) *Academic Rewards in Higher Education,* Cambridge, MA, Ballinger.

McMahon, M., Patton, W. and Tatham, P. (2003) *Managing Life, Learning and Work in the 21st Century*, Perth, Miles Morgan Australia.

Maguire, M. (2005) *Delivering Quality*. London, Department for Education and Skills.

Martin, C. R. (1995) *Looking at Type and Careers*, Gainesville, FL, Center for Applications of Psychological Type, Inc. Available at www.capt.org/catalog/MBTI-Book-60060.htm.

Maslow, A. H. (1943) 'A Theory of Human Motivation'. *Psychological Review*, 50, 370–96.

Maslow, A. H. (1954) *Motivation and Personality*, New York, Harper Row.

Maslow, A. H. (1968) *Towards a Psychology of Being*, Princeton, NJ, Van Nostrand Reinhold.

Maslow, A. H. (1970) *Motivation and Personality*, 2nd edn., New York, Harper Row.

Mason, G., Williams, G., Cranmer, S. and Guile, D. (2003) *How Much Does Higher Education Enhance the Employability of Graduates*? Bristol, Higher Education Funding Council for England.

Miles Morgan Australia (2003) 'Australian Blueprint for Career Development: Draft Prototype'. Canberra, Department of Education, Science and Training.

Moon, J. (2004) *Reflection and Employability*, York, Learning and Teaching Support Network, Higher Education Academy.

Moreland, N. (2006) *Entrepreneurship and Higher Education: an Employability Perspective*, Learning and Employability Series. York, Higher Education Academy.

Morey, A., Harvey, L., Williams, J., Saldana, A. and Mena, P. (2003) *HE Careers Services and Diversity*. Manchester, Careers Services Unit.

Murray, J. P. (1999) 'Faculty development in a national sample of community colleges'. *Community College Review*, 27, 47.

Myers, I. B. and Myers, P. B. (1995) *Gifts Differing: understanding personality type*, Palo Alto, CA, Davies-Black Publishing.

Nardi, D. (2005) 'Eight kinds of smart for all types: psychological type and multiple intelligences'. *British Association for Psychological Type, Typeface*, 16, (Autumn) 23–5.

Nelson-Jones, R. (1989) *Effective Thinking Skills: preventing and managing personal problems*, London, Cassell Educational.

Nicol, D. and Macfarlane-Dick, D. (2006) 'Formative assessment and self-regulated learning: a model and seven principles of good feedback practice'. *Studies in Higher Education*, 31, 199–218.

Nicol, D. and Milligan, C. (2006) 'Rethinking technology supported assessment practices in relation to the seven principles of good feedback practice'. In Bryan, C. and Clegg, K. (eds) *Innovative Assessment in Higher Education*, London, Routledge.

NLWC (1998) *Canadian Blueprint for Life/Work Design*, Ottawa, National Life/Work Centre, Canada Career Information Partnership and Human Resources Development Canada. Available at http://blueprint4life.ca/.

NOICC (2001, 2004) *National Career Development Guidelines*. Washington DC, National Occupational Information Coordinating Committee.

NTL (undated) *The Learning Pyramid*. Alexandria, VA, National Training Laboratories, Institute for Applied Behavioral Science. Copy of image available at http://homepages. gold.ac.uk/polovina/learnpyramid/about.htm.

O'Neill, L. (1999) *Matching Multiple Intelligences to Careers*, Tucson, AZ, Zephyr Press.

Parsons, F. (1909) *Choosing a Vocation*, Boston, MA, Houghton Mifflin.

Patton, W. and McMahon, M. (1999) *Career Development and Systems Theory: a new relationship*, Pacific Grove, CA, Brooks/Cole.

Pedagogy for employability group (2006) *Pedagogy for Employability*, '*Learning and Employability Series*'. York, Higher Education Academy.

Pierce, D. (2002) 'Employability: higher education and careers services'. Paper prepared for the Association of Graduate Careers Advisory Services.

Prosser, M. and Trigwell, K. (1999) *Understanding Learning and Teaching*, Buckingham, SRHE and Open University Press.

Proust, M. (1982) *Remembrance of Things Past*. In Moncrieff, C. K. S. and Kilmartin, T. (eds and trans), New York, Vintage Books.

Purcell, K. and Pitcher, J. (1996) *Great Expectations: the new diversity of graduate skills and aspirations*, Warwick, Institute for Employment Research, University of Warwick; AGCAS; CSU.

Purcell, K., Elias, P., Davies, R. and Wilton, N. (2005) *The Class of '99: a study of the early labour market experiences of recent graduates*, Warwick, University of Warwick and University of the West of England.

Purcell, K, Pitcher, J. and Simm, C. (1999) *Working Out? Graduates Early Experiences of the Labour Market*, Manchester, IER for AGCAS, HECSU and DfEE.

QAA (2001a) *Code of Practice for the Assurance of Academic Quality and Standards in Higher Education: career education, information and guidance*, Gloucester, Quality Assurance Agency for Higher Education. Available at www.qaa.ac.uk/academicinfrastructure/benchmark/default.asp (accessed 20 November 2007)

QAA (2001b) *Guidelines for HE Progress Files*, Gloucester, Quality Assurance Agency for Higher Education (UK). Available at www.qaa.ac.uk/academicinfrastructure/progress Files/guidelines/progfile2001.asp (accessed 15 October 2007).

Quenk, N. L. (1996) *In the Grip: our hidden personality*, Oxford, Oxford Psychologists Press.

Race, P. (1994) *Never Mind the Teaching Feel the Learning*, Birmingham, SEDA Publications.

Ramsden, P. (2003) *Learning to Teach in Higher Education*, London, Routledge Falmer.

Reich, R. B. (1991) *The Work of Nations: preparing ourselves for 21st century capitalism*, New York, Vintage Books.

Reich, R. B. (2002) 'Managing in Uncertain Times'. 19 February 2002. *The Times*.

Rifkin, J. (1995) *The End of Work: the decline of the global labour force and the dawn of the post market era*, New York, Tarcher/Putman.

Robbins, A. (1986) *Unlimited Power*, New York, Fireside, Simon & Schuster.

Roberts, K. (1977) 'The Social Conditions, Consequences and Limitations of Careers Guidance'. *British Journal of Guidance and Counselling*, 5(1): 1–9.

Rogers, C. (1965, first published 1951) *Client Centred Therapy*, Melksham, Redwood Press.

Rubin, T. I. (1990) *Overcoming Indecisiveness: the eight stages of effective decision-making*, London, Cedar.

Schein, E. H. (1993) *Career Anchors: discovering your real values,* London, Jossey-Bass/Pfeiffer and Co.

Senge, P. M. (1990) *The Fifth Discipline. The art and practice of the learning organization*, London, Random House.

Simon, H. (1976) *Administrative Behavior*, New York, Free Press.

Spearman, C. (1927) *The Abilities of Man, their Nature and Measurement*, New York, The Macmillan Co.

Spry, D. and Cripps, B. (2007) *The Psychometric Testing Management Pocketbook*, Alresford, UK, Management Pocketbooks.

Sternberg, R. J. (1997) *Successful Intelligence: how practical and creative intelligence determine success in life*, New York, Simon & Schuster.

Straby, R. (2002) *Life Works by Design,* Ontario, Elora.

Strategis (2004) *Maximising Your Graduate Pipeline*, Ottawa, Strategis.

Super, D. E. (1953) 'A theory of vocational development'. *American Psychologist*, 8, 185–90.

Super, D. E. (1957) *The Psychology of Careers*, New York, Harper Row.

Super, D. E. (1980) 'A life-span, life-space approach to career development'. *Journal of Vocational Behaviour*, 16, 282–98.

Super, D. E. (1990) 'Assessment in career guidance: a life-span, life-space approach to career development'. In Brown, D., Brooks, L. *et al.* (eds) *Career Choice and Development*, 2nd edn. San Francisco, CA, Jossey-Bass, pp. 197–261.

Taylor, K. M. and Betz, N. E. (1983) 'Applications of self-efficacy theory to the understanding and treatment of career indecision'. *Journal of Vocational Behavior*, 22, 63–81.

Terman, L. M. (1975, first published 1916) *The Measurement of Intelligence*, New York, L L Arno Press.

Tiedeman, D. V. and O'Hara, R. P. (1963) *Career Development: choice and adjustment*, Princeton, NJ, College Entrance Examination Board.

Toffler, A. (1970) *Future Shock*, New York, Random House.

Tracy, B. (1984) *Psychology of Achievement*, Paignton, UK, Nightingale-Conant Corporation (DVD and workbook).

UNITE (2005) *The 2005 UNITE Student Experience Report*. Bristol, Unite/MORI/Higher Education Policy Institute.

Universities UK (2002) *Modernising HE Careers Education: a framework for good practice*. London, Universities UK.

Vandevelde, H. (1997) *Beyond the CV*, Oxford, Butterworth Heinemann.

Vygotsky, L. S. (1978) *Mind in Society: the development of higher psychological processes*. In Cole, M., John-Steiner, V., Scribner, S. and Souberman, E. (eds) Cambridge, MA, Harvard University Press.

Ward, R., Jackson, N. and Strivens, J. (2005) *Progress Files: are we achieving our goal?*, Wigan, Centre for Recording Achievement.

Watkins, J. and Cooperrider, D. (2000) 'Appreciative Inquiry: a transformative paradigm'. *Journal of the Organization Development Network*, 32, 6–12.

Watkins, J. and Mohr, B. (2001) *Appreciative Inquiry: change at the speed of imagination*, San Francisco, CA, Jossey-Bass/Pfeiffer.

Watts, A. G. (1999) *Reshaping Career Development for the 21st Century*, Derby, Centre for Guidance Studies, University of Derby.

Watts, A. G. and Hawthorn, R. (1992) 'Careers Education and the Curriculum in Higher Education'. NICEC Project Report. Cambridge, Careers Research and Advisory Centre.

Watts, A. G., Law, B., Killeen, J., Kidd, J. M. and Hawthorn, R. (1996) *Rethinking Careers Education and Guidance: theory, policy and practice*, London and New York, Routledge.

Watts, A. G., Super, D. E. and Kidd, J. M. (eds) (1981) *Career Development in Britain*, Cambridge, CRAC.

Weisinger, H. (1985) *Anger Work-out Book: step-by-step methods for greater productivity, better relationships, healthier life*. New York, William Morrow and Company Inc.

Whyte, W. F. (1991) *Participatory Action Research and Action Science Compared*, Newbury Park, CA, Sage.

Wolf, A. and Kolb, D. A. (1980) 'Career development, personal growth, and experimental learning'. In Springer, J. W. (ed.) *Issues in Career and Human Resource Development*. Madison, WI, American Society for Training and Development.

Woolf, M. (2006) 'The obesity time bomb'. *The Independent*. London. 20 August. Available at http://news.independent.co.uk/uk/health_medical/article1220494.ece.

World Bank (2001) *Globalization*. Available at www1.worldbank.org/economicpolicy/globalization/.

Yorke, M. (2004) *Learning and Employability – pedagogy for employability*, York, ESECT and The Higher Education Academy.

Yorke, M. (2006) *Employability in Higher Education: what it is – what it is not*. 'Learning and Employability Series'. York, Higher Education Academy.

Yorke, M. and Knight, P. T. (2006) *Embedding Employability into the Curriculum*, York, ESECT and The Higher Education Academy.

Zimmerman, B. (2001) 'Theories of self-regulated learning and academic achievement: an overview and analysis'. In Zimmerman, B. and Schunk, D. (eds) *Self-regulated Learning and Academic Achievement: theoretical perspectives*. Hillsdale, NJ, Lawrence Erlbaum Associates.

Index

Page references in italics indicate illustrations.